# Value and Profit

The measurement methods used in finan[...]
our perception of the value and performanc[...]
determining the amount of the reported profit [...] [...]e
resources of the business. Thus, measurement a[...] [...]hareholders
and other stakeholders in the business. It has even been suggested
that the Global Financial Crisis of 2007–10 was partly due to the
mismeasurement of financial instruments.

As a follow-up to his previous book *Inflation Accounting*,
Geoffrey Whittington provides a unique survey of the theory and
practice of measurement in financial accounts. It seeks to define and
illustrate alternative methods, using simple numerical examples,
and to analyse their theoretical properties. Also, it summarises
extensive empirical evidence and the historical development of ideas
and practice. It is essential reading for advanced undergraduate and
postgraduate students studying financial accounting, as well as
practitioners and policy makers concerned with accounting
standards.

GEOFFREY WHITTINGTON is a Senior Research Associate of the
Cambridge Centre for Finance, Judge Business School, and a founding
member of the International Accounting Standards Board (2001–6).
He is the author of numerous publications and essays on financial
accounting, including *The Elements of Accounting* (Cambridge
University Press, 1992) and *The Debate on Inflation Accounting*
(with David Tweedie, Cambridge University Press, 1984).

# Value and Profit

## An Introduction to Measurement in Financial Reporting

GEOFFREY WHITTINGTON

*Judge Business School, Cambridge University*

CAMBRIDGE
UNIVERSITY PRESS

# CAMBRIDGE
### UNIVERSITY PRESS

University Printing House, Cambridge CB2 8BS, United Kingdom

Cambridge University Press is part of the University of Cambridge.

It furthers the University's mission by disseminating knowledge in the pursuit of education, learning and research at the highest international levels of excellence.

www.cambridge.org
Information on this title: www.cambridge.org/9780521155885
DOI: 10.1017/9781139022378

First published 2017

Printed in the United Kingdom by Clays, Ltd.

*A catalogue record for this publication is available from the British Library*

*Library of Congress Cataloging-in-Publication data*
Names: Whittington, Geoffrey, author.
Title: Value and profit : an introduction to measurement in financial reporting / Geoffrey Whittington, Judge Business School, Cambridge University.
Description: Cambridge, United Kingdom : Cambridge University Press, 2017. | Includes bibliographical references and index.
Identifiers: LCCN 2017006036 | ISBN 9780521190978 (hbk : alk. paper) | ISBN 9780521155885 (paperback)
Subjects: LCSH: Accounting. | Valuation. | Profit.
Classification: LCC HF5636 .W593 2017 | DDC 658.15/12 – dc23 LC record available at https://lccn.loc.gov/2017006036

ISBN 978-0-521-19097-8 Hardback
ISBN 978-0-521-15588-5 Paperback

*To Caspar, Hamish and Xander*

# Contents

# Preface

In 1983, I published *Inflation Accounting: An Introduction to the Debate*, on which this book is based. This earlier book was intended to introduce the basic framework of inflation accounting as a preparation for reading the study of the inflation accounting debate which David Tweedie and I published in 1984. However, it was also intended to stand on its own as an introduction to the measurement concepts underlying financial accounting as it is currently practiced, which are extremely important in determining economic decisions. Such issues as how profit is measured in the profit and loss account and how assets and liabilities are measured in the balance sheet affect our perception of the performance of businesses and, increasingly, of other entities, including public-sector bodies. This became alarmingly obvious during the Financial Crisis of 2007 onwards.

When the original book was written, inflation was a major economic concern throughout the world economy, so the book emphasised inflation accounting, whilst acknowledging that inflation is only one aspect of the measurement problem: individual prices typically change relative to one another even when inflation (the change in the general price level) is negligible. Since that time, the world economy has changed in a way that emphasises the importance of specific, rather than general, price changes. Notably, the recession following the Financial Crisis has been characterised by low inflation accompanied by some large changes in the prices of some goods and commodities, such as oil.

This book reflects this shift of emphasis from inflation to individual price changes, although it is based on the earlier one and, in particular, uses the same fundamental framework of accounting identities and numerical examples. The text has been re-written and re-ordered to emphasise specific rather than general price changes, and in particular, the detailed discussion of inflation is now deferred until Chapter 5. It also attempts to reflect the enormous amount of relevant research that has been published since the original book appeared. Much of this research is empirical, whereas the framework of this book is essentially theoretical, focusing on how accounting statements are, or might be, constructed rather than on what methods are actually adopted and how they are received by users of accounts. The style of the book may therefore seem to be a little old-fashioned. I make no apology for this, because theory and empirical studies must surely be essential companions rather than competitors: empirical studies cannot yield sensible answers if they are not based on theoretically sensible questions, and, of course, policy choices involve choosing between theoretical models on the basis of their empirical feasibility and consequences. My perception (despite having started academic life as an empirical researcher working on a large database of company accounts) is that the welcome expansion of empirical accounting research has started to crowd out theory to an unhealthy extent. As a result of this, there is a serious danger that knowledge gained in the past will be lost and will have to be rediscovered when it becomes relevant in the future. Therefore, if I can persuade a few accounting researchers to work through my simple, but fundamental, accounting identities and numerical examples, I will be more satisfied than if I had written a more popular survey of recent empirical work alone.

That is not to say that the book is aimed solely at accounting researchers. I have tried to make it readable and accessible, but the reader's task will be helped by having a basic knowledge of accounting, such as might be obtained from an introductory course. Beyond that, the stronger the readers' background in accounting and finance, the more they are likely to understand, but understanding is relative. Even as the author, I cannot claim to understand fully all of the apparently simple but often subtle problems posed by the subject. That is why I am still attempting to explain it to myself, a third of a century after the original book was published.

It is a pleasure to acknowledge and thank all those who have helped me in the long process of writing this book. Apart from those acknowledged in the preface to the original book, I have benefitted from the support and comments of friends and colleagues too numerous to list here. However, special thanks should be accorded to Richard Barker and Geoff Meeks, professors at Oxford and Cambridge, respectively (and my PhD students long ago), each of whom gave very helpful comments on the penultimate draft. Also, thanks to Dr William Peterson of Christ's College, Cambridge, who made some astute comments on the treatment of index numbers in Chapter 5 and saved me from at least one foolish error. Needless to say, I retain sole responsibility for the remaining errors and deficiencies. Finally, since I left the International Accounting Standards Board in 2006, my work has been supported by the research facilities provided by the Cambridge Endowment for Research in Finance (CERF) at the Judge Business School, and I wish to thank its trustees for their support and its successive directors, Professors John Eatwell and Bart Lambrecht, for their unfailing encouragement.

It is a mark of the passage of time that I dedicated the original book to my children, Alan and Richard, who were then both under ten years old. The present book is dedicated to my grandchildren, who, by the time the book appears in print, will each be at least ten years old. If somebody in their generation reads the book, the effort of writing it will have been worthwhile.

# Abbreviations

INSTITUTIONS

AARF     Australian Accounting Research Foundation

AICPA     American Institute of Certified Public Accountants

APB     Accounting Principles Board (predecessor of the FASB in the US)

ASB     Accounting Standards Board (the UK standard-setting body since 1990)

ASC     Accounting Standards Committee (previously, until 1975, the ASSC; the professional standard-setting body in the UK until 1990)

ASR     Accounting Series Release (a statement on accounting published by the SEC)

ASSC     Accounting Standards Steering Committee (became the ASC in 1975)

CCAB     Consultative Committee on Accountancy Bodies (a committee of professional institutes which supervised the ASC in the UK)

ED     Exposure Draft (a draft accounting standard, issued for discussion)

FAS     Financial Accounting Standard (issued by the FASB)

FASB     Financial Accounting Standards Board (the private-sector standard-setting body in the US)

FRC     Financial Reporting Council (the UK body overseeing the Accounting Standards Board and, latterly, the Accounting Council)

IAS     International Accounting Standard (issued by the IASC)

| | |
|---|---|
| IASB | International Accounting Standards Board (replaced the IASC in 2001) |
| IASC | International Accounting Standards Committee |
| ICAEW | Institute of Chartered Accountants in England and Wales |
| ICAS | Institute of Chartered Accountants of Scotland |
| IFRS | International Financial Reporting Standard (issued by the IASB) |
| IPSASB | International Public Sector Accounting Standards Board |
| PSSAP | Provisional Statement of Standard Accounting Practice (issued by the ASSC) |
| SEC | Securities and Exchange Commission (the US government agency responsible for supervising securities markets and financial information disclosure) |
| SSAP | Statement of Standard Accounting Practice (issued by the ASC) |

## TECHNICAL

| | |
|---|---|
| ARR | accounting rate of return |
| CCA | current cost accounting |
| CoCoA | continuously contemporary accounting |
| CPI | Consumer Price Index (compiled by the UK Office of National Statistics) |
| CPP | constant (or current) purchasing power accounting |
| DV | deprival value (also known as VTB) |
| FV | fair value |
| GNP | gross national product |
| HC | historical cost |
| IRR | internal rate of return |
| MCRV | Making Corporate Reports Valuable (a proposal by ICAS) |
| MWCA | monetary working capital adjustment |
| NRV | net realisable value |
| PV | present value |

RC      replacement cost

RPI     Retail Price Index (compiled by the UK Office of National Statistics)

VTB    value to the business (also known as DV)

# I    An Introduction to the Measurement Problem in Financial Accounting

## I.I INTRODUCTION

The objectives of this chapter are to explain why measurement in accounting matters and to give a broad survey of the problems that will be analysed in more detail in subsequent chapters. First, we discuss accounts, particularly financial accounts, and their uses, and then we shall consider the impact of measurement on accounting numbers. The variety of methods of measurement that have been proposed are then illustrated by means of simple numerical examples, and the quantitative importance of the various adjustments is illustrated by using data from UK companies. Finally, the course of the argument of the rest of the book is outlined.

## I.2 FINANCIAL ACCOUNTING

Accounting can be defined broadly as the provision of information relating to the economic activities of any *accounting entity*, that is, an individual, organisation or group which is accountable to others. For present purposes, we shall narrow this to exclude the special problems of national income accounting and of non-business organisations. We shall be concerned primarily with the accounts of business entities, which are usually corporate bodies, and the field will be further narrowed by being concerned only with the financial accounts and not with the management accounts of these organisations. Financial accounts are the financial statements which have traditionally been drawn up on a periodic basis, usually at least annually, mainly for the benefit of the owners and providers of finance of the firm, i.e. the shareholders and the creditors in the typical case of a company. As we shall see, the range of users and uses has widened in recent years.

We shall not be concerned specifically with management accounts that are prepared for the internal use of the management of the firm, to help them with their decision-making and control activities. The range of management accounting information is very broad, and its form is not specified by statute, so that management accounting practice is more heterogeneous than that of financial accounting. The correct selection of measurement basis for management accounts is obviously important because misleading information could lead to bad management, and the financial accounts complement the management accounts in giving an aggregate view of the outcome of management decisions.[1] The reason for avoiding special analysis of management accounting problems here is merely one of simplicity:[2] financial accounting has quite enough problems to suffice for present purposes.

Financial accounts play an important part in the working of market economies by providing financial information to those outside the accounting entity that helps them to make decisions in relation to it. The most obvious of these decisions is the decision to invest, and investors are usually regarded as primary users of accounts in legal requirements (such as company legislation), accounting regulations (such as the standards of the International Accounting Standards Board, IASB) and other regulatory requirements (such as the listing requirements of stock exchanges). Amongst investors in corporate enterprises, equity shareholders have a particularly important role, enshrined in companies legislation, which typically gives them the right to vote at company meetings that elect directors, accept the accounts, approve dividends, appoint auditors and conduct other important business. They usually share the profits of the entity through dividend payments and bear the residual risk when there are losses, subject to the constraint of limited liability. For these reasons, shareholders are often regarded as the proprietors of the company and a group whose information needs are essential, although the accounts also need to inform other users. Apart from non-equity investors, such as bond holders and banks, these other users include suppliers, customers, employees and others with an economic relationship with the reporting entity, and intermediaries such as credit rating agencies and financial analysts, who provide advice and information to others. They also include a wider range of stakeholders whose interests may be broader and who may not have a direct economic relationship with the entity.[3]

Governments also rely on accounts for taxation purposes, for national income statistics which form the basis of macro-economic management and for regulatory purposes. The regulatory use of accounts has increased in recent years, particularly in competition policy and the regulation of prices in privatised public utilities.[4] Measurement has been a particularly contentious issue in the latter use: the method used to measure the asset base can make a substantial difference to the prices to consumers and the profits to the shareholders of the regulated entity. Another regulatory use, by bank regulators, has become very important during the recent international credit crisis that started in 2007. Here again, measurement has been a critical issue. In particular, some commentators have claimed that the use of 'fair value' (estimates of current market selling price) to measure financial instruments has amplified the apparent volatility of the profits and balance sheet solvency of banks, causing an inappropriate breach of regulatory targets, and has thus magnified the crisis.[5]

Nevertheless, the main focus of financial reporting[6] is on investors, particularly equity shareholders, reflecting their role as proprietors and ultimate risk-bearers. The conceptual frameworks of the leading accounting standard-setters, such as the International Accounting Standards Board (IASB), identify investors (both current and potential) as the principal users of financial reports and express the view that other users will also benefit from the same information, although it is not designed specifically for them.

In serving the needs of investors, the conceptual frameworks usually distinguish between two primary purposes: *decision-usefulness* and *stewardship* (sometimes more broadly described as *accountability*). Decision-usefulness relates to the investor's decision to invest or to disinvest and is therefore served best by forward-looking *ex ante* information directed towards valuing the entity and its share capital. Stewardship is concerned with the accountability of directors or other senior internal managers to external stakeholders, particularly equity shareholders and other long-term investors, for the performance of the entity. Stewardship is therefore more concerned with the *ex post* evaluation of the past performance of the reporting entity. It may lead to decisions about rewarding or disciplining directors (who, under UK law, present the financial accounts to the annual shareholders' meeting of a company as part of their duty of accountability), and it may have implications for investment decisions (e.g. by signalling the quality of management), but it is less directly concerned with the future than is decision-usefulness. A recent proposal by the IASB to exclude stewardship as an objective distinct from decision-usefulness in its conceptual framework was controversial and has been withdrawn,[7] thus reaffirming the importance of the stewardship function of financial reports.

These examples of the range of users and uses of financial accounts should serve to demonstrate that financial accounting is important because of the economic consequences that follow from its use. Matters such as the level of share prices, taxation, dividends, directors' remuneration and product prices have direct consequences for the economic welfare of individuals, and it is therefore not surprising that the debate on different methods of accounting has often been very spirited, even passionate, despite the superficial appearance of the subject as being somewhat dry and technical. The various parties affected have a strong and direct incentive to advocate the accounting technique that seems to favour them most. This has certainly been true of the debate on measurement in accounting.[8]

Before discussing measurement and its effects on accounts, it is important to consider another implication of the widening range of users and uses of financial accounting. It is unlikely that one particular type of information, such as a single profit figure, will meet the needs of all potential users. For example, it is not necessarily the case that the measure of profit used for assessing profits tax should be the same as that used for setting an upper limit on the dividends that can be distributed to shareholders: the fact that the definitions of taxable profit and distributable profit differ under current British legislation is evidence of this. Moreover, even within the narrower confines of serving the specific needs of investors, as preferred by accounting standard-setters, there is a variety of information require-ments, depending upon the preferences of different investors, who may have different degrees of risk aversion and different models of how to evaluate the reporting entity. Despite this, the debate on accounting, and particularly on measurement, has been bedevilled by the implicit belief on the part of many participants that a single number or method can be found that will provide 'all the answers'. This problem is compounded by the fact that most of the separate questions potentially have a number of answers: for example, it is by no means clear that corporation tax should be based on profits rather than net payments to shareholders,[9] and it can be argued that the dividend decision should be constrained by consideration of liquidity as well as profit.

## 1.3 MEASUREMENT IN FINANCIAL ACCOUNTING

Measurement in financial accounting is the process of attaching numerical amounts to items in the accounts. In order to achieve this, two separate choices have to be made: first, selection of the *unit of measurement*, and second, selection of a method of *valuation*. The choice of valuation method will involve the selection of the *attribute* to be measured, such as historical cost (what was actually paid to acquire the item), or a current market value, such as replacement cost or sale value. It will also require a choice of levels of *aggrega-tion* at which measurement is determined: for example, do we value individual items of plant separately or as part of a total value of the factory, or do we attempt a single valuation of the whole business?

The *unit of measurement* for the core financial accounts is *monetary units*. This may seem to be an obvious and uncomplicated decision, but in reality, it raises two difficult problems.

First, a currency has to be chosen. In some cases, this is straightforward, but it is not so in the case of those entities that operate in more than one currency area. In the case of international groups of companies, the choice of a *functional currency* for accounting purposes and the problems of *foreign currency translation*, converting items to the functional currency from other currencies, are sufficiently complex to require extensive guidance in accounting standards.[10]

Second, having selected a currency, there is the problem of *inflation*; nominal currency units, such as pounds sterling or dollars, rarely maintain a constant real value, in terms of purchasing power, over time. Thus, the accountant will find that the nominal currency measurement unit, unlike physical units such as weight or length, does not have identical values at different times, reducing the comparability of accounting numbers across periods. This can also lead to inconsistency within the accounts of a single period, when, as is typical, they measure items by reference to past values or costs or at different times within the reporting period, as in the case of historic cost accounting. In such cases, the accounts will aggregate items measured at different times when the currency unit had different purchasing power, a process sometimes described as 'adding apples to pears'. This problem becomes particularly important in periods of high inflation. A possible solution, which has been used in economies with high inflation rates, is to find a constant, or relatively constant, unit of value and translate variable nominal currency units into this new unit. This process is the same as for foreign currency translation: sometimes the constant unit of value is actually another, more stable currency, such as US dollars or, in Germany in the 1920s, the gold mark. More commonly, the constant measurement unit is created by applying price indices to an existing currency to create, for example, a new 'constant dollar' measure.[11] This is discussed later, in Chapter 5.

The *valuation* problem is the problem of measuring individual items in the accounts in terms of the chosen currency unit. Here also there are difficult choices between different economic attributes of an item in the accounts. The traditional method preferred by accountants was *historical cost*, the amount originally paid for an asset or received for a liability. More recently, *current values* have been adopted in some circumstances: in particular, *fair value*, which is used by the IASB for certain financial instruments,[12] has attracted much attention in the debate on the Financial Crisis. There are three categories of current value: *entry values* (current cost of acquisition), *exit values* (current receipts expected from disposal, of which fair value is a specific variant) and *value in use* (the present value of the future benefits expected from continuing use in the business).

The measurement question is not confined to measuring assets and liabilities at a point in time, as in a balance sheet (illustrated in Section 1.4). It is also concerned with measuring changes over time, as captured by the income statement, which provides measures of profit. The proprietor's capital that has to be maintained before recognising a profit will be affected by inflation (the unit of measurement problem) and by specific price changes (the valuation problem). This is demonstrated by the following simple numerical illustration, which also illustrates the wider problems of measurement.

## 1.4 A NUMERICAL ILLUSTRATION

This example originated in an address by a leading member of the accounting profession to a group of industrial accountants, in an attempt to persuade them to adopt a system of current cost accounting (CCA) which had recently been adopted by the Accounting Standards Committee (SSAP 16, 1980). Current cost accounting replaced[13] the traditional historical cost with current replacement cost[14] and therefore represented a significant change in the measurement basis of financial accounting. The example is extremely simple in terms of transactions, but it demonstrates some quite subtle problems.

The example is as follows:

Fred is a street trader. One morning, he goes to the wholesale market and buys a hundred pineapples for £1 each. He sells 80 for £1.50 each, so he works out his profit for the day by the traditional historical cost method, as follows:

Income Statement[15] (for the period)

|  |  | £ |
|---|---|---|
| Sales |  | 120 |
| *Less* Cost of goods sold |  | 80 |
|  | Profit | 40 |

Note that he has recorded the cost of goods sold as £80, the cost of 80 pineapples. This implies that the 20 remaining pineapples are worth £20, which is what he paid for them. This is historical cost.

Corresponding to his income statement is a *statement of financial position*, traditionally known as the *balance sheet*.[16] This shows his asset and liability positions at a point in time. At the beginning of the day, he had cash of £100, which was equal to his own capital, so that his opening balance sheet only had two items:

Balance Sheet (beginning of period)

|  | £ |
|---|---|
| Assets: |  |
| Cash | 100 |
| Total | £100 |
|  |  |
| *Financed by:* |  |
| Proprietor's Capital: |  |
| Opening Capital contributed | 100 |
| Total | £100 |

At the end of the day, his capital had grown by £40 (the profit) to £140, and this was represented by cash, plus the stock of pineapples, as follows:

Balance Sheet (end of period)

| | £ |
|---|---|
| Assets: | |
| Cash | 120 |
| Stock of Pineapples | 20 |
| Total | £140 |
| | |
| *Financed by:* | |
| Proprietor's Capital: | |
| Opening Capital | 100 |
| Plus Profit | 40 |
| Total | £140 |

This result is based on two measurement assumptions:

1. *Historical cost accounting* is used to measure the assets whose value is not fixed in money terms ('non-monetary assets': in the present case, the stock of pineapples).
2. *Money capital* (sometimes called 'nominal capital') is the capital maintenance concept, i.e. the amount of opening proprietor's capital to be deducted from closing capital before a profit is recognised.

The best way to understand these assumptions is to look at the consequences of varying them.

First, we shall vary the historical cost assumption. Let us assume that the pineapples that remained unsold could not be sold the next day so that they are effectively worthless. This would increase costs of stock consumed by £20 and reduce closing assets by £20, so that profit would now be £20 and total assets £120. This is an application of the conservative valuation rule, 'cost or market value, whichever is the lower', which is often used to modify historical cost in practice.

An alternative measurement rule would be to abandon conservatism and record current market value, irrespective of whether that was higher or lower. If we look to the *exit* (sale) value in this case, and make the revised assumption that the unsold pineapples can be sold on the next day at the same price, we might consider recording them at the current selling price of £1.50. This would be a case of *marking to market*, and the valuation would be consistent with *fair value* as currently defined by the IASB.[17] This would give a total profit of £50 and closing assets (equal to the proprietor's capital) of £150, including stock of £30. Where there were significant costs of realising this profit, accountants and standard-setters might be reluctant to recognise the full profit implied by the change in the selling price alone, so that valuation would be at 'fair value less cost to sell' and the recorded profit would be therefore be reduced by expected selling costs.

The income statement on the 'marking to market' basis, with no adjustment for selling costs, would include the unrealised gain in value of stock, as follows:

Income Statement

| | £ |
|---|---|
| Sales | 120 |
| *Less* Cost of sales | 80 |
| Profit on sales | 40 |
| *Add* Gain on unsold stocks | 10 |
| Total Income | 50 |

The bottom line of the statement is now called 'income' rather than 'profit' because it includes the unrealised gain on unsold stocks in addition to the profit realised by sale. The recognition of unrealised gains arising from revaluation is a controversial issue in financial accounting, as is the method of reporting such gains. There is an ongoing debate about the merits, and methods, of distinguishing between operating profit and other gains which would be included in a total measure of 'comprehensive income'. This issue is explored further in later chapters.

Table 1.1 *Outcome of Alternative Asset Measurement Methods (Nominal Money Capital Maintenance)*

| Measurement Method | Income (£) | Closing Stock (£) | Closing Assets (£) |
|---|---|---|---|
| Historical cost | 40 | 20 | 140 |
| Sale (exit) price | 50 | 30 | 150 |
| Replacement (entry) price | 45 | 25 | 145 |

The corresponding changes to the closing balance sheet would be total assets increased to £150 (reflecting the £10 revaluation of closing stock) and a corresponding increase in the proprietor's capital (reflecting the £10 gain due to the revaluation).

A different approach to current market value would be to look at *entry* values (replacement costs) in the wholesale market that supplies the stock. The replacement cost valuation represents the current cost avoided by owning the asset rather than having to buy it in the market. If we assume that, by the end of the day's trading, the wholesale price of pineapples had risen to £1.25, then the closing stock would be valued at £25, the closing assets would be £145, and income would be £45, including the £5 revaluation of closing stock.

Table 1.1 summarises the alternative representations of Fred's financial position at the end of the day and the profitability of his economic activities during the day.

Income, under different measurement conventions but assuming the same facts, varies from £40 to £50 even in this simple example, which contains only two assets (cash and trading stocks) and no liabilities. The variation would be wider if we were to include the 'lower market value' variant of HC, but that was based on a different factual assumption (a lower market value) so that it is not a valid comparison. However, more alternative measurement conventions, which introduce more variation even with the same factual assumptions, are discussed later. The present example should suffice to show that measurement matters (Table 1.1).

There is, however, one important further issue that needs to be illustrated: the concept of *capital maintenance*. This is concerned with the measurement of the capital figure that has to be preserved (or 'maintained') before income is recognised. In the example so far, we have adopted a *money* capital maintenance concept, which is intuitively so natural that it almost passes unnoticed. In other words, we regard the £100 that Fred started with as the natural base for measuring profit so that any closing assets[18] in excess of £100 are regarded as profit. This does not have to be the case: maintaining capital at a fixed nominal monetary amount can lead to a failure to preserve the economic substance of the business.

To illustrate this in Fred's case, let us consider the original Fred story,[19] which proceeded as follows:

> Suppose that Fred measures his profit on the traditional historical cost basis. He sees a £40 profit at the end of the day and goes out and spends it, saving £80 to replace the pineapples that he has sold. He goes to the wholesale market on the next morning and finds that the price of pineapples has risen to £1.25. This means that he can buy only 64 pineapples, so that he cannot replace his original physical stock of 80 (plus the 20 that he has left from the previous day). Thus, the physical size of Fred's business has been impaired by his basing his consumption (in the case of a company, this would be a dividend) on an income measure that did not allow for the rising cost of replacement.

In order to maintain his *physical capital* in terms of pineapples, Fred would have had to charge *replacement cost* (£100 = 80 × £1.25) for those that he sold, reducing his profit to £20. He would also revalue his closing stock at replacement cost (£25), but this would be regarded as an increase in capital value rather than income. It would not appear in the income statement, although it could additionally be reported (as in the Sandilands model, discussed later) in a supplementary 'statement of gains and losses', in which capital appreciation could be added to profit to give a comprehensive income (or 'total gains') based on maintaining money capital. His closing assets on a replacement cost basis would be £145 (as in the final line of Table 1.1), which would be attributed to capital of £125 (the replacement cost of his capital of 100 pineapples, at £1.25 each) and profit of £20. He could spend the £20 without impairing his ability to maintain the capital stock of the business in physical terms (number of pineapples). This is the approach adopted by *current cost accounting*, which was a method supported in the UK by the Sandilands Committee (1975) and the Accounting Standards Committee (1980) at a time of rapidly rising prices,[20] although its relevance depends upon changes in specific prices (the cost of pineapples) rather than changes in the general price level (inflation). It is sometimes described as an *entity* approach, because it considers the maintenance of capital from the perspective of the business entity (maintaining its physical operating capability) rather than of investors in it. As the primary investor (through the equity capital that he has contributed), Fred may well object that he does not see the point of adjusting for the specific cost of buying pineapples, because he runs the business to make money rather than to preserve stocks of pineapples. If the pineapples appreciate in value, that increases his potential earning power. If he spends this and his physical stock of pineapples is reduced, that does not impair his earning power if he can continue to make the same profit margin, which will, in turn, maintain his sales revenue. If the profit margin on pineapples does fall, he can diversify into other fruit which may offer better margins. Hence, maintaining a particular physical stock is of no interest to him.

Fred's view is known as a *proprietary* view, which is not surprising, because he is the proprietor. This view is concerned to maintain *financial capital* rather than physical capital. It is a natural perspective for the investor, whose ultimate interest is in the flow of cash from the business for personal consumption. This was the view implicit in the use of nominal money capital in the initial illustration and in Fred's subsequent expenditure behaviour, which preserves a nominal money capital of £100 in the business.

The use of *nominal* money capital, preserving a nominal cash value, may not satisfy the objectives of the proprietor when there is *inflation*, which reduces the purchasing power of money. In that case, Fred's objective might be better served by maintaining *real* rather than nominal capital, i.e. by maintaining the command over goods and services (not merely pineapples) that is represented by the value of capital to be maintained. To achieve this, opening capital would be adjusted by a general price-level index. This might not seem to be realistic in our example of a single day's trading, because changes in the general price index over such a short time might be expected to be so small as to be immaterial. However, financial reports are typically prepared annually, and inflation over a whole year can be expected to have a significant effect on the measurement of profit. Moreover, in hyper-inflationary economies, inflation can be significant even for a single day. Hence, if we assume either that Fred's transactions were for a whole year or that he operates in a hyper-inflationary economy, we can assume plausibly that inflation over the period was 10 per cent. In this case, we would adjust the opening capital of £100 to a purchasing power equivalent £110 (£100 plus 10 per cent) at the end of the year. The adjustment of £10 would be an addition to capital and a deduction from profit. This deduction would preserve the real purchasing power of capital, reducing Fred's temptation to spend beyond his means.

Adjusting opening capital to allow for inflation suggests that we should look at other items in Fred's accounts to ensure that they also are adjusted appropriately for inflation. Fred has only two assets at the end of the period, cash and stock. The cash is of fixed monetary amount, so, if we are translating all values into £s as of the end of the period (as we did for capital) no adjustment is appropriate: £120 remains £120 even when prices change.[21] The other asset is stock, and, under the historical cost system, this is valued in beginning of period monetary units, but, unlike cash, it does not have a contractually fixed monetary value. We might therefore wish to make a constant purchasing power (CPP) adjustment to the historical cost of the stock to bring it to its equivalent in terms of currency units of current purchasing power, £22 (or £20 plus 10 per cent). This increase of £2 in the stock measurement offsets the adjustment of £10 to opening capital to produce a net adjustment for inflation of £8. Note that this is not a revaluation of stock in terms of current *specific* price, but a re-statement of historical cost in terms of current measurement units.

The income statement would now be

Income Statement

|  | £ |
|---|---|
| Sales | 120 |
| *Less* Cost of Sales (in current £'s) | 88 |
| Profit (in current £'s) | £32 |

and the closing position, at historical cost re-stated in current £s, would be:

Balance Sheet (end of period)

| Assets: | £ |
|---|---|
| Cash | 120 |
| Stock of Pineapples (in current £'s) | 22 |
| Total | £142 |

| *Financed by:* | |
|---|---|
| Proprietor's Capital: | £ |
| Opening Capital | 100 |
| *Plus* Inflation Adjustment | 10 |
| Opening Capital in current £'s | 110 |
| *Plus* Profit | 32 |
| Total | £142 |

The profit of £32 is the original historical cost profit of £40, less the capital adjustment of £10 and plus the stock adjustment of £2.

If we apply the inflation adjustment to the cases in which the stock is valued at current market values (selling price and replacement cost, respectively), the stock valuations are already expressed in end-of-period units and no further adjustment for inflation is needed. In both of these cases, the only adjustment required is the capital

Table 1.2 *Outcome of Inflation Adjustment ('Real Financial Capital Maintenance')*

| Measurement method | Income (£) | Closing Stock (£) | Closing Assets (£) |
|---|---|---|---|
| Historical Cost (inflation adjusted) | 32 | 22 | 142 |
| Sale (exit) price | 40 | 30 | 150 |
| Replacement (entry) price | 35 | 25 | 145 |

maintenance adjustment, which reduces profit by £10 in each case. The results of inflation adjustment are summarised in Table 1.2. The capital maintenance adjustment would have been different in each case had there been opening stocks because different measurement conventions for stocks would have given different measures of opening capital, which would have led to different adjustments for inflation (the adjustment being opening monetary amount multiplied by the inflation factor).

Table 1.2 demonstrates that applying an adjustment for inflation to opening capital (and, in the case of historical cost asset measurement, adding a similar adjustment to the asset) gives us three new measures of income, in addition to the three in Table 1.1. Taking account also of the physical capital maintenance adjustment (to preserve the number of pineapples available for sale) which could be applied when replacement cost was used as the asset measure, gives us a total of seven different alternative measures of income for this very simple example.

Further variations on asset measurement and capital maintenance are possible, and we have not yet introduced liabilities into the example, but further complications will be left to later chapters. The present example should suffice to demonstrate that measurement issues in accounting are quite complicated and can have a significant impact on the apparent performance and financial state of a business entity. Our example was based on assumed facts, so we turn now to some real evidence of the importance of price changes and their consequences for financial accounts.

## 1.5 SOME EMPIRICAL EVIDENCE

The numerical examples have demonstrated the potential importance of alternative measurement systems. Here we offer practical examples from recent decades that show their importance in the real world.

### 1.5.1 CCA in the UK

The first example is from the period when current cost accounting was required for large companies in the UK. Table 1.3 shows the effect of current cost accounting, CCA, (in the form required by SSAP16, 1980) on the profits and net assets recorded in the accounts of companies which complied with the new standard and included in the Business Statistics Office survey.[22] The number complying is recorded in line 11. The number complying with the standard increased to a peak in 1982. It declined from 1983 onwards, reflecting the increasing unpopularity of CCA as the rate of inflation (row 12) declined.[23] By 1985, only seventeen companies in the sample produced CCA information and the standard was no longer a requirement. The CCA method of SSAP16 required that stocks consumed and depreciation of fixed assets should be based on their current replacement cost rather than historical cost, reducing profit by the excess of current cost over historical cost (row 2 of Table 1.3). The offsetting 'holding gains' from the appreciation in value of stock and fixed assets were not treated as part of profit but were instead added as an adjustment to capital. Thus the current cost profit measure is based essentially on a physical capital maintenance concept of the 'entity' variety, similar to Fred's case of maintaining the stock of pineapples.[24] The CCA balance sheet (statement of financial position) included stocks and fixed assets at their current cost rather than historical cost.

The effect of CCA on profit is shown in rows 1 to 3 of Table 1.3. The percentage decrease in historical cost profit resulting from

Table 1.3 *Profitability of Large UK Companies, 1980–85*

| | | 1980 | 1981 | 1982 | 1983 | 1984 | 1985 |
|---|---|---|---|---|---|---|---|
| **Profit (£ million)** | | | | | | | |
| 1. | Historical cost profit (HC) | 12,997 | 16,857 | 15,503 | 14,764 | 9,021 | 1,702 |
| 2. | *Less* current cost adjustments | 5,431 | 6,067 | 5,152 | 4,541 | 1,930 | 247 |
| 3. | Current cost profit (CCA) | 7,566 | 10,790 | 10,351 | 10,223 | 7,091 | 1,455 |
| 4. | Row 2/Row 1 (%) | 41.8 | 40.0 | 33.2 | 30.8 | 21.4 | 14.5 |
| **Net tangible assets (£ million)** | | | | | | | |
| 5. | Historical cost (HC) | 75,494 | 105,057 | 109,805 | 91,165 | 49,206 | 10,471 |
| 6. | *Add* current cost adjustments | 23,249 | 29,720 | 29,369 | 25,299 | 12,515 | 1,357 |
| 7. | Current cost (CCA) | 98,743 | 134,777 | 139,174 | 116,464 | 61,721 | 11,828 |
| 8. | Row 6/Row 5 (%) | 30.8 | 28.3 | 26.7 | 27.8 | 25.4 | 13.0 |
| 9. | HC Rate of return (Row 1/Row 5) (%) | 17.2 | 16.1 | 14.1 | 16.2 | 18.3 | 16.3 |
| 10. | CCA rate of return (Row 3/Row 7) (%) | 7.7 | 8.0 | 7.4 | 8.8 | 11.5 | 12.3 |
| 11. | Number of companies reporting CCA | 323 | 468 | 705 | 445 | 177 | 17 |
| 12. | Rate of inflation (%) | 15.1 | 12.0 | 5.4 | 5.3 | 4.6 | 5.7 |

Definitions

Row 1, Historical cost profit: Gross trading profit plus other revenue, less depreciation, but before interest and taxation.

Row 2, Current cost profit adjustments: Depreciation, cost of sales and monetary working capital adjustments.

Row 5, Net tangible assets: Net assets, plus bank loans and overdrafts and certain other liabilities, less intangible assets and investments.

Row 7, Current cost adjustments: CCA revaluation of net tangible fixed assets and stocks.

Row 12, Rate of inflation: Change in the Retail Price Index, December on previous December.

More precise definitions are given in the source books.

*Source:* Business Statistics Office, *Business Monitor, MA3, Company Finance,* seventeenth issue 1986 and nineteenth issue 1988, HMSO.

Inflation rates are from Table 18.8 of the *Annual Abstract of Statistics, 1990,* HMSO.

current cost adjustment varied from 41.8 per cent in 1980 to 21.4 per cent in 1984 (the last year in which there was significant compliance with SSAP16). This magnitude of overall decrease is obviously important. The relative decline in its magnitude over time is related to the decline in the general inflation rate (row 12) from 15.1 per cent in 1980 to 4.6 per cent in 1984. Although CCA reflects *specific* rather than *general* changes in prices, a general inflation index does capture the average of a selection of specific prices, so that we might observe that high general inflation was associated with a higher average change in the specific prices used in CCA, if these are affected by similar economic factors.[25]

Rows 5 to 7 show the effects of CCA adjustment on net tangible assets in the year-end balance sheet. Again, the adjustment for current cost is of significant proportions: row 8 shows that the resulting increase in net tangible assets varied from 30.8 per cent in 1980 to 25.4 per cent in 1984. The decline over time can again be related to the decline in general inflation, but the decline is not so marked as in the case of profit because it is dominated by the re-measurement fixed assets, which last for many years so that their adjustment reflects the price changes over multiple years rather than just the most recent year.

The CCA adjustments decrease profit and increase assets relative to historical cost. Hence, the two types of adjustment reinforce one another in lowering the rate of return. Row 9 shows the historical cost rate of return and row 10 shows the CCA rate of return. The CCA return is always lower to a striking extent: less than half the historical cost rate in 1980 and three quarters of the historical cost rate in 1985. The rate of return is a popular measure of corporate performance, and the large and variable differences between rates of return based on different accounting measurement methods demonstrate the practical importance of the choice of method.

### 1.5.2 CPP in Turkey

A second illustration of the importance of accounting measurement uses an entirely different method, the use of general price-level indices

Table 1.4 *Accounting Performance Measures of Turkish Companies, 1982–90*

| Measure | Growth of Net Assets | Growth of Sales | EBIT/Net Assets | EAT/Net Worth | Long-term Debt/Net Assets |
|---|---|---|---|---|---|
| | % | % | % | % | % |
| Unadjusted | 57.7 | 56.2 | 32.4 | 25.5 | 22.8 |
| CPP-adjusted | 28.7 | 3.2 | 12.3 | 9.4 | 9.7 |

*Note:* EAT is Earnings after tax and interest; EBIT is Earnings before interest and tax. Net Assets includes long-term liabilities. Net Worth excludes long-term liabilities. All of the percentage rates are annual rates averaged across the thirty-seven companies in the sample.

to translate historical costs into units of current purchasing power, which is known as CPP accounting. This was explained briefly in Section 1.5.1 and is explored more fully in a later chapter. For the present, it is worth noting two important features of this method. First, it relies solely on general price-level indices rather than the changes of the specific prices of the individual items in the accounts, so that it is methodologically different from CCA. Second, it is concerned with adjusting for the changing purchasing power of the measurement unit, money, and is therefore more likely to be most relevant when inflation is high. In fact CPP accounting has been used in practice in hyper-inflationary economies, notably those in Latin America.[26] The present example is drawn from Turkey which suffered an average annual inflation rate of 49 per cent on the period 1982–90. Table 1.4 records the unadjusted historical cost results reported by thirty-seven of the largest Turkish companies during this period. These are then compared with results adjusted for inflation using a CPP method. The methodology is fully explained in Whittington et al. (1997), from which Table 1.4 is derived.

The first two columns of Table 1.4 show how growth rates can be affected by the change in the value of the measurement unit (money). Both growth measures are exaggerated by inflation, the greater distortion being that of growth of sales, which, unlike the net assets measure, does not reflect monetary values over a number of different years. The rate of return measures in the next two columns also suggest a drastic distortion due to inflation, with unadjusted average profit rates of 32.4 per cent and 25.5 per cent, whereas the adjusted levels are a more plausible 12.3 per cent and 9.4 per cent. The final column shows the gearing ratio, a popular measure of exposure to long-term borrowing, and this also appears to be distorted by inflation. The adjusted measure shows gearing less than half of the unadjusted measure. The difference is attributable to the fact that assets are measured in historical currency units, and adjusting them to current currency units increases the measure. Borrowing, on the other hand, is expressed in fixed amounts of monetary units, so that it is not appropriate to re-state its amount: if I borrowed £1, I have to repay £1 later, even though the purchasing power of £1 may be less at the time of repayment. This is the source of the 'gain on borrowing' that occurs in inflationary times, although the gain will be offset by interest payments if lenders anticipate inflation correctly at the inception of the loan.

### 1.5.3 Replacement Cost Profit in BP's Annual Report

Our final example of the practical importance of measurement comes from the accounts of BP, one of the largest oil companies in the world. Current accounting standards require that stocks (or in US and international terminology 'inventories') are measured at historical cost, on a FIFO (first-in-first-out, so that the oldest stocks are assumed to be used first) basis. Because the price of oil is volatile, BP believes that its operating margins are best measured by charging the replacement cost of stocks, rather than historical cost, against revenue from operations. Hence, it shows replacement cost profit per ordinary share as a key performance measure in its Annual Report (BP, 2015, p. 26) and provides a reconciliation of historical cost profit for the year to replacement cost profit (BP, 2015, p. 216). The difference between

Table 1.5 *BP's Reconciliation of Historical Cost Profit to Replacement Cost Profit*

| Year (ending 31 December) | 2011 | 2012 | 2013 | 2014 | 2015 |
|---|---|---|---|---|---|
| | | ($million) | | | |
| Profit for the year (historical cost) | 25,212 | 11,017 | 23,451 | 3,780 | (6,482) |
| Inventory holding (gains) losses | (1,800) | 411 | 230 | 4,293 | 1,320 |
| Replacement cost profit | 23,412 | 11,428 | 23,681 | 8,073 | (5,162) |

*Source:* BP Annual Report and Accounts.

the two profit measures is the 'holding gain or loss' on inventories (stocks) that is the difference between their historical cost and the replacement cost at the time when they were sold or used in production. The deduction of holding gains from historical cost profit will cause replacement cost profit to be lower and the removal of holding losses will raise it. The key components of the reconciliation are shown in Table 1.5.

BP's replacement cost adjustment is applied only to stocks and not to the depreciation of fixed assets, as would be required for a complete replacement cost measure of profit. Nevertheless, the result of this limited adjustment is significant, reducing the historical cost loss by more than one fifth in 2015, and more than doubling the profit in 2014. In the earlier three years, the adjustment is not as large as a proportion of historical cost profit, but it is variable in amount and direction. The variability of the direction is of particular interest. This arises because the price of oil and related products fluctuates and can go down (giving rise to holding losses in four of the five years) as well as up. This demonstrates the inadequacy of using general price-level indices as a proxy for specific prices (rather than as general adjustments for changes in the measurement unit, as in the CPP system). All of these years saw rises in general price indices (as shown in

Table 5.2), albeit typically at much lower levels than those experienced at the time of the CCA experiment, shown in Table 1.3, and the adjustment of stocks by general indices would have shown holding gains, at a low but steady rate, in all five years, rather than holding losses in four years and a holding gain in another. However, such 'gains' would have borne little relationship to the price of oil.

The three preceding examples should suffice to demonstrate the importance of the choice of measurement method in financial reporting. They also illustrate that the issue is important in different countries and in different economic conditions. The rest of this book is devoted to explaining the alternative measurement systems and analysing the rationale for choosing between them.

## 1.6 RELEVANCE TO CURRENT ISSUES

We have seen that measurement is an important issue in financial accounting. The choice of measure is by no means a simple matter even in apparently simple situations. Moreover, the choice has significant effects on key accounting measures, such as profit or assets employed. It is not surprising, therefore, that measurement has been hotly debated not only by accountants but also by all stakeholders in business enterprises whose interests are affected by the measures reported in the accounts. These include shareholders, lenders, regulators and tax authorities.

One of the earliest and probably the most long-running debate has been that over the appropriate measurement method for price regulation. This emerged in the US late in the nineteenth century when railroad prices were regulated and railroad companies sought to use replacement cost rather than the traditional historical cost to measure their assets in the accounts that were used as the basis for regulation (Boer, 1966). Replacement cost was typically higher than historical cost and so offered a higher asset value to be used to assess the profit and the depreciation that could be recovered in the price. Similar debates still continue today, for example in the privatised utility companies that are subject to price cap regulation in the UK (Whittington, 1998a) and in Australia.

Another topic of debate in many countries and at many times is the adjustment of accounts for inflation. We have seen that the problem of inflation is that the value of the measurement unit, money, changes significantly over time (declining in the case of inflation, and rising in the rarer case of deflation). As we have seen in the case of Turkey, this can result in significant distortions of asset values, profits and other measures that are used to evaluate the performance and state of the business entity. One solution to this problem is CPP accounting, which was illustrated earlier. The problem will be discussed further in Chapter 5. Extreme inflation emerged in Europe, notably in Germany, in the 1920s, when the basic ideas of the CPP method were developed, but it has occurred since in many countries, particularly those of Latin America, where CPP methods have been widely used.[27] There was worldwide inflation in the 1960s and 1970s, but mainly at less extreme levels than those that gave rise to the CPP system. This led to a fierce debate on 'inflation accounting' (more correctly 'price-change accounting') in which current cost accounting (CCA), as illustrated in Table 1.3 emerged temporarily as the officially favoured system. As we have seen, support for CCA evaporated in the UK (and in the other, mainly English-speaking, countries that had proposed to adopt it) when the rate of inflation subsided. In the case of the UK, the defection from CCA was also encouraged by the government's announcement that it did not propose to base Corporation Tax on the CCA results. The use of CCA would have increased deductible expenses for tax purposes for most companies, as indicated by the current cost adjustments in Table 1.3.[28] In debates over accounting, implications for wealth transfers, as in the case of price regulation, taxation, dividend payments and valuation by the financial markets, are never far away and tend to add passion to the argument.

More recently, there has been another fierce public debate about accounting measurement, that concerning fair value (FV). When the rate of inflation declined and CCA went out of fashion, there was still a need for some method of current valuation in accounts. Demand was increasing for accounts that reflected the current situation rather than the past, as embodied in historical cost. Thus, accounting standard-setters sought to introduce current values either as supplementary information (in the notes to the accounts) or, in some circumstances, as the measurement method used instead of historical cost. This was particularly true of accounting for financial instruments, whose use and variety expanded hugely in the last decade or so of the twentieth century. The complexity of these instruments sometimes made historical cost difficult to determine or (because of the high gearing involved and the volatility of market values) historical cost was patently inadequate as a means of describing the asset or obligation. The standard-setters decided that, in many circumstances, a current market value provided a more relevant measure of such assets (and liabilities). In the post-CCA period (the mid-1980s onwards) they chose to describe such a market value as *fair value* (FV), perhaps because the term had been used in the US for some time, but perhaps also partly because it avoided the adverse connotations of CCA, a current value method that had failed to gain support. The FV concept was first used in US standards (developed by the FASB) but was subsequently adopted by the international body, the IASC and its successor (from 2001) the IASB.[29]

If the standard-setters hoped that using FV rather than CCA would avoid controversy, they were sadly disappointed. There were two waves of controversy. The first was on a more technical level. It became apparent (after FASB published its standard on fair value measurement, FAS 157, in 2006 and the IASB endorsed its approach) that FV was assumed to represent a selling price. This was strongly opposed by preparers of accounts, particularly in Europe (where the EU required listed companies to adopt IASB standards from 2005 onwards), who objected to the idea of recording assets that they did not intend to sell (or obligations that they did not intend to settle) at market prices that were irrelevant and possibly non-existent. In particular, there was criticism of the 'day 1' profits that were recorded as a result of measuring assets (and in some cases liabilities) at fair value, rather than cost, at the point when they were acquired.

Some of these objections were based on the misapprehension that the IASB intended to require universal FV, whereas in fact FV applied in only a limited area and was often optional.[30] Nevertheless, they did raise questions about both the relevance and the reliability of FV.

These objections were usually directed at applications of FV other than to financial instruments, which were often assumed to have deep and liquid markets in which prices could be established reliably. However, the second, more serious wave of criticism of FV emerged from the Financial Crisis of 2007 onwards and was directed at the use, or alleged misuse, of FV to measure financial instruments. In a liquidity crisis, there may be no opportunity to sell, so the selling price will strictly be zero, despite an asset (such as a mortgage portfolio) having a value if it were retained (by letting the mortgages run off through repayment). Hence, some asserted that FV was irrelevant, and the IASB was persuaded to relax its restrictions on transferring financial instruments from its FV category to its amortised cost category. Others also argued that FV was unreliable, especially when 'marking to model' (using a valuation model to estimate the market price when no market price was directly observable) was used rather than 'marking to market'(using prices currently observed in active markets). It was believed this generated artificial volatility of asset values and profits, including 'day 1' profits which might never be realised. Some went further and argued that the artificial volatility generated by FV might have combined with the use of regulatory or contractual accounting ratios to cause the crisis itself. This may be a case of blaming the messenger for misinterpretation of the message, but at least it elevated the public's appreciation of the importance of accounting, and particularly accounting measurement, to new heights. The reader should, by now, be persuaded of the importance of measurement in financial accounting. FV and other current value measures will be discussed further in Chapters 4, 6 and 7.

## 1.7 PLAN OF THE REMAINING CHAPTERS

Chapter 2 discusses in greater depth the purpose and structure of financial statements. Chapter 3 discusses historical cost, the traditional measurement basis used in accounts. Chapter 4 then discusses and illustrates current value accounting, which has challenged historical cost in recent years. Chapter 5 then discusses the distinct problems of inflation and CPP accounting, which were introduced briefly in this chapter, and shows how inflation adjustment and current value are complementary rather than competing techniques. Chapter 6 returns to the theme of current value and discusses the many alternative measures of current value that are available. Chapter 7 then attempts to review the earlier discussion and concludes with an account of the current state of accounting practice with respect to measurement, particularly as embodied in International Financial Reporting Standards (IFRS).

NOTES

1 For example, Edwards and Bell (1961), in their classic treatise on the measurement of business income, stress the relevance of financial accounts to management's appraisal of its performance.

2 Introductions to management accounting will be found in Horngren et al. (2013), a popular introductory text, and Hopper et al. (2007), a collection of introductory essays on various aspects of the subject.

3 For example, the UK Accounting Standards Board's *Statement of Principles for Financial Reporting* (Accounting Standards Board, 1999, para. 1.3) lists seven categories of potential users of financial statements.

4 See e.g. Whittington (1994, 1998a).

5 Plantin et al. (2008) examine the potentially destabilising role of fair value accounting in the Financial Crisis.

6 The term *financial reporting* is used to define the financial statements, including narrative reports and supplementary disclosures. *Financial accounting* usually refers only to the principal financial statements (income statement, balance sheet and cash flow statement, together with the accompanying notes).

7 This was part of the proposed revision of the IASB's conceptual framework, the latest version of which is an exposure draft (International Accounting Standards Board, 2015). Stewardship is discussed in the context of the IASB's conceptual framework by Lennard (2007) and Whittington (2008a).

8 Most recently, this has been the case in the controversy surrounding the role of fair value in IASB standards, which has become an issue of international politics. The earlier debate on inflation accounting was equally fierce and was conducted at a political level as well as at the professional level (Tweedie and Whittington, 1984).

9 Meade (1978) discusses the merits of these alternatives, favouring the latter.

10 The current international standard on foreign currency translation, IAS21 (International Accounting Standards Board, 2005a), demonstrates these complexities.

11 The constant unit of purchasing power can be measured in a currency unit at any specific date, as a basis for constant purchasing power accounting (CPP). A popular special case is where the unit chosen is that measured at the *current* date, giving rise to *current* purchasing power (which also abbreviates as CPP). In practice, the current unit is almost invariably used because it has an obvious intuitive appeal to current users of accounts.

12 The measurement of financial instruments was prescribed by IAS39, which is currently being replaced by IFRS 9. Fair value is also prescribed or allowed by several other international standards.

13 SSAP 16 proved to be a false dawn. As we shall see later in this chapter, although it required only supplementary current cost disclosures and applied only to very large companies and those listed on stock exchanges, many companies failed to apply the standard. Its unpopularity led to its withdrawal before it became part of established practice.

14 Strictly, the basis of current cost is deprival value (value to the business), which is discussed in later chapters. In practice, for a profitable going concern, deprival value is usually current replacement cost.

15 The income statement is traditionally known as the *profit and loss account*. The new title has been introduced by the IASB to describe more accurately the content of the statement. However, there is still a degree of ambiguity surrounding the distinction between the 'Profit and Loss'

section of the income statement (broadly, the results of routine business transactions) and other gains and losses (such as changes in the value of fixed assets) which, added to profit or loss, give a measure of comprehensive income (i.e. income and gains from all sources).

16 The IASB has also encouraged the use of the description *statement of financial position* rather than the traditional *balance sheet*. However, we shall continue to use the traditional description because it is a more accurate and well-understood term. The balance sheet, as we shall see later, gives a very limited indication of financial position.

17 The measurement of fair value is the subject of an IASB (2011) standard (IFRS 13).

18 If there were liabilities in the example, this would refer to *net* assets, i.e. assets *minus* liabilities.

19 The original story (Whittington, 1981a) was designed to illustrate the problems specifically of inflation and illustrated the capital maintenance problem using a 'cash-to-cash' example in which no assets other than cash were held at the beginning or the end of the period. Even in this simplified case, the accounting options are varied and problematic.

20 The system was also recommended in many other countries, for similar reasons, at around that time. See Tweedie and Whittington (1984).

21 Of course, it will not buy as much, but that is indicated by the capital adjustment. If the £120 had been held over the full period, Fred would require £132 at the end to preserve his real capital. In fact, he has £12 less, and this is what is called a 'loss on holding money' in the more sophisticated price level adjustment systems that are discussed in later chapters.

22 The full sample is described in the *Business Monitor*. It included all companies above a size threshold and a random sample of smaller companies. The smaller companies that did not have stock exchange listings were not required to comply with SSAP16, although they could comply on a voluntary basis.

23 The events surrounding the failure of SSAP16 and similar experiments in other countries are discussed in Tweedie and Whittington (1997).

24 A complication is the 'monetary working capital adjustment', which was one of the more controversial elements of SSAP16. This is discussed in Whittington (1983) and Tweedie and Whittington (1984).

25 The correspondence would be far from perfect because general price level indices are usually based on prices of consumer goods, whereas the CCA adjustments applied by firms will reflect a higher weighting of capital goods, and the prices of these different types of asset do not necessarily move together.

26 Tweedie and Whittington (1984) provide an overview of these developments.

27 The history of inflation accounting is traced in Tweedie and Whittington (1984).

28 The BP example might seem to contradict this, but it relates to a period when prices (more specifically the price of oil) were not rising so rapidly. Also, the BP example refers only to stocks: depreciation of fixed assets would be increased significantly by the use of CCA and, because it reflects prices over a longer period (asset life) would be more likely to generate a more stable CCA adjustment.

29 An important milestone was the international standard IAS39, *Financial Instruments: Recognition and Measurement*, 1998 and subsequently revised, which required certain financial instruments to be measured at fair value. This was the outcome of a fierce debate in which some influential members of the IASC supported 'full fair value' for all financial instruments (Camfferman and Zeff, 2007, Chapter 11).

30 However, support for FV was apparent in much of the IASB's thinking and its decisions. This is discussed critically in Whittington (2008).

# 2 Fundamentals

## 2.1 INTRODUCTION

It was explained in Chapter 1 that this book is concerned with the problem of measurement in the financial accounts of companies, i.e. the accounts which are published, under statutory obligation, for the shareholders and other interested parties external to the company organisation. The two principal statements with which we shall be concerned are the statement of financial position (balance sheet) and the statement of financial performance (income statement).

Our task is to establish the nature of the problem which measurement poses for financial accounts, and to explain and evaluate the various methods which have been proposed to deal with it. The first stage of this analysis must be to establish the nature and purpose of financial accounts: without an understanding of this and the attendant problems, it is unlikely that we will understand the additional problems imposed by measurement. This first step will be attempted in this chapter.

## 2.2 FINANCIAL ACCOUNTS AND THEIR USES

The traditional function of financial accounts is that of *stewardship*.[1] In the case of a company, this implies that the board of directors, who are responsible for the management of the company's assets, gives a periodic account to the proprietors (the shareholders) of how they have carried out this function. In its narrowest traditional sense, this implies a statement of past transactions, in historical cost terms,[2] which provides a check on the honesty of the steward, but not necessarily on efficiency, which might be assessed in terms of how the current value of the company's assets has grown. Therefore, the assessment of efficiency is also an aspect of stewardship, particularly in the assessment of the extent to which past plans and expectations have been fulfilled.[3] For this purpose, current values may provide a better indication of the current state of the business than is provided by historical cost.

Current and prospective shareholders will also use the accounts to estimate future profitability, on which they will base their investment decisions. Long-term lenders will have a similar need. Thus, *decision-usefulness* from the perspective of long-term investors is also an important function of financial accounts. 'Decision-usefulness' has become increasingly important as the size and global reach of companies listed on stock exchanges has increased, thus widening the information gap between management and investors, and, in the view of some leading standard-setters, this is now the primary purpose of financial accounts.[4]

Apart from their use by long-term investors for decision making, accounts have traditionally been used by creditors, to assess the security for their loans, and creditor protection has been an important factor in accountants' application of conservative valuation principles. The perceived reliability of financial accounts that are prepared on the basis of generally accepted standards and certified by independent auditors has led to their widespread use in loan covenants: undertakings by borrowing entities to protect the creditor by keeping to certain levels of financial prudence. In most jurisdictions, the general public also has been given the right of access to company accounts through a public register. This reflects the fact that the general public may transact with the company (as suppliers, customers or employees) but also that there may be a wider public interest in the transactions of some businesses.

In recent years, the range of uses which company accounts are expected to meet has broadened considerably.[5] Some of these uses were outlined in Chapter 1. This development may partly be due to the growth of very large companies with diffused shareholdings and a consequent increase in the separation of ownership (shareholders) from control (directors). This has placed more responsibility on the financial accounts for communication between the two groups, whereas shareholders who exercise direct control, as for example in family-owned businesses, will have access to management information. This situation has been made more acute by the globalisation of capital markets, which means that investors are often not based in the same country or even the same continent as the businesses that they finance: globalisation has been a strong force behind the increasing worldwide adoption of international accounting standards set by the IASB. Another important factor has undoubtedly been the increased concern of government with the affairs of companies. This is most obvious in the field of taxation: income and corporation taxes typically give governments a claim on company profits which is of a similar order of magnitude to that of the dividends paid to shareholders.[6] Governments also create financial interests in companies by various investment incentive and regional development schemes, and accounting information has been used in the implementation of counter-inflationary price and dividend controls, in competition policy and in the regulation of public utility prices. Finally, other groups within the community such as employees and consumers are also showing an increased interest in the financial affairs of companies, which expresses the changing economic, political and social environment in which companies operate. Notably, much attention has been given recently to the concept of sustainability and how this can be supported by financial reporting.[7]

The result of these developments has been the recognition that accounts serve a wide variety of users and uses. This has long been recognised by some academic writers (notably H. C. Daines (1929), who can claim to be a pioneer of the user-oriented approach to the design of accounting information), but it has penetrated professional circles more recently. Historically, *The Corporate Report* (Accounting Standards Steering Committee, 1975) was an important development in the UK (as was its predecessor in the US, the Trueblood Report; Study Group on the Objectives of Financial Statements, 1973) and it provided a good summary of the user-oriented approach and its implications. Although *The Corporate Report* was a discussion document, and was not adopted as a statement of policy, it nevertheless emanated from a professional committee of high standing and provided a sharp contrast with the earlier narrow approach of the accounting profession in the UK.[8] Many of the proposals put forward in *The Corporate Report* were subsequently adopted in the government's Green Paper on *The Future of Company Reports*,[9] although this was not adopted in legislation at the time. However, economic and social pressures for wider disclosure continued and this was reflected in the widening of the disclosure requirements, particularly in the Directors' Report requirements of the Companies' Act (2006), which followed European Union requirements and the *Report of the Company Law Review Steering Group* (2001). There have been similar changes in the orientation of professional and governmental attitudes to financial reporting in the US,[10] although the American legislative framework, with the SEC (Securities and Exchange Commission) as the body that ultimately controls the form of the financial accounts of corporations listed on public exchanges, tends to emphasise decision-usefulness for investors rather than stewardship to shareholders (Bush, 2005).

The user orientation, with the investor seen as the representative user, underlies the conceptual frameworks of the leading accounting standard-setting bodies, notably the IASB which has gained widespread international support for its standards, more than 100 countries making use of them. This objective can embrace the concept of stewardship to shareholders, but it can also be interpreted more narrowly as prioritising *valuation* of the entity, as embodied in information relevant to predicting future cash flows, to achieve decision-usefulness for investors. Adopting the former, more inclusive, interpretation of decision-usefulness, the IASB proposed to withdraw the separate stewardship objective in its preliminary views on the revision of its conceptual framework (International Accounting Standards Board, 2006). Subsequently, following responses from within the European Union in particular, it reinstated stewardship in its exposure draft (International Accounting Standards Board, 2015).

The debate on the relative importance of *ex ante* decision-usefulness for investors and *ex post* stewardship for existing shareholders (or proprietors) continues. However, it is clear that both perspectives are important and are, to a significant extent, complementary: stewardship leads to pressures on management which can affect prospective returns to investors.

The movement towards user orientation has had two consequences. First, it has led to the idea that accounting information should be related to the investment decisions which users will make, and, since decisions are made in the present and relate to the present or future, rather than to the past, this has created dissatisfaction with historical cost as a valuation base (except where it can be shown to provide data which have predictive value) and a greater interest in current market values or values based upon an assessment of present opportunities and future prospects. This in turn has led to a conflict between reliability[11] and relevance. Historical cost data are more easily verified (e.g. by examining documents relating to purchase or sale) and are relatively objective,[12] in the sense that two independent accountants applying the same rules should arrive at a similar measure. Hence, historical cost is relatively reliable,[13] but it is often argued that reliability is of no value when the data themselves are irrelevant.[14] Current value data, obtained from markets which may be illiquid or by estimating 'economic' present values derived by discounting prospective receipts, may be less easy to verify and less objective (since they depend upon what might happen rather than what did happen), but they are obviously relevant to decisions which are made in the present and will have consequences in the future. Historical cost may, of course, have greater relevance in the case of stewardship, where holding management to account for outcomes relative to past expectations is particularly important, and verifiability and objectivity may be particularly desirable properties because the steward (the board of directors that issues the financial reports) may be tempted to use subjective judgement to report performance in a favourable light. However, the differing requirements of value relevance to investors and stewardship to proprietors (existing shareholders) are a matter of emphasis rather than fundamental difference. Stewardship will often require an assessment of the current condition of the business, which will be informed by its future prospects, and decision makers will often have regard to the past record of management and the quality of corporate governance in forming expectations. Moreover, existing shareholders are also investors (they have the option to sell their shares or buy more) so that they need both types of information.

A second consequence of user orientation is the recognition that there is a variety of users and uses, each of which might have different information requirements, as is apparent in the tension between stewardship and investor decision-usefulness. This raises the possibility that there may be a conflict of interest between different users, whose information needs differ, if financial accounts are to be of the 'general purpose' type. A greater degree of disclosure will help to overcome such problems, by providing more detail or even reporting alternative valuation bases, but this will entail additional costs on both the producers of accounts (the cost of producing the additional information) and on the users (the cost of interpreting more complex information).[15] The various options or requirements in current accounting standards that alternative valuations should be provided in the notes to the accounts,[16] rather than as an integral part of the main financial statements, provide an illustration of practical attempts to resolve the latter problem.

It might, of course, be argued that there is a substantial area of overlap between the information requirements of various users, and that it is more fruitful to concentrate on these areas of common interest than on the differences. It is certainly the case that such matters as the value of the economic resources commanded by a business, the means by which this is financed, and the capacity of the business to add to those resources from both internal (retained profit) and external (borrowing and new issues) sources are of interest to a wide variety of users. However, the traditional 'general purpose' financial statements, the balance sheet (position statement) and the profit and loss account (performance statement), calculated broadly on historical cost principles, do not provide complete information. This is partly because historical cost accounts are not well designed to meet decision needs, since decisions are made in the present and have consequences in the future, and the relationship between historical costs and present values will be weakened by changing prices. Another contributory factor, which would apply to any attempt to devise a multi-purpose system, is that the wide variety of uses implies a wide range of additional information requirements which might have little in common. This problem is compounded by uncertainty, which implies that *ex post* measures of income and value do not necessarily equal *ex ante* measures,[17] and that the present economic value of an asset or a firm (i.e. discounted present value of future receipts) cannot be established objectively in the absence of perfect and complete markets.[18] Thus, uncertainty adds to both the variety and the subjectivity of the available valuation methods. The IASB's standard on disclosures relating to financial instruments, IFRS 7 (2005), illustrates the range of alternative disclosures, such as sensitivity analyses, which standard-setters have adopted to address uncertainty. This need for additional disclosures may be reinforced by the existence of disequilibrium or imperfect markets,[19] which will add to the subjectivity of current market values and will imply that replacement cost (buying price) can diverge from net realisable value (selling price).

Thus, an attempt to report the 'true' value of the firm's assets or its profit for the period will encounter the problem of uncertainty, and a single choice from amongst the variety of measures available is unlikely to meet the needs of all potential users. In the face of this difficulty, some writers[20] have concluded that accountants should not attempt to be valuers, but should concentrate on supplying relevant information to the user, who will estimate his own subjective value. An alternative approach would be for the accountant to attempt to calculate such summary variables as accounting income but to provide different measures for different potential uses: this approach is exemplified in the 'different incomes for different purposes' literature.[21] The narrowest approach of all is to report a single measure of income (or similar summary measure of economic performance) and to justify this on the ground that it is the best proxy or 'surrogate' for the 'true' measure, which would satisfy all users in the absence of uncertainty or market imperfections. There has been a considerable debate on the validity of the surrogate approach to measuring economic income.[22] So far, the surrogate relationship has been shown to hold only under circumstances which are so restrictive that the relationship is unlikely to be a suitable basis for accounting practice.[23] There is also a well-developed literature by economists and accountants, exploring the relationship between the accounting rate of return and the economic rate of return (the internal rate of return or IRR).[24] There is an exact relationship, but only over the complete life of the firm: hence, this is not relevant to annual rates of return based on a single year's outcome, which is the usual context of annual financial accounts.

However, although it may not be possible to measure precisely such concepts as income and capital, they are crucial components of the traditional form of accounts (although the substance of the actual measurement has traditionally left much to be desired) and it seems likely that their measurement will be an important step in many uses of accounts. It is therefore important to clarify these concepts and their traditional rôle in accounting before considering the effects on accounts of alternative measurement methods. This is the purpose of the next section of this chapter.

## 2.3 INCOME, VALUE AND CAPITAL

The traditional financial accounts of a business enterprise consist of a statement of financial position (balance sheet) and a statement of financial performance (profit and loss account). We shall refer to these as the *balance sheet* and the *income statement* respectively. The use of the term income statement is intended to convey the fact that this statement can include non-trading sources of income (such as revaluation or gain on the disposal of fixed assets) whereas profit and loss suggests a statement that is restricted to income from trading or other core business activities. The balance sheet and the income statement can be 'articulated' if the income statement reports *comprehensive income*, which includes all gains and losses for the period. Articulation implies that the income for a period recorded in the income statement equals the change in net worth in the balance sheet during the same period, in the absence of capital introductions (such as new share issues) and withdrawals (such as dividends) by the proprietors. This requires that there should be no transfers to or from capital reserves such as are often associated with methods of revaluation. Articulation is possible because both statements are derived from a common double entry system.[25] The comprehensive income measure that achieves this articulation is sometimes referred to as *clean surplus income*. The two basic statements and their articulation are illustrated as follows.

The balance sheet is a statement of assets and claims at a point in time:

Balance Sheet[26] of firm $A$ at time $t$

| *Claims* | £ | *Assets* | £ |
|---|---|---|---|
| Proprietor's | | Non-monetary (i.e. | |
| interest | $P$ | fluctuating money value) | $N$ |
| Liabilities | $L$ | Monetary (i.e. fixed money | |
| | | value) | $M$ |
| | $\overline{P+L}$ | | $\overline{N+M}$ |

Since the proprietor's interest is a residual or 'equity' claim on the assets of the business (sometimes referred to as net worth or net assets), we have the definition:

$$P_t \equiv N_t + M_t - L_t \qquad (2.1)$$

where $t$ indicates the common point in time, and the 'balance sheet identity':

$$P_t + L_t \equiv N_t + M_t \qquad (2.2)$$

which ensures that the balance sheet always balances due to the residual nature of the proprietor's interest, which is increased by any gains and decreased by any losses.[27] There are two features of this identity which are extremely important in considering measurement in accounting.

First, money is conventionally used as the unit of measurement. If, therefore, money fluctuates in value and different components of the balance sheet are measured in units of different value, it might be argued that the residual claim (Proprietors' interest, $P$) is not measured in homogeneous units, so that it is not legitimate to aggregate the components of the balance sheet. Constant Purchasing Power Accounting (CPP) (which is discussed further in Chapter 5) is a system which has been advocated to overcome this difficulty.

Second, the valuation of assets and liabilities is crucial in determining the amount of the residual claim, $P$. Valuation is the process of translating assets into monetary units. We have therefore distinguished between those assets, such as cash or deposits, which have a clearly defined fixed money value, $M$, and those assets whose values in monetary terms will fluctuate, $N$. This distinction is useful in theoretical discussions about measurement, particularly those concerning inflation accounting, although in practice there may be difficulties in assigning certain assets to either category. For the moment, we shall assume that liabilities, $L$, are also of fixed monetary value, although there are certain cases in which this does not occur: most obviously that of long-term fixed-interest loans, whose market value (at which they might be redeemed) fluctuates inversely with the rate of interest.

The balance sheet identity holds at any point in time. We may therefore difference any pair of balance sheets, relating to the same accounting entity at different points in time, to produce a self-balancing statement of how the financial position has changed over the period intervening between the two balance sheet dates:

$$N_{t+1} + M_{t+1} \equiv L_{t+1} + P_{t+1} \qquad (2.3)$$

and deducting (2.2) gives

$$(N_{t+1} - N_t) + (M_{t+1} - M_t) \equiv (L_{t+1} - L_t) + (P_{t+1} - P_t) \qquad (2.4)$$

This relationship is the basis of the flow of funds statement, which can be an important financial statement in its own right,[28] but it is also the basis of a statement which has, historically, been of more importance, the income statement. As stated earlier, in a firm with no withdrawal or injection of funds by proprietors or other 'capital' adjustments to the proprietors' account, the change in proprietors' interest is solely attributable to the income of the period. Rearranging (2.4), 'clean surplus' income may then be defined[29] as

$$(P_{t+1} - P_t) \equiv (N_{t+1} - N_t) + (M_{t+1} - M_t) - (L_{t+1} - L_t) \qquad (2.5)$$

The appendix to this chapter provides a simple numerical illustration of these algebraic relationships.

We should note certain features of this definition of income, which will be of great importance in the subsequent discussion of measurement. Income measurement is dependent upon the measurement conventions incorporated in the balance sheets. Thus, the assumption that the unit of measurement should be homogeneous will be violated if all figures in both balance sheets are not measured in the same units. Equally, the valuation conventions used in measuring the assets and liabilities in both balance sheets will affect the income measure, over-valuation of assets in the closing position statement and under-valuation in the opening statement both leading to the over-statement of profit. It should particularly be stressed that income measurement requires consistent measurement between two balance sheets as well as within each balance sheet. Since the two balance sheets refer to different points in time, there is a possibility (in practice, a probability) that the purchasing power of the monetary unit (as measured by a general consumer price index) will have changed between the two dates, and that the relative prices of specific assets will also have changed. The problems of recording and isolating the effects of general and specific price changes have been the central concern of the debate on inflation accounting. Adherents of various forms of constant purchasing power (CPP) accounting have sought to deal primarily with the general purchasing power problem, and adherents of various forms of current cost accounting (CCA) and, more recently, of fair value have sought to deal mainly with the problem of specific price changes, whilst adherents of real terms accounting have attempted to deal simultaneously with both problems.

The accountant's method of calculating income is, superficially, consistent with that of the economist, described in the next paragraph: income is the surplus net worth (proprietor's interest) accruing during the period after maintaining opening capital (net worth) intact.[30] However, accounting practice has traditionally deviated from the 'clean surplus' approach, adding some gains and losses direct to proprietors' capital rather than passing them through the income statement. Moreover, the valuation conventions used by the accountant in measuring opening and closing net worth have traditionally differed from those of the economist, the former preferring historical cost, modified by conservatism, as being a relatively objective basis for practical implementation, and the latter preferring current market values or net present values based on discounting prospective returns, as being more relevant to decision making.[31]

The most widely quoted economist's definition of income is that of Hicks (1946). His concern is with individual income, defined as the amount that can be spent during a period whilst maintaining intact the economic position (or 'capital') of the consumer at the beginning of the period. Hicks offers three definitions of income, each embodying a different concept of the capital to be maintained:

1. 'Income No. 1 is ... the maximum amount which can be spent during a period if there is to be an expectation of maintaining intact the capital value of prospective receipts (in money terms)'.

2. 'Income No. 2 . . . (is) . . . the maximum amount the individual can spend this week, and still expect to be able to spend the same amount in each ensuing week'.

3. 'Income No. 3 must be defined as the maximum amount of money which the individual can spend this week, and still expect to be able to spend the same amount *in real terms* in each ensuing week'.

The first definition is closest to the accountants approach: the capital value to be maintained at the end of the period is equal to that held at the beginning. However, the method of measuring capital is not that used by the accountant: it is a forward-looking present value based on discounting expected future receipts.

The second definition requires the maintenance of prospective expenditure rather than capital value, so that the capital to be maintained is represented by the expected future stream of receipts rather than its capitalised value. When interest rates remain constant, there is no difference between the two definitions, but when interest rates change, the two resulting measures of income will differ. For example, if interest rates rise, a lower capital value will be required to generate a given level of expected receipts, so that end-of period capital values will be lower, reducing 'No. 1' income by a loss due to interest rate changes. 'No. 2' income will not be affected by the interest change because expected receipts are unchanged.

The third definition allows for inflation: the difference between expenditure in *monetary* terms (as in definitions No. 1 and 2) and *real* terms (command over real goods and services rather than monetary units). This issue is also of concern to the accountant and is discussed in Chapter 5.

Each of these definitions is an *ex ante* concept, adopting the forward-looking approach, using the information and expectations that existed at the beginning of the period, which is ideally relevant to decision making. There is a parallel set of three *ex post* concepts, defining the income of the past week from the perspective of the end of the week, which is clearly of more relevance to the financial accountant, who is typically concerned to report past events in accordance with his traditional 'stewardship' function. However, as Kaldor (1955) points out, even the *ex post* measures involve the estimation of future events, in order to assess 'the capital value of prospective receipts' (No. 1 definition) or the expectation of the amount available for expenditure in subsequent weeks (definitions Nos. 2 and 3). Thus, although the No. 1 definition might superficially appear to be similar to the accountant's traditional method of calculating income for a firm,[32] the underlying valuation methods are very different. Not only is the economist's definition of income more subjective than the accountant's, which leads to greater uncertainty about the valuation of assets at any point in time, but also, under conditions of uncertainty, *ex post* valuations will not necessarily equal *ex ante* valuations. Thus the estimate of the income for a period will depend upon the state of knowledge at the time when the estimate is made. In the case of an *ex post* measure made at the end of a period, at, say, time $t + 1$, this means that the estimate of opening net worth at time $t$ may be different when viewed from time $t + 1$ than it was when viewed from the state of knowledge at time $t$. Thus, the capital to be maintained intact (net worth at time $t$) is not unambiguously determined and we have to make a decision as to how to treat the windfall gain or loss,[33] which is the source of the discrepancy between the two evaluations of opening net worth.

It might seem that the treatment of windfalls is a trivial issue, but in fact it is central to the economist's model of income, because, apart from windfalls and assuming a constant rate of discount, the income of a period is simply the opening present value, multiplied by the discount rate. The formal definition of present value (PV) is

$$V_0 = \sum_{t=1}^{n} \frac{Q_t}{(1+r)^t} \tag{2.6}$$

where  $V_0$ = present value at time zero

$Q_t$ = cash receipts (positive)

or payments (negative) $t$ periods hence

$r$ = discount rate per period

If we assume certainty or correct expectations, one period hence, and if the cash receipt of the period $Q_1$ is not consumed, we will have

$$V_1 = \sum_{t=2}^{n} \frac{Q_t}{(1+r)^{t-1}} + Q_1 = V_0(1+r) \tag{2.7}$$

This demonstrates that, in these circumstances, closing present value is opening present value increased by the discount rate, and that income, which is the difference between the opening and closing present values is therefore

$$Y = V_1 - V_0 = V_0 r \tag{2.8}$$

Thus, from knowledge of the net present value and the discount rate, we can infer the income for the period (and, with additional assumptions about reinvestment, for all future periods) in the special case in which initial expectations are fulfilled.

When expectations are not fulfilled, windfalls will play a crucial rôle in *ex post* evaluation, since they comprise deviations from previously planned returns. The construction of an *ex post* accounting income measure suitable for the evaluation of deviations from previous plans is one of the objectives of financial accounts assumed by Edwards and Bell (1961) in their classic work on business income measurement. This comparison of outcome with previous expectation is primarily a *stewardship* use of accounts.

Another important feature of the economist's definition of income is now apparent. If we know present value, it seems likely that, for many purposes, notably for *valuation* of the business for *investor decisions*, we shall not require an income measure, since present value summarises in present terms all the future flows which are expected to occur.[34] The investment decision rule derived from capital budgeting theory is to accept investments whose present value exceeds initial cost: no estimate of income is required. Attempts to make investment decisions on the basis of expected profits or rates of return are cumbersome and less satisfactory from a theoretical standpoint.[35] Even the internal rate of return method of investment appraisal, which is derived from the basic discounting relationship,[36] is generally less satisfactory than the net present value method.[37] An important example of a case in which knowledge of net present value would render income measurement redundant is share valuation, if we assume that the shareholder's valuation is the present value of the future dividends which he expects to receive from ownership of a share.

However, the fact that knowledge of net present value under conditions of certainty might make income measurement redundant for some purposes does not make it redundant under conditions of uncertainty or for all purposes. We have already seen that, in conditions in which expectations are not fulfilled, windfall gains and losses measure the effect of these changes in expectations, so that they (and therefore their separation from anticipated income) provide information relevant to *ex post* evaluation and control. More importantly, we do not usually know net present value because that requires knowledge of future returns which are uncertain and require estimation which may involve the use of past income data. Hence, an income measure may be an important input into the estimation of present value. This takes us away from the realm of the 'Hicks No. 1' capital maintenance approach, and towards that of the 'Hicks Nos. 2 and 3' consumption maintenance approach stated earlier and described briefly, in the context of accounting, in Chapter 1. If we can estimate a 'standard stream' of constant periodic consumption, in the case of individuals, or distributions to shareholders, in the case of companies, which is expected to be maintainable[38] over the definite future, we have a very simple means of assessing present value. It is well known that, in the case of a perpetual constant stream of expected receipts, at the rate of $\bar{Q}$ per period, expression (2.6) reduces to

$$V_0 = \frac{\bar{Q}}{r} \tag{2.9}$$

Thus the present value of the equity interest in the firm is the standard stream income per period, attributable to equity, divided by the appropriate discount rate, $r$. The estimation of the appropriate discount rate is, of course, a difficult problem, especially when we introduce risk into the analysis[39] Therefore, it is possible to argue that the accountant's role should stop with the estimation of $\bar{Q}$, leaving the valuation problem to the shareholder. Furthermore, it is possible that the accountant should concentrate on providing information relevant to the estimation of $\bar{Q}$, rather than attempting a precise estimate.[40]

The design of the accounting system explicitly to report a measure of Hicks No. 2 or 3 standard stream income is a formidable undertaking because of the subjectivity involved in estimating future returns. Scott (1976) and Black (1980, 1993) have made some suggestions as to how this might be done in order to help investors, although they inevitably involve a large dependence on assumptions about the future, which would be difficult for auditors to verify and would be particularly troublesome in stewardship uses.[41] The difficulties inherent in this approach have led others to advocate some form of cash flow reporting,[42] although this still encounters the problem of forecasting future events. Some of the contributors to the debate on inflation accounting in Britain, particularly as regards the gearing and monetary working capital adjustments (such as Gibbs, 1976), seemed to be concerned with liquidity rather than profitability and came close to advocating forms of cash flow accounting,[43] although they continued to use the language of income measurement (e.g. referring to the variable of central interest as a profit measure). However, if they *were* really concerned with income measurement it seems to be with a 'standard stream' measure of the Hicks No. 2 or 3 variety, rather than with the Hicks No. 1 capital maintenance type which emerges more naturally from the methods used traditionally by accountants. The Sandilands Report's emphasis on the predictive value of current cost operating profit might be interpreted in this light, as an example of standard stream income measurement.[44]

We may summarise the main points of the preceding discussion of business income measurement as follows:

1. There are two basic models of income, one based upon capital maintenance and one based upon consumption maintenance, or, in the case of a company, dividend maintenance.

2. The former model, capital maintenance, is, formally at least, consistent with the manner in which accountants have traditionally measured income, but the valuation basis used by accountants has traditionally been historical cost, whereas economists based their model on current values. In a world characterised by uncertainty and imperfect markets, the economist's ideal method of calculation is ambiguous and we face a choice between various current entry values (purchase prices, or replacement costs), current exit values (selling, less costs of disposal) and present values (discounted present values of returns expected from use in the ordinary course of the business). All of these measures involve a degree of subjectivity, which is particularly acute in the case of present values. The choice between measures might be expected to differ as between different individual users and different uses.

3. The latter model, consumption maintenance, is burdened with a strong element of expectations. Clearly, the maximum amount which can be consumed (or distributed) per period over an indefinite future depends crucially upon expectations about purchase prices, selling prices and productivity. The capital maintenance approach can at least hope to use current market prices, which are observable, but the consumption maintenance approach is entirely dependent upon subjective expectations, unless it is to resort to arbitrary assumptions.[45] On the other hand, the consumption maintenance approach does avoid the problem of assessing current values where reliable market prices are not observable. An alternative route out of this dilemma might be to abandon accruals-based income measurement entirely and resort to a performance statement based on cash flows, with both *ex ante* projections and *ex post* statements of actual cash flows, such as those proposed by Ijiri (1979) and Lee (1979), although this might raise a number of new problems.[46]

4. The reservations about income measurement expressed earlier indicate that we are unlikely to be able to measure a single general purpose income number under the conditions which prevail in the real world in which practising accountants operate. Moreover, if markets were sufficiently complete and reliable to yield the valuations necessary to measure such a number, there would be a strong case for using the balance sheet (based on appropriate current market measures) rather than the income statement to value a business or a share in it, which is the central concern of the 'decision-usefulness' approach to assessing the usefulness of financial accounts. Thus, we do not have a simple standard by which to judge alternative measurement techniques. It is quite possible that different techniques will be satisfactory in different circumstances or for different purposes, so that the choice of accounting technique can be viewed as a problem of social choice, involving judgement between the competing claims of different users of accounts. However, we can at least hope to ascertain whether particular techniques live up to the claims made for them and to identify the precise assumptions which are necessary for this to be the case.

## 2.4 CONCLUSION

In this chapter, we have considered some of the central problems of financial accounting. It is clear that, even in the absence of changing prices, accounting faces serious difficulties in a world characterised by uncertainty and imperfect markets and by the competing claims of different users of accounting information. Thus, it is not surprising that the debate on measurement has become inextricably linked with the debate on the other problems of accounting. Such questions as how to value fixed assets are related both to our fundamental model of how to measure capital and income and to our view on how to allow for the effects of price changes on those measurements.

It is also clear that there is not a single model of accounting, or a single summary measure, such as an income number, which will meet the needs of all users and uses of accounts in all circumstances.

Thus, our subsequent review of the techniques of measurement, and of the debate on the subject, is not likely to lead to the emergence of an ideal general solution. Indeed, one possible criticism of the conduct of the debate on measurement, and indeed on other aspects of accounting, is that the participants have tended to cling rigidly to their own narrowly based 'solutions', without recognising the merits of alternative methods in alternative situations. What we can hope to do is to identify the assumptions upon which alternative techniques are based, to consider the soundness of the reasoning which derives them from those assumptions, and to consider the uses and the circumstances in which they are appropriate.

### APPENDIX: A NUMERICAL EXAMPLE

This numerical example is an extension of that given in Chapter 1. We continue to assume that Fred has a stock of 20 pineapples at the end of the period. These stocks are assumed to be worth £20 at historical cost (both selling value and wholesale value being higher). We add a liability to the example by assuming that Fred financed his business partly by borrowing £50 from his Aunt Mabel. This additional claim reduces the amount of Fred's own residual claim as proprietor of the business.

The relevant facts are now:

1. Fred has started the period with £100 in cash, of which £50 was lent by Aunt Mabel and £50 was his own (proprietor's) capital.
2. He then bought 100 pineapples for £1 each.
3. The wholesale price of pineapples then rose to £1.25p each.
4. He then sold 80 pineapples for £1.50p each, yielding £120 in cash.

The algebraic accounting relations stated in equations (2.1)–(2.5) in the text are neutral as to the valuation system used. We shall illustrate them using the historical cost method since this is still the most widely practiced system, and is also simple in application, avoiding such problems as the re-statement of proprietor's interest to allow for changing prices.

Historical Cost Accounts

Balance Sheet at $t$ (start of period)

| Claims | | £ | Assets | | £ |
|---|---|---|---|---|---|
| Proprietor's Capital | $P$ | 50 | Cash | $M$ | 100 |
| Loan (Aunt Mabel) | $L$ | 50 | | | |
| | | 100 | | | 100 |

Balance Sheet at $t + 1$ (end of period)

| Claims | | £ | Assets | | £ |
|---|---|---|---|---|---|
| Proprietor's Capital | $P$ | 90 | Stock | $N$ | 20 |
| Loan (Aunt Mabel) | $L$ | 50 | Cash | $M$ | 120 |
| | | 140 | | | 140 |

It can easily be seen that the balance sheet identities (2.1), (2.2) and (2.3) hold for both balance sheets. The horizontal (side-by-side) format used here emphasises the identity. The vertical format used in the previous chapter is possibly more easily understood and is commonly used in practice.

Flow of Funds Computation (period $t$ to $t + 1$)

| Sources | £ | Uses | £ |
|---|---|---|---|
| $(P_{t+1} - P_t)$ | 40 | $(N_{t+1} - N_t)$ | 20 |
| $(L_{t+1} - L_t)$ | 0 | $(M_{t+1} - M_t)$ | 20 |
| | 40 | | 40 |

This demonstrates that identity (2.4) holds. A simple rearrangement in vertical format is:

Flow of Funds Statement (period $t$ to $t + 1$)

| | £ |
|---|---|
| *Source of Funds* | |
| Net funds from trading operations | 40 |
| *Uses of Funds* | |
| Increase in stocks | 20 |
| Increase in cash balance | 20 |
| | 40 |

There are no transactions on the proprietor's capital account, so the increase in its balance (£40) must be the trading profit (identity (2.5)).

Income Statement for the period $t$ to $t + 1$

|  |  | £ |
|---|---|---|
| Sales |  | 120 |
| *Less* Cost of goods sold* |  | 80 |
|  | Profit | 40 |

\* Purchases £100, less closing stock £20. Note that, because the historical cost basis has been used, the accounts do not reflect the change in the wholesale price of pineapples subsequent to their purchase.

The cash flow statement has recently been established as an additional financial statement, preferred to the flow of funds statement because it offers a different view of the entity's performance, free of the accrued assets and liabilities reported in the balance sheet and therefore free of the problems of measuring them. As its name suggests, the cash flow statement summarises the entity's cash transactions for a period. In its purest form, the so-called direct method, it summarises the cash transactions:

Cash Flow Statement for the period $t$ to $t + 1$

|  | £ |
|---|---|
| Cash Balance at $t$ | 100 |
| *Add*: Cash received from Sales | 120 |
|  | 220 |
| *Less*: Cash paid for Stock | 100 |
| Cash Balance at $t + 1$ | 120 |

In more complex businesses, the 'indirect method' is sometimes a more convenient way of deriving the cash flow statement. This involves starting with the accrual-based income statement and adding back the accrued assets and liabilities, as follows:

Cash Flow Statement for the period $t$ to $t + 1$

|  | £ |
|---|---|
| Cash Balance at $t$ | 100 |
| *Add*: Net Cash Inflow from Operations | 20 |
| Cash Balance at $t + 1$ | 120 |

In this simple case, net cash from operations is calculated as operating profit (£40), less the amount invested in stocks during the period (£20). In more realistic cases, there will be adjustments for depreciation and other accruals that affect the profit calculation but not cash flow.

Another complication of cash flow statements is the definition of cash. This will invariably include current bank balances, but other short-term financial instruments may be regarded as having equivalent liquidity and these 'cash equivalents' are sometimes included in the 'bottom line' balance of the cash flow statement, rather than as investments.

NOTES

1 It is notable that the first study of inflation accounting, an important measurement issue, published by the Institute of Chartered Accountants in England and Wales, was entitled *Accounting for Stewardship in a Period of Inflation* (Institute of Chartered Accountants in England and Wales, Research Committee, 1968).

2 The historical cost convention is usually modified by the conservative principle of 'cost or market value, whichever is the lower' in the case of stocks and work-in-progress and more recently 'impairment tests' for certain other assets have been required by accounting standard-setters such as the IASB.

3 This aspect of the role of accounting features particularly in the work of Edwards and Bell (1961), which is one of the most important contributions to the theory of measurement in accounting and will be discussed in later chapters.

4 For example, in the IASB's proposed revision of its conceptual framework (International Accounting Standards Board, 2015).

5 Although this is written mainly with the UK in mind, the history of accounting in the US is very similar, as is that in the rest of the English-speaking world, and more recently the forces of globalisation and the consequent spread of international regulation have extended the similarities to many other regions of the world.

6 Taxes on company profits usually take two forms: profit taxes levied directly on company profits (as in the case of the UK Corporation Tax) and income taxes levied on the dividends and interest payments to investors.

7 Sustainability includes environmental sustainability but also social and economic sustainability. It was strongly advocated by the Brundtland Report (United Nations, 1987) and sustainability reporting guidelines have been developed subsequently by the independent GRI group. These developments are summarised in Jones (2010).

8 For example, the recommendations on accounting principles (ICAEW, 1952) which were still used at the time.

9 Secretary of State for Trade (1977).

10 The Trueblood Committee Report (Study Group on the Objectives of Financial Statements, 1973) was in many respects the US counterpart to *The Corporate Report* and served as a starting point for most subsequent developments in financial reporting in the US, notably the Financial Accounting Standards Board's Conceptual Framework programme. Zeff (2016) provides a comprehensive history of the evolution of the objectives of financial accounting, particularly with respect to accounting standards in the US. More recent corporate social responsibility disclosures have been a direct response of preparers of accounts to user demand (Moser and Martin, 2012).

11 The IASB, in its revision of its conceptual framework, has chosen to replace reliability with 'representational faithfulness (International Accounting Standards Board, 2015). This has proved to be controversial (Whittington, 2008), so here we retain the previous description, reliability, as being clearer.

12 The most noted advocate of historical cost on this and related grounds is Ijiri (1971).

13 But not an identical measure, because the application of accrual conventions, such as the matching of costs to revenues, and the recognition of revenue itself, usually involves a degree of subjective judgement.

14 See R. L. Mathews (1965) for a well-known statement of this view in the context of inflation accounting.

15 A critique of reporting a variety of valuation bases, on the grounds that this leads to unacceptable complexity for the user of accounts, was provided in a classic work by Chambers (1966, particularly Chapters 7 and 8). A useful summary of the information economics approach to accounting, which treats accounting information as an economic commodity, will be found in the American Accounting Association Statement (1977, pp. 21–25).

16 For example, IFRS 7, the current IASB standard (2005) on disclosures relating to financial instruments, requires that the fair value of each class of financial instruments be disclosed (para. 25).

17 Barton (1974) provides a critique of the economist's income concept as a model for accountants, under conditions of uncertainty.

18 See Bromwich (1977a) and Beaver and Demski (1979). Complete markets exist when there are markets for all commodities in all possible states of the world, so that all uncertainties can be insured against by dealing in futures markets.

19 Bromwich (1975a) examines some of the implications for current value accounting of imperfect markets. More recently, the debate on fair value accounting has led to discussion of the consequences of illiquid markets (Plantin et al., 2008).

20 Bromwich (1977a), Peasnell (1977) and Beaver and Demski (1979) were early advocates of this view.

21 See Whittington (1981a) for a survey of literature on income measurement.

22 See Barton (1974, 1976), Revsine (1970, 1976),Cook and Holzmann (1976), Kay (1976), Peasnell (1982) and Edwards et al. (1987).

23 See Revsine (1976).

24 Path-breaking studies were Kay (1976) and Peasnell (1982), and there was a series of papers in the *American Economic Review* following a paper by Fisher and McGowan (1983). This literature is surveyed in Whittington (1997).

25 G. Macdonald (1974a) suggests that this articulation of accounts has had a restrictive influence on the development of accounting, by preventing the use of different valuation bases for different statements. He argues that a statement of financial position (balance sheet) might be most

informative if it reported current sale values, whereas a performance
statement might be more informative if it were on a current cost basis
(deprival value, which is discussed in later chapters). There was a shift in
the focus of accounting and auditing, from the balance sheet, which was
regarded as the primary financial statement during the first three decades
of the twentieth century, to the profit and loss account, which receives
primary emphasis today (Chatfield, 1974). More recently, the IASB has
been criticised for allegedly attempting to reintroduce a 'balance sheet
approach' through its emphasis on fair value (Penman, 2007). The 'clean
surplus' models associated particularly with Ohlson (1995), on the other
hand, demonstrate how the balance sheet and the income statement can
be complementary to one another, if prepared on a consistent basis.

26 The format adopted here is the traditional horizontal form as used in the
UK, with claims on the left side and assets on the right. In the US,
traditional practice has been to put assets on the left and claims on the
right. More recent practice in all countries has favoured the vertical
format, which sums assets, deducts liabilities to produce a 'net assets'
figure and then presents the equity (proprietors') interest as a balancing
item, equalling net assets. The later approach is widely used and probably
informative to readers, but the horizontal format has advantages for
pedagogic purposes.

27 The notation used here was originated by R. J. Chambers, but Chambers
would not have approved of all the uses to which it would subsequently
be put, because he was strongly committed to certain stringent
measurement criteria which he claimed to be met only by his 'CoCoA'
(Continuously Contemporary Accounting) method, based on
contemporary realisable market values (Chambers, 1978).

28 See e.g. *Statements of Source and Application of Funds*, Accounting
Standard No. 10, issued by the Accounting Standards Committee in July
1975. More recently, standard-setters have preferred what they describe
as cash flow statements, as in the IASC's standard IAS 7 (revised in 1992)
to convert from funds flow to cash flow. As illustrated in the appendix
to this chapter, cash flow statements summarise the cash receipts and
payments of a business, rather than summarising changes in balance
sheet items, which include non-cash accruals. However, in practice, the
'cash flow' standards typically allow diversions from pure cash flow
(which would require the use of the unpopular 'direct method' of

measuring cash flows and would focus on cash rather than 'cash equivalents') and retain elements of funds flow.

29 The income statement will, of course, record gross flows, such as sales and purchases, whose net effect is reflected in the identity which follows. Profit is calculated as revenues (which are increases in assets or decreases in liabilities), less expenses (which are decreases in assets or increases in liabilities): the net profit is therefore an increase in net assets attributable to the proprietor. This relationship emerges clearly from the numerical illustrations given in the preceding chapter and in the appendix to this chapter.

30 This is not, of course, consistent with the economist's notion of 'pure profit', which is the residual after deducting a notional interest charge for 'normal profit'.

31 Useful analyses of the different approaches to income measurement of the accountant and the economist will be found in R. S. Edwards (1938), Alexander (1948), Solomons (1961) and Barton (1974). A survey of the literature and a bibliography will be found in Whittington (1981a), a collection of readings on the subject is Parker et al. (1986), and a textbook with clear numerical illustrations is Lee (1985).

32 The Hicks definitions are, of course, definitions of personal income. To translate them into appropriate definitions of the profits of a business, we must substitute 'distributed to the proprietors' for 'spent'.

33 The two sources of such gains, or losses, are changes in actual or prospective receipts from those originally expected, and changes in the discount rate which is applied in calculating the net present value of those receipts. Some writers define interest rate changes as being separate from windfalls.

34 This argument is stated more fully in Whittington (1974).

35 This is discussed in any good textbook such as Bierman and Smidt (2007).

36 Calculate that discount rate $r'$ which makes $V_0 = C_0$ where $C_0$ is the initial cost. The decision rule is then: invest when $r' \geq r$ ($r$ being the market discount rate used in the net present value calculation).

37 Hirshleifer (1958) gives an elegant demonstration of this.

38 Note that it does not actually have to be maintained *ex post*. Returns could be reinvested in the business, which should lead subsequently to increased returns. The standard stream represents the sustainable earnings from the resources invested in the business at the time of

measurement, on the assumption that the earnings are distributed to proprietors rather than reinvested.

39 A useful survey of the problem is provided by Armitage (2005).

40 This point is made cogently by Peasnell (1977) and by Bromwich (1977a).

41 The type of criticism, made by Nobes (1977) of the Sandilands 'deprival value' proposals for valuation, could also be made of Scott's (1976) proposals, particularly in relation to the treatment of monetary assets: the method of valuation to be used depends upon the intended use of the asset, which adds a further degree of subjectivity. However, this approach is consistent with the IASB's treatment of financial instruments (IFRS 9, 2009), and with its current stance on measurement (International Accounting Standards Board, 2015).

42 Notable advocates of cash flow accounting are Lawson (1971), Lee (1972) and Ijiri (1979).

43 This point is made by Edey (1979).

44 A good critique of the use for share valuation of Sandilands' operating profit, is provided by Kennedy (1976).

45 Kennedy (1976) points out that the valuation of shares based upon discounting Sandilands operating profit by an earnings yield obtained in the market would involve making the assumption that there would be no more inflation: surely an inappropriate assumption for an accounting system which purports to be 'inflation accounting'!

46 Practical experience suggests that cash flow information is used as a supplement to rather than a substitute for accrual accounting. Even the academic proposals for cash flow do not envisage the complete loss of accrual information. Lee (1979) for example advocates a balance sheet on a current cash equivalent (net selling price) basis.

# 3   Historical Cost Accounting

Historical Cost (HC) is the basis of traditional accounting, although it is not usually applied in its pure form. Common modifications are *ad hoc* revaluations of fixed assets and the doctrine of conservatism, which encourages a downward bias in valuation practices by valuing certain assets, such as stocks, at historical cost or market value whichever is the lower. In this chapter, we shall consider some of the properties of HC accounting.

This is a necessary prelude to the study of alternative measurement methods in accounting, for two reasons. First, it is important to establish why there has been dissatisfaction with HC, particularly in periods of rapidly changing prices: if such dissatisfaction is ill-founded, then there is no reason to tamper with traditional methods which have stood the test of practical application. Second, it is important to discover the properties of HC in the absence of changing prices. If these are desirable properties of a financial accounting system, then it might be thought that the object of accounting should be to adjust HC to eliminate the effects of changing prices so that it retains the properties which it possesses when prices are stable. This has indeed often seemed to be the reasoning used, in the context of changes in the general price level, by advocates of Constant Purchasing Power Accounting (CPP), who seek to eliminate the distortionary effect introduced into HC measurements by inflation. On the other hand, if, as some have suggested,[1] HC accounts have little meaning even in the absence of price changes, it would seem futile to base an accounting system on the principle of restoring to HC accounts a significance which they never had.

## 3.1 THE STATIONARY STATE

One of the hypothetical situations in which historical cost accounting has a clear significance is a stationary state,[2] in which all prices are constant through time, and are expected to remain so, and in which each asset has a single, unambiguous price (i.e. there is no divergence between buying price, selling price and present value in use) and there are no transaction costs (so that, for example, selling price equals the amount that the owner can realise by disposal of an asset). The existence of the stationary state ensures that there is no divergence through time between HC and current costs, and that the currency unit in which they are measured maintains a constant value. However, cost could still differ from exit value (net realisable value on sale, or present value of future cash flows if retained for use by the business). This would be ruled out if there were complete and perfectly competitive markets, such that there was one unique price for each asset (or liability).The existence of only one price for each asset ensures that there is no problem of choice between entry values (replacement costs, which are assumed in these circumstances to equal HC), exit values (selling prices), or value in use, as all are equal. We therefore have a single unambiguous current value for each asset and liability which is equal to HC. In these circumstances, if we add the assumption that all assets and liabilities have identifiable historical costs that can be recognised in the accounts,[3] HC profit will be equal to economic profit, i.e. the increase in net worth measured by HC accounting will equal the increase in the sum of present values of the assets of the firm.[4] Thus, it is not necessary to go beyond HC accounting, as it can provide all of the information provided by these alternative valuation systems.

The assumptions required for this situation to exist are, however, stringent and unrealistic. The requirement that both absolute prices and relative prices remain constant assumes an equilibrium world in which nothing changes. In practice, levels and patterns of both demand and supply change continuously, leading to price changes of both types, so that the value of the currency unit in terms of a standard basket of commodities (such as the Consumer Price Index) changes through time, as do the relative values of different commodities. The assumptions necessary to achieve one price for each asset are equally unrealistic. They include:

1. Perfectly competitive long-run equilibrium in all markets, with all the assumptions which this entails.[5]
2. The existence of such a market in all assets and liabilities ('complete markets'), so that, for example, all part-used fixed assets have a market price.
3. No transaction costs, so that the price equals both the cost of buying an item and the proceeds of sale.
4. The accrual conventions used in the application of HC are such as to value all assets and liabilities, including part-used assets and self-generated intangible assets (such as customer goodwill), at amounts that reflect the cost of resources expended to obtain them (including accumulated interest costs on capital invested), less the proportion of the economic benefit or burden (in the case of liabilities) that has expired since the date of acquisition, thus equalling their competitive market price.

The latter assumption is necessary because, although HC accounting may appear superficially to be objective, the accrual process (the allocation of revenues and expenses to periods) gives rise to the allocation problem, which has been explored rigorously by Thomas (1969, 1974), i.e. when goods or services are purchased in a group for multiple uses, how should we allocate the costs of the group to individual uses, and when only part of an item is used up in a period, how do we allocate the cost between cost charged against profits of the period and cost accrued as an asset to be used in future periods? The obvious example of this problem is the costs of a fixed asset, which are allocated across periods by means of depreciation charges: conventional methods of depreciation, such as straight-line or reducing balance, would typically not meet requirement (4).[6]

The perfect competition assumption ensures that no asset[7] can trade for two separate prices (a condition sometimes described as 'the law of one price'), so that replacement costs equal selling prices, and each cost or price is independent of the quantity sold. The assumption that there are no additional transaction costs ensures that there is no divergence between price and value to the owner or to the prospective purchaser of an asset. In combination with the stationary state (a form of long-run equilibrium) these assumptions also ensure that there are no excess profits (sometimes called 'pure profits') in the economy, each asset earning only a normal rate of profit (equal to the discount rate, $r$, of Chapter 2) and present value equalling market price. Complete certainty is not necessary for perfectly competitive equilibrium to exist at a particular point in time, but correct expectations are necessary if the equilibrium is to be sustained. If expectations are not fulfilled, the stationary state is likely to be upset, because *ex ante* plans have not been fulfilled *ex post*, causing disequilibrium.

Even in these stringent conditions, it should be noted that HC is not uniquely suited to be the valuation basis of accounting: it merely happens that there is equality between the alternative values. In these circumstances, we would probably select HC as the chosen basis because of its traditional role in accounting, which makes it acceptable, familiar, and of proven feasibility, and because of its ease of verification and its compatibility with the control function of the firm. HC is readily documented by means of invoices and similar records, and it arises naturally out of the process of recording the physical transactions of the business and controlling the amounts of goods and services under the firm's ownership. It is therefore compatible with the stewardship objective of providing an account of the transactions of the business. This is a central theme in Ijiri's classic defence of HC (Ijiri, 1971). However, in practice, HC is not entirely unambiguous because its accruals may depend on allocation rules which can be subjective and arbitrary.

In reality, the world is characterised neither by stationary state conditions nor by perfectly competitive equilibrium with complete markets. There are also significant additional costs of transacting which lead to different values even when prices are equal (for example, if the costs of buying and of selling are both positive, the total cost of acquiring an asset, the 'entry value', will be higher than the net returns from selling it, the 'exit value', when buying price equals selling price[8]).

We might hope to deal with the price changes resulting from the break-down of the stationary state by adjusting HC records by means of indices: general price indices to deal with general price-level changes and specific indices to deal with cases in which individual prices diverge from the general index. This would lead us to a form of constant purchasing power (CPP) accounting if general indices alone were used, or to a form of real terms accounting when both types of index were applied. However, when the second set of conditions (complete perfectly competitive markets) breaks down, we are faced by a more fundamental problem: that income and value are no longer uniquely defined. Thus, we face a choice between HC, replacement cost, current selling price, or present value in use (and possibly a variety of choices within each of these categories), reflecting different assumptions about how assets are deployed, and we are forced to consider the possibility, discussed in Chapters 1 and 2, that different types of information will serve different purposes.[9] This situation has given rise to the wide range of alternative accounting theories and systems which are discussed in subsequent chapters.

## 3.2 PROFITS ON COMPLETED PROJECTS

An alternative situation in which HC yields an unambiguous measure of profit which might be considered useful is in the case of the lifetime profit on completed projects, starting with an initial cash injection and finishing with completed liquidation, i.e. realisation in cash. If we assume, for illustrative purposes, that such a project extends over two accounting periods, we might demonstrate this result as follows, using the notation of Chapter 2. Assume an initial cash subscription at time $t$ of $M_t$. The balance sheet equation is then

$$P_t = M_t \tag{3.1}$$

Assume that, at the end of Period 1 (time $t + 1$), the cash $M_t$ has been exchanged for stocks $N_{t+1}$ and there have been no other transactions. The balance sheet equation is now

$$P_{t+1} = N_{t+1} \tag{3.2}$$

Because the stocks are valued at HC, $N_{t+1} = M_t$ and $P_{t+1} = P_t$. The profit for Period 1 is therefore

$$P_{t+1} - P_t = N_{t+1} - M_t = 0 \tag{3.3}$$

At the end of Period 2, at time $t + 2$, the venture is liquidated by the exchange of the stocks $N_{t+1}$ for cash $M_{t+2}$. The balance sheet equation is now

$$P_{t+2} = M_{t+2} \tag{3.4}$$

and the profit for Period 2 is therefore

$$P_{t+2} - P_{t+1} = M_{t+2} - N_{t+1} \tag{3.5}$$

Clearly, the periodic profits depend crucially upon the valuation of stock at the end of the first period, $N_{r+1}$. If this had been at market value, it is possible that this would have exceeded the HC valuation, so that a positive profit would have appeared in period 1, but this would have been exactly offset by a lower profit in period 2, when the stock was written off against profit, leaving total profits for the lifetime of the venture unchanged. This latter result is easily demonstrated. The lifetime profit of the venture is the sum of the profit for the two periods

$$P_{t+2} - P_{t+1} + P_{t+1} - P_t = M_{t+2} - N_{t+1} + N_{t+1} - M_t \tag{3.6}$$

or

$$P_{t+2} - P_t = M_{t+2} - M_t \tag{3.7}$$

Thus, the intermediate valuation attaching to the assets is of no consequence for the lifetime profit calculation and HC is as acceptable as any other basis for intermediate valuation, if we are not concerned with periodic profits within the full lifetime. However, some important reservations must be made:

1. The accountant is typically concerned with *going concerns*, not with self-liquidating ventures, and cannot, therefore, make the convenient 'cash-to-cash' assumption.

2. Even in the case of a self-liquidating venture, the accountant is usually concerned with *periodic* evaluation of the entity, not with its performance over its lifetime. The intermediate valuation $N_{t+1}$ will clearly have a crucial bearing on how the relative performance of the entity is measured within each period.

3. The equivalence of alternative lifetime profit measurements was obtained by assuming that $P_t$ was to be the capital to be maintained. The importance of the capital maintenance concept was illustrated, in a 'cash-to-cash' business, in Chapter 1. As we saw there, a *real* (inflation adjusted) capital maintenance system would adjust $P_t$ by the change in a general purchasing power index over the relevant period, in order to define capital to be maintained. Thus, in our simple example, real lifetime profit would not be $P_{t+2} - P_t$, but would rather be $P_{t+2} - P_t(1 + p_1)(1 + p_2)$ where $p_1$ is the percentage increase in the general index during period 1 and $p_2$ the increase during period 2.[10] Equally, an entity-based replacement cost measurement system might involve writing up the initial capital by changes in a specific index, $s$, relating to the type of goods traded by the entity, yielding a lifetime profit of $P_{t+2} - P_t(1 + s_1)(1 + s_2)$, where $s$ is the percentage change in the specific index over the relevant period.

Thus the 'cash-to-cash' long-run equivalence of HC with other asset valuation systems has little bearing on how the periodic accounts of continuing entities should be drawn up, since it ignores the essential asset valuation problem of periodic reporting. Furthermore, the problem of measuring the capital to be maintained before recognising a profit is inadequately dealt with by HC in a period of changing prices.

## 3.3 THE EQUIVALENCE OF THE 'BOOK YIELD' AND THE INTERNAL RATE OF RETURN

Another possible defence of HC is that it yields an accounting rate of return (ARR) or 'book yield' which is a good approximation to the internal rate of return (IRR) used in capital budgeting theory. It will be recalled (Chapter 2, note 31) that the IRR is that rate of return, $r'$, which, when used as a discount rate, renders the net present value of an investment equal to zero:

$$\text{NPV} = \sum_{t=1}^{n} \frac{Q_t}{(1+r')^t} - C_0 = 0 \tag{3.8}$$

where   $C_0$ = initial net cash outlay
        $Q_t$ = future net cash inflows
        $n$ = number of periods in the life of
             the investment

The ARR is simply the accounting profit for a period divided by the average accounting value ('book value') of the net assets employed to earn that profit. It might be thought that, as accounts are often used for purposes of *ex post* appraisal, it is desirable that the rate of return measured by the accounts (ARR) should equal, or at least approximate, the IRR, which is the 'true' *ex post* yield derived from economic theory, and maximisation of which is, in most cases, consistent with economic decision-making models.

There is a considerable literature on this subject, starting with papers by Harcourt (1965) and Solomon (1966), which demonstrated that wide divergences were possible between ARR and IRR. A series of papers followed, which served to identify how the relationship between ARR and IRR was affected by various conditions, such as aggregation across numbers of projects (i.e. measurement at the firm level or the project level), additional investment, different periods of measurement (e.g. taking average ARR rather than annual ARR), and different lengths of life of investment. All of this has been neatly encapsulated in an analytical paper by Kay (1976)[11] which demonstrates the general relationship between ARR and IRR. It appears that *over the lifetime* of a project or firm (i.e. from initial flotation to final liquidation), IRR is a weighted average of ARR. Kay demonstrates a method of calculating the appropriate weights. Thus, *over long periods*, average ARR may be a good approximation to IRR. Certain other conditions (such as steady growth of the firm at something close to the rate of profit), which improve the approximation, are also specified.

From the point of view of annual reporting of company performance, this is not encouraging, and certainly does not justify the view that HC accounting is adequate, for the following reasons:

1. The ARR/IRR equivalence holds exactly only over the complete life cycle of a firm. Thus, for reporting the performance of a continuing entity, the valuation of assets at the end of a period is crucial, and HC may not prove to be as good a proxy, or 'surrogate', for economic value as some current valuation basis, such as replacement cost.[12] This is another example of the weakness of the 'cash-to-cash' assumption discussed in Section 3.2.

2. The equivalence holds strictly only for *averages* (weighted in a specific manner) over the lifetime of the firm, or, as an approximation, over long periods. Thus, it is of little use in supporting the use of ARR as a measure of economic return in a single period, which is presumably one of the principal functions of the annual accounts of companies, providing a prompt signal of good or bad profitability. This deficiency of the ARR is recognised by Kay (1976, 1978) and is another illustration of the weakness of the lifetime 'cash-to-cash' approach.

3. A fundamental issue, which was raised early in the debate by Vatter (1966), is the appropriateness of the IRR as an ideal standard. The IRR is itself a calculation of the average compound rate of return earned

over the lifetime of an investment or venture. It is based upon the assumption of constancy of the rate of return over all periods and does not allow for the fact that the opportunity cost of capital may vary between periods, or for the fact that the returns themselves may be concentrated in various periods. Thus, the IRR is really an expression of rate of return *over the lifetime as a whole*. It may, for convenience or for comparative purposes, be expressed as an annual rate, but it does not record the profitability of a particular year or other period shorter than the full life cycle. In other words, it solves the allocation problem by means of the arbitrary assumption that an equal rate of return was earned in each period. This makes it an inappropriate standard by which to judge the performance of the firm over any period shorter than the full life cycle.

Another defence of the use of ARR in empirical studies across firms, which is made by Whittington (1979), is that many types of error in ARR (viewed as an approximation to IRR) can be expected to average out in such a way as to impart little or no bias to statistical studies. This argument relates specifically to large-scale studies involving many firms and assumes that the rate of return is averaged over a number of years. It is therefore relevant to certain economic studies of the structure and performance of industries, or larger groups of firms, over fairly long periods, but it does not purport to be a valid defence of ARR as a measure of the performance of an individual firm in a single year. It is thus not of direct relevance to the problem of producing annual financial reports to the shareholders or other interested parties of a particular firm.

Thus, the ARR based on historical cost (HC) can be informative as an estimate (but not an exact measure) of the *ex post* economic rate of return (IRR) of an accounting entity when averaged over a number of periods (Kay, 1976) and when averaged across a number of entities (Whittington, 1979). It is therefore incorrect to assert that HC is meaningless. The real weakness of the case for HC based ARR as a proxy for IRR lies in the limitations of IRR, which reflects returns over a long period, giving equal weight to each year. Financial accounts typically report performance over a single year or less, and recent performance is the central concern of users, whether for stewardship purposes by shareholders (indicating action that should be taken to improve financial performance) or for valuation by investors. For both of these purposes, users of accounts will need to assess the current financial state of the business, giving greater weight to recent events, as reported in the latest accounts. The accountant is unlikely to be able to provide them with a precise measure, such as present value (PV), but the accounts may provide information that assists users in their own estimates of PV. A critical component of this will be the estimation of future cash flows and, with this in mind, we now consider the possibility that HC profit may assist in the prediction of these.

### 3.4 SMOOTHED CASH FLOW

An alternative approach to evaluating HC accounting is to take as our model not conformity with the type of valuations proposed by economists but consistency with the 'Hicks No. 3' consumption maintenance approach, defined in Chapter 2. This interpretation emphasises the HC profit and loss account rather than the balance sheet. The profit and loss account is seen as measuring the sustainable net cash flow which the firm derives from its operations. Accruals are seen to be necessary in order to eliminate abnormal cash flows, e.g. due to the acquisition of a fixed asset, and the writing-off of accruals (e.g. by charging depreciation) is interpreted as a device for smoothing out the impact of the cost of such lumpy items, so that the profit figure is a measure of the maximum sustainable dividend.[13] Such a measure, apart from its relevance to dividend policy, might be a basis for valuing the equity shares of business by calculating the discounted present value (PV) of the sustainable earnings, an approach that is consistent with the widespread use of price/earnings (P/E) ratios by investors.[14] In this approach to income measurement, the balance sheet is interpreted simply as an accrual sheet, recording those cash outlays (at HC) which have not yet been charged to profit and loss. Examples of such an interpretation are the Trueblood Report (Study Group on the Objectives of Financial Statements, 1973) and Whittington (1974), but this approach has roots in the earlier history of accounting thought, e.g. Schmalenbach (1959) adopts this interpretation in his *Dynamic Accounting*, which first appeared in 1919, and which justifies the approach by reference to historical precedents.

More recently, a defence of historical cost accounting as a basis for assessing sustainable earnings has been developed by Penman (2007).[15] He argues that for conventional businesses that buy inputs, utilise them to add value, and sell the finished product at a profit, the transactions record that is the basis of historical cost accounting provides important information about the ability of the business to generate an operating surplus. In such a business, the discounted present value of the sustainable operating surplus will be a sounder basis for valuation than estimating the fair value (interpreted as selling price) of the assets of the business. He illustrates his argument with an analysis of the value of the Coca Cola Corporation, using both the balance sheet approach and the income statement approach (based on historical cost). He suggests that fair value is of greater relevance to the valuation of businesses or segments of businesses that hold assets passively for gain in market value rather than actively adding value, especially where those assets have a reliably measurable market selling price.

The main problem with the 'Hicks No. 3' income measurement approach is that we may have to make strong assumptions in order for the single year's profit figure to be a useful measure of sustainable future distributions. If everything (demand, output, prices, and costs) remained constant, as in the steady state, we might regard the profit figure as 'standard stream' income which could be divided by an appropriate discount rate to give a valuation of the firm at the end of the period.[16] This, however, is an unreasonably stringent assumption, and it is likely in practice that each period's performance will have unique features which are unlikely to be repeated. Some of these features will improve the firm's prospects for the future, and others will worsen them. We might hope that some of these changing prospects would be reflected in changing end-of-period values of assets and accruals (although, as we shall see later, it is unlikely that even current values will correspond with the economist's measure of present value), but accrued historic costs do not seem likely to be appropriate values for this purpose outside the stationary state conditions described earlier. There will be some features of a particular year which have no bearing whatsoever on future prospects but which will affect historical cost profits, unless some highly subjective adjustments are made, e.g. exceptionally low demand leading to low sales and poor capacity utilisation. Thus, it seems unlikely that pure HC accounting can reasonably be interpreted as an ideal measure of 'Hicks No. 3' standard stream income. It is, of course, possible to estimate a standard stream income even when there are annual fluctuations, if future outcomes are known. In such a case, it is possible to calculate a constant annuity which is of equivalent value to the fluctuating expected annual stream of returns.[17] This annuity would equal the discount rate multiplied by the discounted present value of the future expected receipts. However, such a measure would be critically dependent on estimates of future events; it would thus lose the relative objectivity of being grounded in past transactions, which is one of the main attributes of historical cost. Furthermore, if it is possible to calculate the discounted present value of the business, or its share capital, there seems little purpose in the additional step of calculating standard stream income. A more practical approach is that of Nissim and Penman (2008), who use current income as input to a model which incorporates smoothing and growth factors to *estimate* future income, rather than assuming prior knowledge of it.

Thus, it is possible that HC accounting can produce information that assists the estimation of a 'smoothed cash flow' measure. The common practice of using accounting earnings, often with additional adjustments by the user, to assess share values is an example of such a use (Black, 1980). The Nissim and Penman (2008) study is an example of how HC earnings data can be used as an input to the projection of distributable cash flows, rather than a precise measure of those cash flows. Hence, rather than providing precise 'pure' income measures, an HC profit and loss account may provide useful information for decision making in an uncertain world.

Hence, despite the difficulties of estimating standard stream income, the idea of an earnings-based approach to valuation is an attractive one, particularly for the added value type of activity identified by Penman, where it will at least be a cross check on other methods of valuation and may, in an imperfect world, be the best single method, since all measures are subject to error. The approach has also been supported by economists such as Scott (1976) and Black (1980, 1993). A common difficulty of their different approaches and that of Penman is that of defining earnings, particularly the separation of non-recurring gains from sustainable earnings. Each suggests a different approach to this problem and none suggests pure historical cost as the appropriate measure for all assets, liabilities and costs. The more general problem of disaggregating comprehensive income (including all gains) into meaningful components was encountered by the IASB in its attempts to separate profit from gain within its comprehensive income statement (Barker, 2004).

It might seem that the introduction of general and specific price changes would weaken the possible link between HC accounting and standard stream income, but this is not necessarily the case. Much depends upon the precise assumptions made about the future course of general and specific prices. For example, if we were able to accept the view that, in the absence of inflation, HC profit was a good approximation to standard stream income, and if we further assume general price inflation at a constant annual rate with real variables unchanged and a balanced age structure of assets, HC profit under inflation becomes a measure of standard stream income in current prices, or 'real' standard stream income. If we wished to estimate money standard stream income for future periods,[18] we would simply multiply by the inflation factor appropriate to a particular future year. Specific relative price changes would give rise to more subtle problems. A crucial factor would be how and when specific price changes were reflected in selling prices: if pricing were always conducted on the basis of recovering HC rather than current costs, then HC accounting would still yield a measure of standard stream profit.[19] On the other hand, if pricing were on the basis of current cost, current cost accounting (CCA) might give a more appropriate measure.

In summary, it seems that, under realistic conditions of uncertainty and market imperfection, it is difficult to sustain the standard stream income interpretation of historical cost profit in a precise sense. However, in appropriate circumstances, HC earnings and profit margins may be useful as inputs to the estimation processes of individual users of accounts. although, as we shall see later, other measurement methods, such as current replacement cost, might also be of potential use.

### 3.5 OBJECTIVITY AND STEWARDSHIP

Hitherto, we have been concerned with the extent to which HC accounts match up to some ideal standards derived from economic theory, but it was argued in Chapter 2 that the achievement of such standards usually requires conditions which do not prevail in the real world. It is therefore not particularly surprising that HC fails to *measure* economists' concepts for profit or value, under realistic conditions. However, it can also be argued that, in some circumstances, HC fails to provide *information* relevant to the measurement of such concepts, so that current value, reflecting the most up-to-date market evaluation of the firm's assets, might be more appropriate to the assessment of the economic progress of the business.[20] This possibility will be explored in subsequent chapters.

There is, however, one other important line of defence of HC accounting which has been put forward trenchantly by Ijiri (1971). The basis of this defence is that the unique property of HC is that it is based on the recording of events which have actually occurred, rather than upon contingent events, such as the price which an asset would obtain in the market were it sold or its cost in the market were it replaced. This gives basic HC data a unique claim to objectivity, although in the actual practice of HC accounting an important element of subjectivity creeps into the operation of the accrual system, since, as Thomas (1969) has shown, the rules for allocation of costs to time periods (as, for example, in depreciation charges) and between activities (as, for example, in the allocation of marketing costs between current sales and future customer relationships) are 'incorrigible' and arbitrary.[21] Ijiri argues that its relative objectivity gives HC a unique advantage in resolving potential conflicts where there is a problem of dividing claims on the firm between different interested parties (a type of problem which he describes as 'allocation': this is, of course, an entirely different allocation problem from that described by Thomas, and is what economists would describe as a distribution problem, as in the theory of distribution). An example of such a problem is the determination of the corporation tax base. Ijiri also argues that HC records perform a unique control function in keeping a record of the actual external transactions of the business. This is part of the traditional *stewardship* rôle of accounting.[22] Few would deny the value of HC records in this respect, although the keeping of basic HC records for control purposes does not necessarily rule out revaluation at current values for the decision-making or valuation function of financial reporting.[23]

## 3.6 CONCLUSION

We conclude, not surprisingly, that HC accounts do not have an unambiguous significance in terms of economic concepts of value and profit, except in closely defined circumstances which are unlikely to be prevalent in the real world. In a more realistic setting of disequilibrium, imperfect and incomplete markets and changing prices, HC accounts may give useful signals for valuation purposes that have to be interpreted with care, and in conjunction with other relevant information. HC accounts do have value, as records of past events, in fulfilling the traditional *stewardship* role of accounting and this, together with the fact that the system is established in practice, provides motivation for accountants to wish to retain it. It is with respect to *decision making* and valuation, by managers, shareholders and others, that HC is likely to be found inadequate or incomplete. Under stationary state conditions, in which all prices are constant, HC is acceptable as a surrogate for current values, but once prices are (realistically) allowed to change, it is current values rather than HC which will represent economic opportunities available or forgone and which are likely to enter decision or valuation calculations. Of course, it is not obvious which of a variety of current values is likely to be the most relevant: this issue will be taken up in later chapters. Moreover, it is not clear that, in a realistic setting of imperfect and incomplete markets, it will be possible to measure all assets and liabilities at current market values. In particular, valuation of the business as a whole includes the value of goodwill and certain intangible assets that are difficult to identify and even more difficult to value. This opens the possibility that a historical cost earnings measure, as proposed by Penman, might have practical use. What is clear is that HC alone is unlikely to provide complete information, so that the properties of current value accounting deserve exploration.

The next chapter will deal with the measurement of the effects of specific price changes, by means of current value accounting systems. The appendix to this chapter gives some simple numerical examples which illustrate the more general algebraic argument used in the main text of the chapter.

## APPENDIX: A NUMERICAL EXAMPLE

This numerical example is a variant of that given in the appendix to Chapter 2. We here introduce a depreciating asset and follow the course of the business over a three-period life cycle, in order to illustrate some of the concepts introduced in Chapter 3.

The additional facts for period 1 are now:

1. Fred started the period with an additional asset. This was a depreciable fixed asset (a cart) purchased for £100 at the start of the period.
2. This asset is to be depreciated over a ten-period life by the 'straight-line' method (i.e. at $^1/_{10}$ of cost per period).
3. The cart was paid for by the proprietor, so that his opening capital is now £150 (£50 in cash and £100 for the cart).
4. The proprietor withdraws £30 for his own use at the end of the period.

The facts for period 2 are:

1. 80 pineapples purchased for £1.30 each, half for cash and half on credit, payable in the next period.
2. 90 pineapples sold for £1.50 each.
3. 80 of these pineapples were sold for cash and 10 were sold on credit, payable in the next period.
4. The proprietor spends all of his cash for private purposes, other than what he needs to pay his creditors.

The facts for period 3 are:

1. 100 pineapples purchased for £1.80 each on credit.
2. The creditors from the previous day are paid, and the debtors redeem their debts.
3. 90 pineapples sold for £2 each, 80 for cash and 10 on credit.
4. The proprietor spends £10 cash for private purposes.

In period 4, the proprietor decides to liquidate his business:

1. The remaining stock of pineapples is sold for £2.20 each, paid in cash.
2. The cart is sold for £120 cash.
3. The creditor is paid, and the debtor pays, in full.
4. The proprietor pays off the loan and withdraws the remaining cash for his own use.

## A.I HISTORICAL COST ACCOUNTS

### Balance Sheet at $t$ (start of first period)

| | £ | | | £ |
|---|---|---|---|---|
| Proprietor's Capital | 150 | *Fixed Assets* | | |
| Loan (Aunt Mabel) | 50 | Cart (at cost) | | 100 |
| | | *Current Assets* | | |
| | | Cash | | 100 |
| | 200 | | | 200 |

### Income Statement for period 1, $t$ to $t + 1$

| | £ |
|---|---|
| Sales | 120 |
| *Less* Cost of goods sold* | 80 |
| Trading profit | 40 |
| *Less* Depreciation[†] | 10 |
| Profit | 30 |

\* Cost of goods sold is purchases £100, less closing stock £20, both at historical cost.

[†] Depreciation is $^1/_{10} \times £100$ (historical cost).

### Balance Sheet at $t + 1$

| | £ | | £ | £ |
|---|---|---|---|---|
| *Proprietor's Capital* | | *Fixed Assets* | | |
| Opening balance (at $t$) | 150 | Cart (at cost) | 100 | |
| *Add* Profit for the | | *Less* depreciation | | |
| period | 30 | to date | 10 | |
| | 180 | | | 90 |
| *Less* Drawings | 30 | *Current Assets* | | |
| Closing balance | | Stock (at cost) | 20 | |
| (at $t + 1$) | 150 | Cash | 90 | |
| *Loan* | 50 | | | 110 |
| | 200 | | | 200 |

Income Statement for period 2, $t + 1$ to $t + 2$

|  | £ |
|---|---|
| Sales | 135 |
| *Less* Cost of goods sold* | 111 |
| Trading profit | 24 |
| *Less* Depreciation | 10 |
| Profit | 14 |

* On the FIFO (first-in-first-out) principle: opening
  stock (20 pineapples at £1 each) £20 + purchases (80
  pineapples at £1.30) £104 – closing stock (10
  pineapples at £1.30 each) £13.

Balance Sheet at $t + 2$

| Proprietor's Capital | £ | Fixed Assets | | £ |
|---|---|---|---|---|
| Opening balance | | Cart (at cost) | 100 | |
| (at $t + 1$) | 150 | *Less* depreciation | | |
| *Add* Profit for the | | to date | 20 | |
| period | 14 | | | 80 |
| | 164 | Current Assets | | |
| *Less* Drawings | 106 | Stock (at cost) | 13 | |
| Closing balance | | Debtors | 15 | |
| (at $t + 2$) | 58 | Cash | 52 | |
| Loan | 50 | | | 80 |
| Current Liabilities | | | | |
| Creditors | 52 | | | |
| | 160 | | | 160 |

Income Statement for period 3, $t + 2$ to $t + 3$

| | £ |
|---|---|
| Sales | 180 |
| *Less* Cost of goods sold* | 157 |
| Trading profit | 23 |
| *Less* Depreciation | 10 |
| Profit | 13 |

\* Opening stock £13 + purchases £180 – closing stock (20 pineapples at £1.80 each) £36.

Balance Sheet at $t + 3$

| *Proprietor's Capital* | £ | *Fixed Assets* | | £ |
|---|---|---|---|---|
| Opening balance | | Cart (at cost) | 100 | |
| (at $t + 2$) | 58 | *Less* depreciation | | |
| *Add* Profit for the | | to date | 30 | |
| period | 13 | | | 70 |
| | 71 | *Current Assets* | | |
| *Less* Drawings | 10 | Stock (at cost) | 36 | |
| Closing balance | | Debtors | 20 | |
| (at $t + 3$) | 61 | Cash | 165 | |
| *Loan* | 50 | | | 221 |
| *Current Liabilities* | | | | |
| Creditors | 180 | | | |
| | 291 | | | 291 |

Income Statement for period 4, $t + 3$ to $t + 4$

|  | £ |
|---|---|
| Sales | 44 |
| *Less* Cost of goods sold* | 36 |
| Trading profit | 8 |
| Realised Holding Gain[†] | 50 |
| Total Profit | 58 |

* Opening stock (20 pineapples at £1.80 each).

† Sale of cart £120, less written-down value £70.

Note that the bottom line of the income statement is now described as 'total profit' (rather than, as previously, 'profit'), because it includes a realised gain on the fixed asset (the cart), which is not part of normal operating profit. These two components of income may be used differently in the estimation of future returns.

Balance Sheet at $t + 4$*

|  | £ |  | £ |
|---|---|---|---|
| *Proprietor's Capital* |  | Cash | 169 |
| Opening balance $(t + 3)$ | 61 |  |  |
| *Add* Profit for the period | 58 |  |  |
|  | 119 |  |  |
| Loan | 50 |  | — |
|  | 169 |  | 169 |

* This balance sheet is drawn up prior to the final payment of £50 to redeem the loan, the remaining £119 being available for the proprietor.

A.2 ILLUSTRATION OF SOME POINTS MADE
IN THE CHAPTER

### A.2.1 Equivalence of 'Cash-to-Cash' Income Measures (equations (3.1)–(3.7))

The reported profits in this example are:

|          | £    |
|----------|------|
|          |      |
| Period 1 | 30   |
| Period 2 | 14   |
| Period 3 | 13   |
| Period 4 | 58   |
|          | £115 |

This is equal to what the proprietor put in, less what he took out, in cash, over the whole period from flotation to liquidation of the business.

His drawings, less contributions, over the whole period were:

|                          | £    |
|--------------------------|------|
|                          |      |
| $t + 1$                  | 30   |
| $t + 2$                  | 106  |
| $t + 3$                  | 10   |
| $t + 4$                  | 119  |
| Total                    | 265  |
| *Less* capital introduced $(t)$ | 150  |
|                          | £115 |

If we vary the asset valuation conventions in the intermediate balance sheets $(t + 1, t + 2$ and $t + 3)$ we will shift profits between periods, but the total profits over the lifetime of the business will be the same, provided that we follow the 'clean surplus' rule of reporting all recorded gains and losses in the income statement.

For example, if we varied the depreciation method, to write off the asset over a 5-period life, we would charge £20 per period rather than £10, so that profit of each of the first three periods would be lower by £10. However, the realised holding gain in the final period would now be £30 higher (£120 less written-down value £40 = £80), exactly compensating for the lower profit in earlier periods. A higher depreciation rate in the earlier periods produces a lower written-down value in the final period and therefore a correspondingly higher gain when the asset is sold. The change in the depreciation method could also shift the relative profitability of the first three periods, e.g. by employing the reducing balance method which charges the earlier years relatively heavily, but there would always be the same net result over the asset's lifetime. This is because the net cost of the asset from purchase to sale is always original cost, less sale price. Depreciation is merely a device for allocating this total cost between periods.

The choice of stock valuation method could also affect the relative profitability of different periods. We might, for example, use the last-in, first-out (LIFO) method, which assumes that those goods acquired most recently are the ones sold first. This has the possible advantage of more closely approximating a replacement cost charge against profit, and has found favour in the US (largely because of tax advantages that it brings), but it can lead to very low valuations of stock, and may not be a very realistic representation of stock movements especially in the case of a perishable commodity, such as pineapples, where it would be a perverse policy to sell the freshest stock first. In our illustration, the alternative stock valuations are as follows:

| Time | FIFO | LIFO | |
|------|------|------|------|
| $t+1$ | 20 | 20 | (20 at £1 each) |
| $t+2$ | 13 | 10 | (10 at £1 each) |
| $t+3$ | 36 | 28 | (10 at £1 each, plus 10 at £1.80 each) |

Substituting the LIFO values into the calculation of costs of goods
sold gives us the following profit figures:

|  | £ |
| --- | --- |
| Period 1 | 30 |
| Period 2 | 11 |
| Period 3 | 8 |
| Period 4 | 66 |
|  | £115 |

The total lifetime profit is unchanged, but the profit in periods 2
and 3 is reduced (reflecting rising costs of replacing stocks). This is
exactly compensated by a higher profit in period 4, when the stock is
liquidated and the cost charged in calculating profit is based on the
lower LIFO valuation. This must always be the case over a 'cash-to-
cash' life cycle. The closing stock of one period serves to reduce the
cost of sales in that period but will increase the cost for subsequent
periods in which the stocks are sold. A lower valuation of closing
stocks implies a higher cost of sales for the current period, but a lower
cost for subsequent periods. So long as stocks are held, a lower value
will imply lower profits to date and a higher value will imply higher
profits to date, but when the stocks are finally liquidated the value
is their realised cash value, whatever the previous basis of valuation.
Thus, accumulated profits were different (by the difference in stock
values at the end of each period) under the two valuation schemes, at
the end both of period 2 and period 3, but in period 4, when stocks are
no longer held, total profits once again become identical.

### A.2.2 Non-equivalence of 'Cash-to-Cash' Income When Inflation Adjustments Are Introduced (Section 3.2, (3.3))

Suppose that there was inflation of 10 per cent in period 1, 20 per
cent in period 2, 10 per cent in period 3 and 5 per cent in period
4. If the proprietor had not withdrawn any money, his capital to be
maintained before recognising a profit on final liquidation would be
$[£150(1.1)(1.2)(1.1)(1.05)]$ if he were to maintain the purchasing power
of his funds, i.e. £228.69p. Hence, 'real' profit for the lifetime of the

business, expressed in purchasing power of the monetary unit at the end of the period (the $t + 4$ £) might seem to be £36.31p (or £265–£228.69).

In fact, the proprietor's position is rather more complicated, because he has withdrawn money at each period end rather than as a lump sum at the end of the final period, so that the capital contributed changes between periods. His periodic profit, applying a 'real' capital maintenance concept would be as follows:

| Period | Original 'money' profit £ | Re-stated opening capital Calculation | Re-stated opening capital Amount (£) | 'Real' profit £ |
|--------|---------------------------|----------------------------------------|--------------------------------------|-----------------|
| 1 | 30 | £150 × 1.1 | 165 | 15 |
| 2 | 14 | £150 × 1.2 | 180 | −16 |
| 3 | 13 | £58 × 1.1 | 63.80 | 7.20 |
| 4 | 58 | £71 × 1.05 | 74.55 | 54.44 |
| Total | 115 | | | 60.65 |

The sum of the 'real' periodic profits, £60.65, is substantially below that of the unadjusted 'money' profit measure, as would be expected in a period of inflation. Each period's opening capital is increased in proportion to the rise in the price index during the period. This results in a 'real profit' calculation, based on maintaining capital in 'end-of-period' £s rather than 'beginning of period' £s, although the unit of measurement is still not strictly comparable between periods, as would be the case with the CPP system, described in the next paragraph. The periodic adjustment of opening capital now means that life cycle profits, even in the 'cash-to-cash' case, will depend upon the valuation scheme: a different valuation scheme will lead to different measurements of opening capital in each period and, therefore, different amounts of re-statement to allow for inflation. For example, suppose that the stock was valued £10 higher at the end of period 1 and that this revalued stock was consumed in period 2, leaving later valuations unchanged. This would imply profit higher by £10 in period 1 and this would be added to opening capital for period 2, which would now be £160. However, at the end of period 2 this capital would be re-stated ($\times$1.2) to give £192 to be maintained before recognising a profit, an increase of £12 over the previous figure. Thus, the increased profit of £10 in period 1 would be offset by a £12 reduction in the profit (actually an increase in the loss to £28, in this example) for period 2, causing a reduction of £2 in total life cycle profit.

The 'real' profit calculated earlier is not a full constant purchasing power (CPP) measure such as will be discussed in Chapter 5. The full CPP system would involve an alternative valuation scheme, re-stating the historical costs of assets in terms of £s of constant purchasing power. Furthermore, CPP would require re-statement of the periodic profit figures in constant £s, so that that the total profit for the life cycle of the firm would be an aggregation of homogeneous units of measurement. At present, the periodic profits are measured in end-of-period £s for each separate period, and a CPP purist would object that these figures are not comparable or aggregable across periods because they are expressed in different units of measurement. A CPP adjustment to re-state the 'real' profit figures in current (end of period 4) £s would be as follows:

| Period | 'Real' profit | Re-statement calculation | CPP profit (end of period 4 £s) |
|--------|--------------|--------------------------|--------------------------------|
| 1 | 15 | £15 (1.2) (1.1) (1.05) | 20.79 |
| 2 | −16 | −£16 (1.1) (1.05) | −18.48 |
| 3 | 7.20 | £7.20 (1.05) | 7.56 |
| 4 | 54.44 | £54.44 (1) | 54.44 |
| Total | 60.64 | | 64.31 |

It should be noted that this re-states the 'real' profit figures without adjusting the underlying valuation scheme (for depreciation and stock valuation) which would also be affected by full CPP adjustment: the full adjustment is illustrated in the appendix to Chapter 5. However, the present illustration is sufficient to demonstrate that we can obtain yet another different life cycle profit figure if we measure in units of constant purchasing power. We would, of course, obtain a different number for each different CPP measuring unit: for example, if we measured in base-year $(t)$ pounds, lifetime profit would be £42.18 $(= 64.31 \div [(1.1)(1.2)(1.1)(1.05)])$.

### A.2.3 'Book Yield' as a Measure of the Internal Rate of Return

The accounting rate of return (ARR), or 'book yield' in the preceding example is calculated as follows:

*Accounting Rate of Return calculation*

| Period | Average capital employed Calculation | Amount (£) | Profit (£) | Rate of return (%)* |
|---|---|---|---|---|
| 1 | $[150 + 180] \div 2$ | 165 | 30 | 18.18 |
| 2 | $[150 + 164] \div 2$ | 157 | 14 | 8.92 |
| 3 | $[58 + 71] \div 2$ | 64.50 | 13 | 20.16 |
| 4 | $[61 + 119] \div 2$ | 90 | 58 | 64.44 |
| Total | | 476.50 | 115 | 24.13 |

\* Rate of Return is Profit divided by amount of Capital
  Employed.

We have a choice of two measures of rate of return: the arithmetic average of the separate ratios for periods 1 to 4, which is 27.93 per cent, or the weighted average, obtained by calculating the ratio of the totals over the whole period, which is 24.13 per cent. The latter corresponds more closely with (but is not identical with), the weighting scheme proposed by Kay (1976).

If we take 24 per cent as our estimate of the internal rate of return $(r')$, we can test this by the following discounting calculation, based on equation (3.8) in the text:

*Discounted Cash Flow Calculation, with r' = 0.24*

| Time | Cash flow | Discount factor $\left(\dfrac{1}{(1+r')^t}\right)$ | Present value |
|------|-----------|-----------------------------|---------------|
|      | (£) |      | (£) |
| $t$     | −150 | 1.00     | −150  |
| $t+1$   | 30   | 0.806452 | 24.19 |
| $t+2$   | 106  | 0.650364 | 68.94 |
| $t+3$   | 10   | 0.524487 | 5.24  |
| $t+4$   | 119  | 0.422974 | 50.33 |
| Total   | 115  |          | −1.30 |

The cash flows are the actual cash contributions and with-drawals by the proprietor. These are multiplied by the discount factor to yield a present value as at time $t$. The sum of the final column is the net present value (NPV) of the business to the proprietor at time $t$, discounting at 24 per cent per period. This is very close to zero, indicating that 24 per cent is a good approximation to $r'$. The fact that the NPV is negative shows that 24 per cent is an over-estimate of $r'$, since a slightly lower discount rate would increase the present value of the positive cash flows, bringing NPV closer to zero. A precise solution, calculated by a computer programme using iterative methods,[24] shows that IRR is 23.58 per cent.

Despite the relative accuracy of ARR as a measure of IRR in this instance, the example also serves to illustrate the limitations of this property. ARR fluctuates widely between periods and the assessment of the performance of the business within each separate period is one of the main concerns of periodic accounts. If this assessment is based on ARR, then the valuation and allocation methods used to measure capital employed and profit for the individual period become crucial, and correspondence of life cycle ARR with *ex post* IRR becomes irrelevant.

It should be noted that the IRR calculated here is unadjusted for inflation, i.e. it is based upon the comparison of nominal cash outlays with nominal future cash flows, no attempt being made to adjust the cash flows for inflation. It is therefore a money rate of return rather than a real rate of return, and is suitable for comparison with the 'nominal' rates of interest actually observed in markets (which are fixed in terms of monetary units and incorporate an element to compensate for anticipated inflation), rather than 'real' rates of interest (such as those on index-linked bonds, which attempt to eliminate the inflationary element by indexation of the money return).

NOTES

1 E.g. Rayman (1980).

2 For an alternative discussion of this, see Edwards and Bell (1961, Chapter 1).

3 The identification of the cost of intangible assets arising from the entity's operations, particularly business goodwill, poses acute difficulties. Equally, the measurement of liabilities such as provisions for future restitution of damage (as in environmental clean-up costs of mineral extraction) involves estimation of future costs rather than being grounded in historical transactions.

4 We are assuming that all assets, whether tangible or intangible, are recorded in accounts (there being a complete set of perfect markets in which they can be valued) and that pure goodwill (i.e. an excess of the economic value of the whole firm over the aggregate value of its individual assets) cannot exist, because long-run perfectly competitive equilibrium precludes the existence of pure profits.

5 These are discussed in any good micro-economics textbook.

6 Harcourt (1965) demonstrates how the economist's 'Golden Age' equilibrium can be upset by arbitrary accounting rules based on historical cost.

7 The argument applies equally to assets and liabilities: the term 'asset' is used merely for convenience, just as economists often use the term 'good' to describe any traded item.

8 In some markets, particularly those that use brokers as intermediaries, transaction costs are included in the price through a difference between the purchase price (the 'bid' price) and the selling price (the 'offer' price), the difference between the two being referred to as the broker's 'turn'

(effectively a dealing commission). The terms 'entry value' and 'exit value' were introduced by Edwards and Bell (1961).

9 This argument is expounded rigorously and at greater length by Beaver and Demski (1979).

10 Where there are intermediate repayments to the proprietor, the formulation is more complicated. This is illustrated in the appendix to this chapter.

11 A subsequent paper by Peasnell (1982) proved many of Kay's results in discrete form, as used in this book, rather than the continuous form (based on integral calculus) used by Kay. The discrete form has a greater intuitive appeal in accounting applications because accounting is concerned with recording discrete transactions and events. The academic debate on the economic significance of the accounting rate of return is surveyed in Whittington (1997).

12 This point was made by Wright (1978) in his comment on Kay's paper, and by Whittington (1979).

13 A similar interpretation can be made of current cost profit, as, for example, in Sale and Scapens (1978), which analyses the Sandilands concept of Distributable Operating Flow.

14 This approach to accounting measurement was also supported by two eminent economists: Fischer Black (1980, 1993) and Maurice Scott (1976).

15 This is elaborated in Nissim and Penman (2008).

16 One adjustment that need not be made is for growth of future profits due to incremental investment. By using current earnings as the basis of valuation, we are implicitly assuming that all income is distributed as dividends. Any retained profit and other new finance would be expected to require a normal rate of return on the additional investment. It is only super-normal (or sub-normal) future profits that pose a problem for valuation using the standard stream approach. This is a problem only if the standard stream profit measure cannot be adjusted in such as way as to capture the value of the prospect of future super-normal profits (these would be included in goodwill in a balance sheet approach to measurement). Penman's model does incorporate a growth factor, estimated from past performance, which could be regarded as a proxy measure of such a prospect.

17 This is the theoretical ideal proposed by Scott (1976).

18 This would, for example, be necessary if we wished to value the firm by dividing standard stream income by a market discount rate, which included the market's anticipation of inflation.

19 For an analysis of the effects of pricing policy on profitability in periods of inflation, see R. N. Anthony (1976).

20 Mathews (1965) provides a strong statement of this view, in a critique of the HC basis of CPP accounting.

21 Thomas' criticism also extends to replacement cost systems, when depreciation is based upon allocations of the replacement cost of new assets rather than second-hand market values of used assets. The reporting of historical cash flows is one method of avoiding the accrual problem (Thomas, 1979).

22 Stewardship has recently been a contentious issue in the IASB's conceptual framework project (Whittington, 2008a; Zeff, 2007).

23 This, and a number of other telling criticisms of Ijiri's argument, will be found in MacNeill (1971).

24 I am grateful to my former colleague, Ian Davidson, for providing this.

# 4 Current Value Accounting 1: Valuation

The earlier discussion (Chapter 1) has shown that it is possible to separate the problem of valuation from that of inflation, if we accept that inflation implies a decline in the general purchasing power of money.[1] Even in the absence of general inflation, it is likely that individual prices will change, and in the presence of inflation it is likely that individual prices will not move directly in line with the rate of inflation, as measured by a general index. Thus, in the first case, historical cost will not be an accurate representation of current value, and, in the second case, neither historical cost nor historical cost adjusted by a general index (CPP) will give an accurate representation of current value. Therefore, if some indication of current value is considered to be an important feature of accounts individual assets and liabilities (liabilities being negative assets) will require revaluation. An obvious example is that of commodities such as oil (illustrated by the BP example in Chapter 1), whose prices fluctuate strongly both in nominal (money) terms and relative to the general price level.

The case for reporting current values is strong, but not overwhelming. If accounts are supposed to give information relevant to decisions about the allocation of assets and liabilities or claims on them (such as the proprietor's net worth), or if they are intended to meet the needs of stewardship (giving an account of how effectively the entity has been managed), then current values are relevant information because they represent the value of opportunities which are currently available, whether it be replacement (in the case of replacement cost, RC), sale (in the case of net realisable value, NRV) or value in current use (discounted present value of future cash flows,

PV). This immediately raises the problem of whether to choose any single current valuation method and, if so, which one. Alternatively, it would be possible to choose different valuation methods for different assets (as in the case of value to the owner, which is discussed later in this chapter), or a variety of current values could be reported for each asset in the balance sheet. This topic will be discussed further in a later section. The questions of aggregation and the converse problem of allocation also arise, but the main practical objection to current valuation is usually the subjectivity involved in estimating current values, in the absence of deep, liquid and complete markets. This was an important issue in the worldwide debate of the 1970s and 1980s on current cost accounting, particularly in relation to estimating value in current use (PV). More recently, the same issue has been hotly debated in relation to fair value and its possible role in fuelling the Financial Crisis of 2007 onwards.

The preceding argument relates to the reporting of current values in the balance sheet. There could also be benefits to be obtained from income statements based on current values. However, we saw in Chapter 2 that current value income is equivalent to ideal economic income only under very restrictive conditions, and Revsine's (1970) demonstration that, under certain conditions, current value holding gains on assets would measure windfall gains, whilst current operating profit would measure sustainable income, serves to demonstrate the restrictive nature of the conditions, rather than to encourage the belief that it is possible to measure economic income under more realistic conditions.

A less ambitious but more plausible reason for basing income measures on current values is that advanced by Edwards and Bell (1961),that current values provide a means of providing an *ex post* account of the economic progress of the firm to date, using the latest available market-validated information. Tippett (1979) provides an elaboration of this point of view. An assessment of economic income, or the economic value of the firm as a whole, requires taking a view as to the prospective cash flows of the firm. Current values may be a relevant input in forming such a view, particularly in providing current cost measures which are informative about profit margins, but will not provide a direct valuation of the whole firm. This will require an assessment of the value of the firm by discounting the prospective cash flows. The excess of this valuation over the current value of the net assets of the firm is a measure of goodwill, which is the present value of the expected future returns in excess of normal returns on the net assets invested. Thus the current value of assets (less liabilities) enables a separation to be made between the firm's achievements to date (reflected in the current value of net assets) and the value of its future prospects (reflected in goodwill).[2]

An alternative case for current value based income measures might be in terms of the maintainable consumption or 'standard stream' (Hicks No 3) concept of income. This type of concept often seemed to underlie the debate on current cost accounting (one possible form of current value accounting), especially in the discussions of 'distributable profit' or 'distributable operating flow', which can be interpreted as being close to Hicks' idea of maintainable consumption (e.g. Sale and Scapens, 1978), although the Sandilands Report (paras. 100–103) based its central concept of income on the 'Hicks No. 1' capital maintenance model (maintenance of the value of initial capital, rather than future consumption levels). However, if current value income measurements are to be justified on consumption maintenance grounds, the precise assumptions necessary to sustain the case need to be explored more thoroughly than is typically the case in published work on the subject. It seems probable that a precise measure of 'Hicks No. 3' income will emerge only under fairly restrictive assumptions about the future course of individual asset prices, the general price level and interest rates and will therefore rely heavily on subjective expectations. The most thorough attempt to apply the standard stream model to business accounting is by Scott (1976): this demonstrates clearly the importance of expectations in this approach, e.g. the appropriate treatment of real holding gains on stocks depends upon the extent to which the increase in the real cost of stocks will be passed on in the selling price. Another interesting exploration by an economist of the consumption maintenance approach (although not explicitly within the Hicksian framework) is by Black (1993).

If the case for current value accounting is based upon its usefulness as an approximation to the 'Hicks No. 1' capital maintenance measure of income, an important issue is the definition of the capital to be maintained intact. There are three broad definitions of capital maintenance which tend to be associated with current value systems, money capital, real proprietary capital and entity capital. Money capital is the value of capital in monetary units, irrespective of fluctuations in the value of money, as in a historical cost system. Real proprietary capital implies the adjustment of money capital by an index reflecting changes in the proprietor's purchasing power. A general index is usually advocated for this purpose, in which case, if assets are valued at current prices, we have a form of 'real terms' accounting, as described briefly in Chapter 1 and discussed more fully in Chapter 6. Entity capital implies the adjustment of money capital to reflect changes in the price of the specific assets held by the firm. It is thereby intended to maintain the accounting entity intact in its specific form. In an extreme approach, this can amount to maintaining the identical physical assets of the entity intact, but this is often moderated, to allow for technical progress and factor substitution due to changing prices, by defining the maintenance of 'operating capacity' as the object of capital maintenance. Another variant of the entity capital maintenance approach is to introduce a proprietary element by means of a 'gearing adjustment'. These alternative concepts of capital maintenance will be discussed in more detail in Chapter 6. For the remainder of this chapter, we shall concentrate upon the basic technique of current value accounting, and the choice of valuation base.

## 4.2 BASIC METHODS OF CURRENT VALUE ACCOUNTING

Current value accounting requires the periodic up-dating of asset (and liability) values. In terms of book-keeping entries, this implies debiting the asset account, to record the increase in value, and crediting the holding gain. If the holding gain is regarded as a profit, it is transferred to the credit of the income statement, thus preserving the 'clean surplus' relationship between the Income Statement and the Balance Sheet, but if it is regarded as a growth of the capital to be maintained intact (as in the case of the entity approach to capital maintenance, described earlier) it is transferred to the credit of proprietor's capital, as an increase in capital reserves, breaking the clean surplus relationship between the Income Statement and the balance sheet. The latter transfer can be carried out via a Statement of Gains, as in the Sandilands Report's proposals, so that the proprietors are made aware of the gains despite the fact that they are not recognised as profit. The total gains figure from that statement (unlike the narrower income measure obtained from the income statement) can then serve as a comprehensive income measure which has a clean surplus relationship with the balance sheet, so that total gains are consistent with the change in net assets recorded in the balance sheet over the period.

In terms of the algebraic notation used in earlier chapters, the current value balance sheets are

$$P_t'' = N_t'' + M_t - L_t$$

and

$$P_{t+1}'' = N_{t+1}'' + M_{t+1} - L_{t+1} \tag{4.1}$$

where $N''$ indicates current value of non-monetary assets at the relevant date, $M$ and $L$ are of fixed money value, and $P''$ is the proprietor's net assets under current valuation. When some liabilities, such as long-term loans, are 'non-monetary', fluctuating in money value, they should be revalued and deducted in calculating $N''$, which should strictly be defined as *net* non-monetary assets. The 'clean surplus' profit measure under current value accounting, assuming money capital maintenance and no dividend distributions or introductions of new capital, is

$$Y_{CVA} = P''_{t+1} - P''_t \tag{4.2}$$

In the transactionless case in which each asset is held throughout the period, we can re-define the closing balance sheet as

$$P''_{t+1} = N''_t(1 + s) + M_t - L_t \tag{4.3}$$

where s is a specific index measuring the value change of the specific bundle of assets $N''_t$. Maintaining the nominal money value of capital, and abandoning the accountant's traditional reluctance to recognise gains on holding assets until they are realised, the total (clean surplus) profit then becomes equal to the sum of the holding gains of the period:

$$Y_{CVA} = N''_t.s \tag{4.4}$$

If we substitute an entity capital maintenance concept, the holding gain $N''_t.s$ will be regarded as an accretion to capital, and profit will be zero, breaking the 'clean surplus' articulation of profit with the change in the balance sheet value of proprietors' capital. This is analogous to the current cost accounting measures of operating profit, proposed by the Sandilands Committee, so we can call it $Y_{CCA}$:

$$Y_{CCA} = P''_{t+1} - (P''_t + N''_t.s) = 0 \tag{4.5}$$

More generally, if we drop the assumption of the transactionless interval, we can define current value income, on a money capital maintenance basis, as

$$\begin{aligned} Y_{CVA} &= P''_{t+1} - P''_t \\ &= (N''_{t+1} - N''_t) + (M_{t+1} - M_t) - (L_{t+1} - L_t) \end{aligned} \tag{4.6}$$

This is broadly what the Sandilands Committee proposed as the basis of its Statement of Gains.[3] The current cost profit proposed by Sandilands uses the entity concept of capital maintenance and is based upon[4] the following model:

$$Y_{\text{CCA}} = P''_{t+1} - (P''_t + N''_t.s)$$
$$= [N''_{t+1} - N''_t(1 + s)] + [M_{t+1} - M_t] - [L_{t+1} - L_t] \qquad (4.7)$$

$N''_t.s$ is the total net holding gain. Since the composition of $N$ can now change through time, this holding gain should be calculated by reference to changes in the value of each specific asset over the period for which it is held. Thus $s$ is now not merely an index of the change in value of the assets held throughout the period expressed as a proportion of the initial assets. The appropriate computational procedure would be first to calculate the total net holding gains on all non-monetary assets held during the period, including those acquired or disposed of during the period. This sum is defined as $N''_t.s$ and could be divided by $N''_t$ to yield a measure of $s$. Thus $s$ is the end product of the calculation rather than an ingredient in making it, and in practice it would be unnecessary to carry the calculation so far as the derivation of $s$, because the total net holding gain, $N''_t.s$ rather than $s$, is the centre of interest. This procedure enables entity capital maintenance to be based upon maintaining the value of a shifting population of capital assets, rather than being tied rigidly to assets held at the beginning of the year.

There are, of course, alternative concepts of capital maintenance. There are variants upon the entity approach, and there is the competing concept of maintaining real proprietary capital. The alternative concepts of capital maintenance will be discussed in Chapter 6. We now turn to the alternative definitions and interpretations of what we have hitherto defined broadly as 'current value'.

## 4.3 THE CHOICE OF CURRENT VALUES

The choice of current valuation base is a very complex issue. Not only are there three basic types of value available (entry, exit and value in use, as discussed earlier), but within each type a number of variations is possible. In choosing between valuation bases we may face the problem that one basis is appropriate for valuing assets in the balance sheet but another basis is appropriate for assessing changes in assets and capital for the purposes of the profit and loss account (Macdonald, 1974b).[5] Thus, if we insist on having articulated accounts,[6] prepared on a single consistent valuation basis to give a 'clean surplus' measure of income, we may be unable to implement our preferred valuation basis for each statement. Alternatively, we may wish to prepare a variety of statements on different valuation bases: this will eliminate the first problem but may raise a new problem of complexity, since the user of accounts will now be faced with a choice of different balance sheets and profit and loss accounts prepared on different valuation bases (Chambers, 1972).

Another approach is to use a valuation rule, such as value to the owner, which selects the valuation of a particular asset according to such circumstances as the relative values arising from the alternative bases, as in the traditional conservative rule 'cost or market value, whichever is the lower'. This does allow more than one valuation basis to be used in the accounts, whilst avoiding the complexity arising from having alternative values of the same asset, but this simplicity may be obtained at the cost of losing valuable information in those cases where more than one value is relevant to users' needs. It may also introduce an aggregation problem, since the aggregate value of assets now represents a collection of values using different bases.

As a prelude to the discussion of the choice of valuation bases, we shall briefly describe the three broad bases and the case for each of them, in turn. Subsequent sections will discuss two specific valuation approaches that have found favour with accounting standard-setters: value to the owner and fair value.

### 4.3.1 Replacement Cost ('Entry' Value)

Replacement cost is probably the basis favoured by the majority of writers on current value accounting and it has found most favour in practice. Early advocates of replacement cost were Schmidt (1921, 1930) in Germany and Limperg in the Netherlands. Schmidt and other members of the German school influenced Sweeney (1936), who advocated replacement cost valuation as the ideal base upon which to implement his system of stabilised accounting (a form of CPP adjustment). Schmidt's ideas were subsequently influential in shaping proposals for a form of current cost accounting in West Germany (Coenenberg and Macharzina, 1976). The Dutch school was influential in the adoption of a form of replacement cost accounting by some companies in the Netherlands, notably by Philips of Eindhoven, whose system of accounting was designed by Limperg's pupil, Goudeket, although strictly the Dutch method was based on replacement *value*, which, as explained later in this chapter, is a form of Value to the Business. Replacement cost was also favoured as a valuation base by Edwards and Bell (1961) and later by Revsine (1973) in the US and was proposed in pronouncements by the Securities and Exchange Commission (1976) and the FASB (1979b).[7] In Australia, Mathews and Grant (1958) and Gynther (1966) were notable advocates of replacement cost accounting, although later professional and official proposals in Australia (e.g. Institute of Chartered Accountants in Australia and Australian Society of Accountants, 1975; Mathews, 1975) and New Zealand (Richardson Committee Report, 1976) tended to follow the 'value to the owner' approach, as advocated by Baxter (1967, 1975) and others (including Wright, 1970, in Australia). Value to the owner was adopted in the Sandilands Report (Sandilands Committee, 1975) and subsequent professional proposals for reform in the UK,[8] culminating in the standard SSAP16 (1980, withdrawn 1988). Value to the owner leads to replacement cost in most circumstances in practice (Gee and Peasnell, 1976) but it is based upon different reasoning and will be discussed separately.[9]

In view of the wide range of writers who have supported replacement cost accounting, and the wide variety of their proposals, it is impossible to do justice to all of their arguments. However, it is clear that, to the individual firm, replacement cost is a cost rather than a value, although it might, under certain circumstances, be equal to a value (such as 'value to the owner', in many cases), i.e.

replacement cost represents the cost of acquiring an asset (which Edwards and Bell describe as an 'entry' value), not the value attaching to an asset already held. It thus has an obvious relevance to the assessment of costs in the profit and loss account. If we adopt a 'Hicks No. 1' capital maintenance approach to income measurement, it seems intuitively reasonable that replacement cost should be charged to profit because this allows for replacement, and hence for capital maintenance, although more thorough investigation raises the problem of defining what is meant by 'replacement'. If, alternatively, we adopt a 'Hicks No. 3' consumption maintenance approach, it again seems intuitively reasonable that we will maintain consumption levels in future if we replace whatever was used up in creating the output, but again the concept of replacement requires closer definition.

There is, in fact, a variety of concepts of replacement. At one extreme, there is the concept of physical replacement (favoured, for example, by Edwards and Bell, 1961, and aptly described by Bell, 1971, as 'reproduction cost') which charges against profit the replacement cost of the assets actually used up in the course of the period. At the other extreme, there is the concept of economic replacement: the money amount necessary to compensate for the loss of the assets' services.

Where there is technical progress or where changes in relative factor prices have caused a change in the optimal productive method (a case discussed by Petri and Gelfand, 1979) there is a divergence between the cost of physical replacement and the cost of replacing the equivalent service. This will be due not only to reduced capital costs but also to more efficient use of associated factors of production, such as labour and fuel. Furthermore, in such conditions, it is quite likely that the firm will not wish to replace the equivalent service, if demand for the product is declining in favour of a substitute product. 'Value to the owner' attempts to deal with this problem by substituting alternative values (the higher of present value in use or net realisable value on disposal) when replacement is not justified.

If we follow the 'economic replacement' argument very far, we shall arrive at a point at which replacement cost is used merely as a surrogate for economic value, a position explored by Revsine (1973, 1976), Barton (1974) and Cook and Holzmann (1976). This implies that replacement cost depreciation or appreciation (holding gains) is a measure of the change in the discounted present value of the firm resulting from owning the asset or assets in question. This equivalence will hold only under highly restrictive conditions and is not, therefore, a sound basis for a practical accounting system.

The alternative approach is to adhere strictly to one of two broad concepts: replacement of the physical object ('reproduction') or replacement of the physical service. Both of these approaches avoid the fundamental difficulties involved in imputing an economic value to services, which would lead inevitably to some attempt to assess economic income. If we adopt the cost of reproduction, the profit and loss account will be charged with the current cost of production under the techniques actually employed (by way of the depreciation charge, and the charge for stocks). Under changing conditions (of prices or technology) this will have poor predictive ability, but it will fulfil Edwards and Bell's objective[10] of providing an *ex post* description of the activities of the firm based upon market purchase prices prevailing at the time of each transaction. It will also lead to a 'holding gain or loss', indicating the difference between historical purchase price and price at the time of use. Thus, the year-end balance sheet will show unrealised holding gains (or losses) representing the excess (or deficiency) of replacement cost over (or under) historical cost of assets carried forward for future use. There is, of course, no reason to believe that these assets will be put to a use which justifies current replacement cost, or that replacement cost will remain the same until the time of use. The uncertainty surrounding future replacement cost at the time of use is one reason which has been advanced for separating unrealised holding gains from realised holding gains.[11]

With regard to the choice of the reproduction cost of the physical service (rather than the specific asset) as the basis of replacement cost, this seems to be the most appropriate method for the calculation of an operating profit which reflects current costs. If the 'reproduction of assets' and the 'reproduction of service' bases are not identical, this implies that the assets currently used by the firm are not those which it would use were it to seek to purchase the services at their lowest current price in the market place. Thus, the physical assets used by the firm have ceased to be 'best current practice' assets and the firm has sustained a holding loss which should be reported when it occurs, the assets being written down to the lower cost of replacing the services embodied in them, which is the opportunity cost of using them. Subsequent use of the assets should be charged to profit or loss on the new, lower 'replacement of service' valuation. In assessing the cost of replacement of the service, an appropriate allowance should be made for changes in the cost of other productive factors which are associated with the use of the asset. For example, if the alternative asset economised on the use of fuel and labour, an estimate of the present value of these savings should be deducted from the cost of the new asset in calculating the replacement cost of the service embodied in the existing asset.

At this point, it might be objected that the physical asset might, in such a case, have maintained its market value because of its value in alternative uses, so that the 'holding loss' is due merely to the firm's mis-management of its resources. An example might be the case of real property, which provides a service for the firm's present activities (e.g. as a warehouse) but which could be put to more profitable alternative uses (such as conversion to residential use) whilst being replaced by cheaper commercial property that is not suitable for more profitable alternative uses. Such mis-management might reasonably result in a 'holding loss' if the asset is kept in its present use, but the balance sheet will show the asset at a lower value than it might command currently in the market. It would clearly be of value to shareholders and other external users of accounts to know that the market value is higher than the balance sheet value of the asset in such a case, in order to assess the effectiveness of management. For example, in calculating a rate of return on capital employed, it would seem appropriate to include in the denominator (capital employed) the asset at its full market value: this represents the revenue forgone by retaining the asset rather than disposing of it in the market.

Two aspects of this argument should be noted. Firstly, it is not an argument about the basis of assessing replacement cost, but about the greater relevance, in some circumstances, of an alternative valuation basis, net realisable value.[12] Secondly, it illustrates the possibility of a divergence between the valuation basis appropriate to a balance sheet and that appropriate to the calculation of operating profit in the income statement. This is because we have imputed different uses to the two statements, but these uses do seem to be plausible. This difficulty can be overcome by means of additional disclosures. For example, a replacement cost balance sheet can be supplemented by a note showing net realisable values, when these are materially higher than replacement costs. Similarly, a supplementary Statement of Gains (as in the proposals of the Sandilands Report) can clarify the interpretation of replacement cost profit. The replacement cost income statement calculates operating profit after charging for replacement of the services used at current costs, and the holding gains (or losses) show how the firm has gained (or lost) by buying assets before the time of their use. These holding gains and losses can be added to operating profit to yield a comprehensive income, having a 'clean surplus' relationship with the replacement cost balance sheet, in a comprehensive income statement.[13] The components of this income statement can be used as inputs to projections of future cash flows for use in valuing the entity.

Whatever the measure of replacement cost used, we are likely, in practice, to encounter the twin problems of allocation and aggregation (Thomas, 1974), although these problems are not unique to replacement cost. Allocation arises in the valuation of individual assets both across assets and through time. Across assets, we have the problem of attributing jointly incurred costs to individual assets, such as work-in-progress, where an allocation has to be made between the cost of finished and unfinished goods. Through time, we have the problem of allocating the capital cost of a durable asset across the individual periods during which it is used. In both cases, the problem could be avoided if there were markets for all of the items for which replacement cost was being estimated, but in practice it is likely to be difficult to establish a market purchase price for part-processed work-in-progress or part-used capital assets. The problem of aggregation also arises when assets are interdependent; replacement cost of one asset individually might be either more or less expensive than if we were to replace it together with all of the other assets with which it is associated in the productive processes.[14] An obvious example is that the cost of a new car is usually much lower than the total cost of purchasing and assembling its component parts. Thus, if we were estimating the replacement cost of a whole factory, as we might for insurance purposes, we would probably use different asset prices from those which would be applied to estimate the replacement cost of those assets which need to be replaced as a result of normal wear and tear in an accounting year. The latter level of aggregation is more likely to meet the needs of users of a profit and loss account based on replacement cost, as it indicates the level of replacement cost which is likely to be incurred in the maintenance of the present level of productive activity.

Another difficulty in implementing certain forms of replacement cost accounting (particularly the Edwards and Bell form) is in making the distinction between 'holding gains' and 'operating gains'. More precisely, the problem is one of establishing the exact meaning of replacement cost, particularly with respect to timing. Since production takes time it is extremely difficult to define a precise moment of 'use' at which replacement cost can be established, particularly in the case of stocks and work-in-progress. The precise definition of replacement cost does, of course, determine the division of realised gains between operating profits (against which replacement cost of assets used is debited) and holding gains (to which the difference between historical cost and replacement cost at the time of use is credited). Moreover, the value of the dichotomy between operating gains and holding gains has been questioned[15] on the ground that production and asset holding are essentially joint decisions in many instances. Whether or not these criticisms invalidate the usefulness of the dichotomy depends partly upon materiality (how important is the arbitrary timing element in replacement cost) and partly upon fact (whether the decisions are in fact separate or joint). A further issue, which is also one of fact, is the question as to whether the dichotomy improves the ability of users of accounts to predict the future course of events.

In conclusion, there are two types of basic approach to replacement cost accounting. One is what was described earlier as a *measurement* perspective on financial accounting and sees it as providing surrogates for economic value (in the balance sheet) and income (in the profit and loss account or income statement). This relationship has been demonstrated to hold only under very restrictive circumstances. The alternative approach is what has been characterised as an *information* perspective and regards replacement cost accounting as providing data relevant to the assessment of the economic progress of the firm and the estimation (but not the precise calculation) of economic value and income by the users of accounts. This approach is probably best characterised by the work of Edwards and Bell. The 'relevant data' provided by the replacement cost profit and loss account are a statement of the operating profit based on current replacement costs and a statement of both realised and unrealised holding gains, due to the change in purchase prices between the time of purchase of assets and the time of use (or, in the case of unrealised gains, the closing balance sheet). The operating profit assesses the *ex post* profitability of operating activities and will be of direct use in predicting the future only if prices, costs and level of activity are expected to remain the same. The precise definition of replacement cost presents a number of conceptual problems, as does the dichotomy between holding gains and operating gains. The replacement cost balance sheet shows the current replacement cost of assets held for future use by the firm. Here also there are conceptual problems, but a more important limitation of the replacement cost balance sheet is that its valuations are based upon the continuity of the business in its present form and do not show the market value of the assets which might be realised by their disposal. Even if we accept the continuity assumption, replacement costs do not indicate the value which the firm will realise from the use of the assets: this will depend upon the operations of future periods.[16] Thus, a replacement cost balance sheet has the advantage over a historical cost balance sheet that it is based upon contemporary rather than historical values, but it shares with it the limitation that, taken by itself, it is based upon costs rather than values and gives no direct indication of the amounts for which the assets of the firm could be sold.

### 4.3.2 Net Realisable Value ('Exit' Value)

One system which remedies this problem, at the price of raising new problems of its own, is net realisable value accounting. In many ways, net realisable value is an intuitively appealing valuation basis for accounts. If accounts purport to report values, then a natural interpretation of value is the amount of money for which an asset can be exchanged in the market place (net realisable value being selling price, less selling costs). The balance sheet lists assets and attributes values to them, and it is not surprising that unsophisticated users tend to assume that its valuations are based on selling prices. Tweedie (1977) refers to net realisable value as an 'intuitive concept', and reports an empirical study which supports this view.

This is not to say that all advocates of net realisable value in accounts are unsophisticated. On the contrary, amongst academic writers, those who have advocated net realisable value have tended to argue with greater-than-average sophistication and at a higher-than-average theoretical level.

One of the earlier advocates of the incorporation of net realisable values in accounts was Canning (1929), who made the first systematic critique of accounting practice from the standpoint of economic theory. Canning proposed that assets should be valued at net realisable values when, as in the case of inventories, a 'direct valuation' is possible. In other instances (as in the case of fixed plant and machinery held for future use). Canning proposed 'indirect valuation' methods based upon 'opportunity differences', which are essentially similar to the 'value to the owner' rules developed by subsequent writers, and discussed later in this chapter. Canning was not, therefore, a single-minded advocate of net realisable value, his main concern being to change the orientation of accounting from backward-looking historical cost to contemporary and forward-looking measures which are more compatible with rational economic decisions. He was aware that different information might serve different purposes and might be subject to different degrees of uncertainty, and he was willing to use a variety of valuation bases, including the use of alternative valuations for the same asset. However, Canning was certainly a pioneer in proposing the incorporation of market selling values in accounts. In this context it is relevant that Canning shared his contemporaries' pre-occupation with the balance sheet as 'the major end-product of accounting' (Canning, 1929, p. 179), although he was true to his Fisherian economic theory in recognising that, even on a current value basis, the sum of the net assets of the firm will not equal the economic value of the firm as a whole (the discounted present value of future net returns), the difference being goodwill.[17]

Perhaps the best-known early advocate of current market value was Kenneth MacNeal, whose *Truth in Accounting* (MacNeal, 1939) has achieved classic status as a polemic in favour of current value accounting. He approached the problem as a practical accountant, rather than a theorist, but his proposals have many features which have been supported by subsequent theoretical writers, notably Chambers (1966). It is notable that MacNeal was financial controller of an investment trust company, and subsequently a property company, both types of activity being associated with investment in durable assets which are held with a view to possible re-sale, not with a presumption that they will be used up in the productive activities of the business. Indeed, the inspiration for MacNeal's work was his (successful) attempt to persuade the auditors of his investment trust to accept accounts based upon current market values of the investments. The background to MacNeal's work has been thoroughly explored by Zeff (1982), who points out that MacNeal stopped short of advocating net realisable values, preferring middle market prices (between buying and selling price) when buying and selling prices differed.

Of later accounting theorists, the two most closely associated with the advocacy of net realisable value are Chambers (1966) and Sterling (1970), although Ross (1969) has provided a practitioner's view of the case for current values, including net realisable values in some cases. Chambers was a particularly prolific writer on the subject, much of his work being listed, with a commentary, in Chambers (1977). He called his system Continuously Contemporary Accounting, and this has been dubbed CoCoA, to differentiate it from the replacement-cost-oriented current cost accounting (CCA). Net realisable value was also considered as a possible valuation base by Edwards and Bell (1961, Chapter 3) who propounded a model of 'realisable profit' on this basis and coined the term 'exit value' to describe it. Their final choice was to favour 'entry value', replacement cost (a decision defended by Edwards, 1975), as incorporated in their model of 'business profit', in preference to net realisable value (which they refer to, somewhat imprecisely, as 'opportunity cost') for general purposes in an ongoing business, but they emphasise that both measures are of potential usefulness.

A notable subsequent advocacy of net realisable value was 'Making Corporate Reports Valuable' (MCRV), a report sponsored and published by the Institute of Chartered Accountants of Scotland (McMonnies, 1988). This was supported by research in the form of case studies and literature searches. It was a wide-ranging examination of the context and process of financial reporting, in the spirit of

*The Corporate Report* (Accounting Standards Steering Committee, 1975) and has subsequently been influential in the thinking of professionals and standard-setters. In Chapter 6 it dealt specifically with measurement and concluded that some form of current measurement (replacement cost or net realisable value) was preferable to historic cost (considered to be less relevant) or net present value of future returns (considered to be relevant to investment decisions but too subjective for use in financial reporting). The current measurement that was preferred was net realisable value, on the ground that a measure of value was more relevant than a measure of cost (p. 103). The latter preference reflected the 'balance sheet' approach that was explicitly endorsed in the report: the balance sheet was regarded as the central financial statement, conveying important information about the value of the business, and the accruals-based income statement was mainly a means of explaining changes in the balance sheet value of the business. The theoretical basis adopted owed a great deal to the previous work of Chambers (1966) and Sterling (1970), which was explicitly acknowledged (p. 61).

The measurement proposals in MCRV did not have the apparent impact on policy that was achieved by some other aspects of the Report, although the increasing adoption of fair value in accounting standards, particularly for financial instruments, might be regarded as consistent with the exit value approach. However, when fair value was finally defined clearly in accounting standards (FAS 157; Financial Accounting Standards Board, 2006) it was based on selling price without deduction of selling costs. Net realisable value, as advocated in MCRV, is defined by the IASB and FASB as 'fair value, less cost to sell'.

Although these various writers emphasise different reasons for using net realisable values, the broad case can be summarised as follows. Firstly, and probably most important, is the usefulness of current net realisable value as an indication of an important opportunity facing the firm, that of disposing of the asset. Chambers refers to this as the 'current cash equivalent' of an asset, and correctly emphasises that this is a relevant value in making a wide range of decisions and appraisals, although he is perhaps at fault in neglecting the merits of alternative valuations: rational economic decisions are usually based upon a *comparison* of values of alternative dispositions of assets, not on the absolute amount of one value in isolation (Whittington, 1974). Edwards and Bell ascribe similar merits to net realisable value by describing it as 'opportunity cost', although in doing this they also are over-stating its merits: opportunity cost uses the *best* alternative revenue forgone, whereas net realisable value represents one of several alternatives any of which may represent the best (see note 28).

Secondly, there is a group of arguments surrounding the measurement properties of net realisable value. These arguments are particularly associated with Chambers (1966) and Sterling (1970). It is claimed that net realisable values have properties of additivity and objectivity which conform with the requirements of measurement theory better than do alternative measures. Powerful support for net realisable values has come from Thomas (1969, 1974), whose incisive work on the allocation problem leads him to the conclusion that net realisable values are the only values which can avoid the allocation problem.[18] However, Thomas does not accept that net realisable values avoid the aggregation problem: the market value of a group of assets valued together is not necessarily equal to the sum of that of the individual assets. Some of the other arguments surrounding the measurement properties of net realisable values are somewhat abstruse (Chambers, 1966), and sometimes appear to involve the imposition of apparently arbitrary criteria for assessing accounting measurements (Chambers, 1978).

Finally, it can be argued that net realisable value has greater intuitive meaning to users of accounts (Tweedie, 1977), and is therefore more likely to communicate more useful information to them, than are various alternative valuation bases. This raises the difficult issue of the extent to which accounts should attempt to accommodate the needs of relatively unsophisticated users. On the one hand, it might be argued that the intuition and common sense of an unsophisticated user should be respected as *prima facie* evidence of the relevance and usefulness of the information. On the other hand, it could be maintained that sophisticated users, such as investment analysts or financial journalists, are the real opinion formers, who influence the less sophisticated users through their advice and comment and who help to make the market share price by their control of institutional investment. Thus, for example, a subscriber to the Efficient Markets Hypothesis[19] would be inclined to regard the information needs of the unsophisticated investor as immaterial: such investors should accept the ruling stock market price as the best indication of a share's worth and select their portfolios merely with a view to obtaining the desired spreading of risk.[20]

The case against net realisable value as a valuation base is usually based upon its apparent lack of relevance to a continuing business, when continuity is assumed either to be axiomatic, accounts being prepared on the 'going concern' assumption, or to be the most profitable option open to the firm. In such a case, net realisable value does not represent the consequences of a course of action which will be taken. Not only, therefore, will it attribute irrelevant values to specific assets, but it will also ignore the 'goodwill' arising from the going concern value of the entity, apart from those limited cases in which it is identifiable as part of a marketable intangible asset such as a brand name. Hence, the sum of the realisable values of the assets, less liabilities, will not equal the value of the whole business, and the balance sheet will not provide a direct valuation. However, the net realisable value of separable assets may give an indication of the amount (excluding goodwill) that could be realised in a liquidation, and this may provide useful information on the risk being borne by creditors and other stakeholders, although liquidation values can be depressed by the 'fire sale' effect (enforced sale rather than disposal in the ordinary course of business).

It was the continuity assumption which led Edwards and Bell (1961) to prefer replacement cost to net realisable value. Where fixed assets are held for use in the firm, they may have very low net realisable values, because of the heavy transaction costs involved in sale, but they may also have high replacement costs which are, nevertheless, justified by the high prospective returns to be earned by using them in the business, so that replacement would be worthwhile. In the extreme, 'non-vendible' assets may have a zero (or negative) net realisable value but be essential to the profitable operation of the firm, for example in the case of highly specific infrastructure assets which have high removal and restitution costs. This type of argument has been used by Baxter (1967) in a review of Chambers' (1966) book, and by Weston (1971) in a commentary on a paper by Chambers (1971a). Chambers originally (Chambers, 1966) dealt with 'non-vendible' assets by valuation at replacement cost but later (Chambers, 1970) hardened the consistency of his approach by advocating that they should be valued on the net realisable value basis, even if this requires a zero value.

Edwards and Bell also claim that, for the continuing business, 'realisable profit' (based on net realisable value) is essentially a short-run measure, since it does not indicate the firm's ability to stay in business by covering the costs of replacement, which must be met if the firm is to stay in business in the long term. This is not an entirely satisfactory argument because the incentive to make replacement investments must depend upon future prospective returns rather than current returns, and Edwards and Bell are concerned with *ex post* performance. Anthony (1976) has suggested that the measure of profit which best indicates the long-term capacity of a steady state firm to survive in an inflationary environment depends upon the firm's pricing policy, replacement cost being an appropriate accounting base only when it is used as the basis for setting selling prices.

Another argument against net realisable value is based upon its contravention of the realisation principle (Edwards, 1975). Traditionally, accountants have been reluctant to recognise selling prices before a sale is actually made. This reluctance is supported by the doctrine of conservatism, the belief that it is prudent to under-estimate rather than to give as accurate as possible an estimate of value, so that prospective sale proceeds will be recognised only when they give rise to a loss (an impairment) and not when they give rise to a pre-sale profit. This has no obvious theoretical justification in terms of relevance, although it would be supported by a requirement for reliability, when the selling price is difficult to establish or the sale is uncertain. This is particularly relevant to the stewardship objective, because accountability of management is likely to be best served by accounting information which is not capable of manipulation by management. Recognition of price changes before realisation is also a feature of replacement cost accounting, which recognises cost increases before the costs are actually paid in the market place, reporting them, in Edwards and Bell's system, as holding gains. Hence, the realisation argument does not seem to favour either of the two current market valuation bases.

Edwards (1975) has suggested that 'exit' values (net realisable values) should not be used when they are derived from markets in which the firm is normally a buyer rather than a seller. This is really an extension of the basic argument that, for assets bought for use rather than re-sale, the proceeds of realisation represent the outcome of an unlikely event, so that replacement cost is probably more relevant to describing the value put on the assets in the usual type of transaction which the firm undertakes. This line of argument leads Edwards to concede that net realisable values might be appropriate in valuing stocks of finished goods. It therefore leads us into the area of multiple valuation bases, which will be discussed later.

The estimation of net realisable values as 'current cash equivalents', in Chambers' system, gives rise to important conceptual difficulties. Chambers emphasised the importance of realisation in the ordinary course of business as being the rule for assessing current cash equivalents. This avoids some of the excessively low valuations which might arise if stock were assessed at its immediate selling value (a problem which led Chambers, 1966, to use a cost basis for calculating stock values, for which he was subsequently criticised by Baxter, 1967). However, especially in the case of certain longer-lived assets, realisation in the ordinary course of business is difficult to apply, without venturing into the difficult and highly subjective area of estimating the present value of future receipts. In such cases, the Chambers system has to use the values which would obtain in an orderly disposal (rather than immediate liquidation), and there is a definitional problem in distinguishing between a current cash equivalent (which Chambers advocated) and discounted present value (which Chambers, rejected). Chambers' answer to this was that he was concerned with current market values, not with estimating future returns (Chambers, 1970), but if this rule is strictly enforced it is difficult to justify current cash equivalents as *realisable* values or as opportunity costs.

In summary, net realisable value clearly has relevance to a wide range of potential uses of accounting data. It is particularly appropriate in the balance sheet, the total of which represents the 'current cash equivalent' of the firm's assets on orderly disposal, although there may, in some instances, be an aggregation problem and there may be problems in valuing assets which are 'non-vendible' in the short term. Furthermore, the value of the firm's goodwill will not be included in this total, so that the value of the firm as a going concern will not normally be equal to the total value of the assets recorded in the balance sheet.[21] However, the sum of net realisable values does represent the value of one important opportunity which is open to the firm, if we can assume that all separately saleable items are recognised in the balance sheet.[22] The relevance of this opportunity and the problems of measurement will depend partly on the type of business concerned: a firm whose main business consists of holding durable assets for capital gain rather than use in operations is likely to find net realisable values relevant to its objectives and relatively easy to implement if (as seems likely in such a case) relevant market prices are available.

The profit and loss account derived from a net realisable value system is less satisfactory, particularly in the case of a continuing manufacturing business. In the case of a commodity trader (such as Sterling's, 1970, dealer in wheat) the problem of substantial fixed assets held for use in the business rather than re-sale may not arise, so that a measure such as Edwards and Bell's 'realisable profit' might be a particularly appropriate measure of the firm's performance. However, when fixed assets are held for use in the business, the depreciation charge on such assets in a net realisable value system will not reflect the current replacement cost of the asset services used during the period. If we accept Thomas' argument that all depreciation allocations are arbitrary and incorrigible, and that this is sufficient reason to abandon attempts at making such allocations, we may be unimpressed by the case for replacement cost depreciation.[23] However, we may still harbour some anxiety about the alternative offered by net realisable value, if this involves the writing-off of the total cost of a new item of plant in its year of installation, even when its replacement cost is rising and its prospects for profitable use are good, but its selling costs are high. Such a treatment may be consistent with the aims of the CoCoA accounting system, but those aims clearly do not encompass the description of the progress of the business as a going concern.

Finally, it is notable that the principal advocate of the net realisable value basis, Chambers, defended net realisable value in financial accounting to the exclusion of alternative measures (Chambers, 1972). It seems from the earlier discussion that net realisable value is one measure which is relevant in a wide range of situations but is not the only relevant measure: in many cases, we will wish to compare alternative measures. It may be that promoting net realisable values as the only measures which should appear in financial accounts has impeded the acceptance of the view that net realisable values are widely relevant and therefore deserve a place in accounts, even if it is not the primary or exclusive place.

### 4.3.3 Present Value ('Value in Use')

The third basic method of valuation to be considered is economic value or present value, i.e. the discounted present value of the future receipts to which an asset is expected to give rise if it is retained for use within the business. This might be thought to be the 'true' value of an asset or a firm, but, as was apparent from the discussions of Chapter 2, this would only be an appropriate description under restrictive conditions which do not hold in the real world in which accountants operate. Present values require two essential pieces of information, the amount of the future cash flows and of the appropriate rate of discount. In a world of uncertainty we would need to have knowledge of the probability distribution of the cash flows,[24] and the degree of uncertainty which this represented would affect the risk-adjusted discount rate. If the economy consisted of a set of complete markets in a state of perfectly competitive equilibrium, we would be able to obtain present values by observing prices in these markets, but a more realistic scenario for the accountant is a disequilibrium economy with imperfect and incomplete markets, in which one rôle of accounts is to provide information on which individual subjective estimates of present value will be made (Beaver and Demski, 1979; Bromwich, 1977a; Peasnell, 1977).

In practice, the measurement of present values by accountants is regarded as too subjective to provide a reliable basis for accounting. Although it has been adopted as one ingredient in the 'value to the owner' rules, which have been adopted for practical application in a number of countries, and in the estimation of fair value when market prices are not available (FRS13; International Accounting Standards Board, 2011), present value has been the most controversial component of these rules and has been discarded in some practical applications. However, this has not prevented 'economic value' from being presented as an ideal to which practical measures should conform as closely as possible. The 'surrogate' argument for replacement cost (discussed earlier) is an example of this approach, although it has, in fact, failed to demonstrate that replacement cost can be used as a surrogate for present value under realistic conditions. The work of Canning (1929) is another example of economic value being used as an ideal. Each of Canning's eclectic range of valuations was chosen to reflect, as nearly as possible, the economic value of a particular type of asset. For short-term assets this led him to a net realisable value approach and for fixed assets his 'opportunity difference' approach was similar to the 'value to the owner' basis,[25] discussed in the next section. Staubus (1971) is a later representative of this approach, seeking to identify the appropriate valuations of particular assets in particular situations which are consistent with the fundamental assumption that 'the most useful meaning of asset and liability quantities is the item's incremental effect upon the net discounted amount of the entity's future cash flow' (p. 50).

A possible criticism of the Staubus approach is that the different valuations which he uses are not additive, i.e. we cannot add together the replacement cost of one asset and the net realisable value of another without violating the criteria for homogeneous measurement, upon which Chambers rests part of his case for net realisable values. This is dismissed convincingly by Staubus on the ground that his measurements are not to be treated as realisable values or replacement cost *per se*, but rather as surrogates for present values, so that in this sense they are homogeneous measurements. However, there is a more difficult problem arising out of the addition of the Staubus surrogates for incremental net realisable value, in the form of the familiar aggregation problem. We have no guarantee, unless we impose severe restrictions such as constant returns to scale,[26] that the sum of incremental present values will equal the present value of the whole firm. Thus, even if we accept the Staubus surrogates as being acceptable estimates of the incremental present value of individual assets, which may be of some use in making decisions about the disposition of those assets, the balance sheet total may not give us a useful measure of the present value of the whole firm,[27] and the related profit and loss account will not give us an estimate of economic income. Furthermore, the twin problem of allocation also arises, if we start with an estimate of the aggregate present value of the firm and try to measure the individual assets and liabilities by allocating the total (or the aggregate cash flows from which the total present value is derived) to individual items.

Finally, if a single present value basis is applied, either by direct estimation or by means of surrogates, to the complete exclusion of alternative methods of valuation, another familiar difficulty arises.

For many economic decisions or *ex post* evaluations a standard of comparison is required. This may consist of past periods' performance or forecast data using the same valuation basis, but it might also involve comparison of data for the same time or period using a different valuation basis. In this situation, present value data will be useful only in conjunction with other types of data, so that the relationship between alternative valuation bases becomes one of complementarity rather than competition. A particularly important practical use of present value in conjunction with other values has been as a component of recoverable amount (the higher of present value and net realisable value) which is used in impairment tests to set an upper limit on cost-based valuations (historical cost or replacement cost) in accounts. If cost measures are not justified by prospective returns, as measured by the recoverable amount, they are reduced to that recoverable amount. An example of this is the use of the impairment test in the measurement of acquired goodwill in current IFRS. The value to the owner (discussed later) can also be interpreted as an application of impairment testing.

It should also be noted that, in some circumstances, more than one estimate of present value may be relevant, e.g. if we wish to compare the present use with an alternative use. In such a case, the present value of the asset (or a group of assets) in the best alternative use within the firm will constitute the relevant standard for comparison, if it exceeds net realisable value and the assets are already owned by the firm. If the assets are not already owned, the opportunity cost calculation will use the highest of replacement cost, net realisable value and present value in the best alternative use, as the standard for comparison.[28]

In general, the dependence of value in use on management's assumptions about the appropriate use and its expected cash flow outcomes raises serious 'moral hazard' problems in the context of accountability (alternatively referred to as stewardship). In some cases, management may have incentives to exaggerate their financial performance by over-stating the prospective returns, whereas in other circumstances they may hide the under-utilisation of an asset by ignoring potentially more profitable uses. Hence, the subjectivity of value in use restricts its utility as a vehicle for accountability.

In summary, present value or 'economic value' is potentially useful information for the purpose of a number of decisions and appraisals. It is difficult to measure, being highly subjective, and various surrogate measurements have been suggested, although the justification for using these, except in very closely defined situations, is purely pragmatic. Moreover, there may be a serious aggregation problem in interpreting the sum of incremental present values or their surrogates, and a serious allocation problem in attributing present value of the whole firm to individual assets.

A common feature of the three 'pure' valuation bases discussed earlier is that each is of potential relevance in particular circumstances and that in some cases we might wish to compare values derived from alternative bases. This raises the important issue of whether it is feasible to produce multiple-column accounts which incorporate alternative valuation bases, and this will be discussed in the final section of this chapter. However, before doing so we must consider two important valuation bases which are derived from the 'pure' bases discussed previously. The first of these, 'value to the owner', makes use of all three 'pure' valuation bases, selecting according to their relative values for the particular asset concerned. The second, fair value, can be regarded as a variant of exit value. Both bases are important because they have become part of accounting practice, as well as receiving considerable attention in the literature.

### 4.3.4 Value to the Owner ('Deprival Value')

Value to the owner, 'value to the business', 'opportunity value' or 'deprival value' (DV) is an eclectic valuation technique, based on the economic behaviour of a profit-maximising owner. It can value an asset at either net realisable value (NRV), replacement cost (RC) or discounted present value in current use (PV). Its basic method is to establish the minimum loss which a firm would suffer if it were deprived of an asset: this is taken as a measure of the value of the benefits conferred by ownership of the asset. These benefits would include the possible proceeds of sale or redevelopment when an asset is currently not deployed in the most profitable manner (Van Zijl and Whittington, 2006). Replacement cost sets a ceiling on deprival value in those cases in which it would be possible and worthwhile to replace the asset (cases 1, 2, 4 and 5 in the following table), so that the deprival value argument is often used to justify replacement cost as a general asset valuation basis (e.g. Parker and Harcourt, 1969). The deprival value principles can be applied to liabilities (Baxter, 1975; Horton and Macve, 1995; Lennard, 2002; Baxter, 2003), in which case the valuation is often referred to as *relief value* because it measures the benefit that a firm drives from being relieved of an obligation.

It is an important feature of the DV approach that the measurements underlying it represent real opportunities facing the reporting entity. To that extent they are 'entity specific', i.e. different entities will report different values according to the specific opportunities available to them. However, this does not imply a free choice that depends on management's choice of policy. The opportunities chosen should be the optimal choices for a profit-maximising entity, so that replacement cost should represent the most economic choice available to the entity and net realisable value and value in use should represent the highest values actually obtainable. The full consequences of a particular course of action should be reflected in the measurements, including, for example, consequential changes in operating costs resulting from a replacement that incorporates improved technology.

The origins of the 'value to the owner' idea in the English-speaking world appear to be in the US in the 1920s, although a single original source has not been established. It is customary to attribute the idea to Bonbright (1937), but Bonbright had been working in the field of asset valuation for some years before the publication of his classic work. Sweeney (1933) (in his paper on capital) cites Bonbright (without reference to any particular publication) as the source of the argument that replacement cost (of the service rather than the specific asset) is normally the appropriate valuation of an item of capital 'under conditions of intelligent free competition'. However, Canning (1929) had also devised rules of the value to the owner type for the valuation of fixed assets, basing his reasoning upon 'opportunity differences'. His work influenced that of Wright (1964, 1965, 1968, 1970), who developed the application of 'opportunity value' rules in the context of depreciation (1964 and 1968), stock valuation (1965), and financial accounting generally (1970). A similar concept emerged in the continental European literature, notably in Limperg's concept of 'replacement value' which was developed in the 1920s but was originally part of a Dutch oral tradition (based on Limperg's lectures at the University of Amsterdam) and appeared in English publications only from 1960 onwards (Goudeket, 1960; Mey, 1966; Burgert, 1972; Camfferman, 1998). German practice and literature dating from the early twentieth century also contained a similar concept (Schneider, 1998), and its theoretical foundations can be traced to the work of the Austrian school of economists. The writers who acknowledge direct allegiance to Bonbright are the LSE triumvirate, Baxter (1967, 1971, 1975, 2003), Edey (1974) and Solomons (1966, 1986), and also Parker and Harcourt (1969) and Stamp (1971). Of these, Solomons was the first to set out the value to the owner rules in the familiar inequality form, later popularised by Parker and Harcourt (1969) and adopted by numerous other writers. This is reproduced in the following table, using the format adopted by Ma (1976).

| Case | Interrelationship | Value to the owner |
|---|---|---|
| Asset in use | | |
| 1 | PV > RC> NRV | RC |
| 2 | PV > NRV > RC | RC |
| 3 | RC> PV> NRV | PV |
| Asset in trade | | |
| 4 | NRV > PV > RC | RC |
| 5 | NRV> RC> PV | RC |
| Asset in divestiture | | |
| 6 | RC > NRV > PV | NRV |

The first column of the table classifies the cases according to three broad categories of asset-holding activity. 'Asset in use' describes the three cases in which a rational, profit-maximising decision would imply that the asset be held for use in the firm, because PV in use in the firm is the most profitable opportunity: it should be noted that in case 3 PV is less than RC, so that the asset would not be replaced after use, but PV is the most profitable opportunity available, given that the asset is already owned by the firm, the two opportunities being hold for use (PV) or sell (NRV). 'Asset in trade' describes an asset which, in a profit-maximising firm, would be held for re-sale, since the re-sale value (NRV) exceeds value in use (PV), but which would be replaced, since selling price (NRV) exceeds buying price (RC), i.e. it would be profitable for the firm to trade continuously in the asset. The final case, 'asset in divestiture' is one in which sale is the most profitable use of an asset held by the firm (NRV > PV), but replacement is not worthwhile (RC > NRV), i.e. once-for-all sale rather than continuous trade is appropriate. It will be observed that the six cases listed exhaust all of the possible relationships between the three values, so that the rules deal with all possible contingencies.

Another way of presenting value to the owner is as replacement cost with an impairment test for recoverability. Value to the owner(or DV) is the lower of replacement cost and recoverable amount (RA), where recoverable amount is the higher of value in use (PV) and net realisable value (NRV). RA represents a cap on the value to the owner of holding the asset, so any asset with a higher RC would not justify replacement and should therefore be measured at the lower RA. Formally:

$$DV = \min \{RC, RA\}$$
$$\text{Where } RA = \max \{PV, NRV\}$$

Cases 3 and 6 are ones in which the RA cap is binding: in case 3, RA is PV and in case 6 it is NRV.

Value to the owner became a hotly debated topic amongst academics and policy makers during the inflation accounting debates of the 1960s, 1970s and early 1980s. Baxter's (1967) advocacy of value to the owner in an influential review of Chambers (1966) led to considerable controversy, especially in the pages of *Abacus*. Chambers (1970) attacked value to the owner as referring specifically to a situation in which the firm was deprived of the asset, a situation which he felt was appropriate to an insurance valuation (which was one of the purposes which Bonbright had in mind) but not to the general problem of financial reporting. He also objected to the subjectivity involved in calculating PV. Chambers was taken to task by Wright (1971) for seeming to identify PV with value to the owner, whereas PV would be the relevant 'value to the owner' only in relatively rare circumstances (case 3 in the table). Stamp (1971) proposed that PV could be dispensed with even in this case by measuring 'netback' (the higher of PV or NRV)[29] as NRV. Stamp's rule was subsequently criticised by Yoshida (1973) on the ground that PV is relevant in determining the final value even when it does not emerge as the final value, so that subjective PV does help to determine the choice of measure under Stamp's system despite never being reported. It was also criticised by Wanless (1974) who maintained that the situation in which PV is the value to the owner might be quite common.[30]

Chambers (1971b) replied to Wright, acknowledging that value to the owner was not always equal to PV, but still maintaining that the use of PV introduced an unacceptable degree of subjectivity and also objecting to the hybrid nature of value to the owner, which was alleged to violate the criteria for homogeneous measurement.[31] Chambers also demonstrated certain ambiguities in Bonbright's definitions, but, as has already been explained, Bonbright was not the exclusive source of the value to the owner principle.[32] Ma (1976) also entered this debate, emphasising the ambiguity of PV when the asset is part of a joint productive process, so that the problem of allocation arises. This criticism seems to be inappropriate: as Edey (1974) points out, if the asset concerned is essential to a joint operation, the PV of the whole operation *will* be relevant to the asset-holding decision, and RC of the whole will become the relevant 'deprival value' ('deprival value' being the description of value to the owner favoured by Baxter and Edey). It might be argued that deprival value is specifically designed to prevent the attribution of an excessive aggregate value in such a case.

In 1975, value to the owner, referred to as 'value to the business', was adopted by the Sandilands Committee and since then it was the asset valuation base of all British proposals for current cost accounting, including the ASC's standard SSAP16 (issued in March 1980).[33] It was also proposed by the Richardson Committee Report in New Zealand (1976) and by the 1975 Australian Preliminary Exposure Draft,[34] both of which adopted Stamp's proposal for avoiding the calculation of PV as value to the owner. These developments gave further impetus to theoretical work exploring the rationale of value to the owner.

Two statements from the LSE school on the use of value to the owner in financial reporting, by Baxter and by Edey, were published in the year preceding the Sandilands Report. Baxter's case was essentially pragmatic ('such a standard is grounded in common sense', Baxter (1975, p. 125), stressing that 'deprival value' avoids certain apparently anomalous valuations which would result from applying a single valuation method (RC, NRV or PV) in all circumstances (hence the apparent irrelevance of Ma's criticism). Edey (1974) dealt particularly with the problem of aggregation and conceded that, for collections of interdependent assets, the only satisfactory method of applying deprival value is in aggregate, i.e. to calculate PV, NRV or RC for the group of assets, which may imply valuing the firm as a whole, a formidable task in practice.

Following the publication of the Sandilands Report, Gee and Peasnell (1976) provided 'A Pragmatic Defence of Replacement Cost' in the context of the Sandilands system. They explored each of the six possible relationships between PV, NRV and RC (given in the earlier table) and appraised them in terms of their likely frequency, the circumstances under which they might arise, and the valuation problems arising from those circumstances. They concluded (with some reservations about case 6, RC > NRV > PV) that RC is likely to be a satisfactory valuation basis in most cases, and that the simplicity resulting from having a single valuation basis is likely to compensate for any consequential loss of accuracy. As this is an extension of Stamp's 'netback' method of simplifying value to the owner, it might be dubbed the Lancaster method.[35] Gee and Peasnell did not produce empirical evidence in support of their assumptions as to the likely frequency of the various cases, and this is an area which still requires empirical investigation.

A second theme in the Gee and Peasnell paper was the problem of aggregation, a problem stated earlier by Edey (1974). They conceded the difficulty of interpreting the sum of the RC of individual assets, bearing in mind that this might well exceed the PV of the whole firm,[36] but they pointed out that this problem of 'over-imputation' of individual values can arise equally under the conventional value to the owner rules (as discussed by Edey, 1974), and so does not invalidate the case for their simplified approach. The theme of aggregation was explored further in Peasnell (1978). This used Thomas' (1969, 1974) arguments concerning the 'incorrigibility' of allocation rules to demonstrate that the total value of a firm's assets under the conventional value to the owner rule (as used in current cost accounting) is rendered arbitrary when there are interaction effects between assets, which make the allocation of PV dependent upon the precise definition and level of disaggregation of deprival. This paper also considered interactions due to risk. The author concluded that the valuation of intangible assets and their separation from the valuation of other assets require urgent consideration in current cost accounting. However, he did not discuss the fundamental issue of what the total value of assets in a 'value to the owner' system *ought* to mean: he appeared to suggest that it should sum to the PV of the whole firm, but the author's own work elsewhere (Peasnell, 1977) suggests that accountants 'do not have a comparative advantage in calculating PV and should not attempt it'. A related question is that, if the aggregate of value to the owner of individual assets is an arbitrary sum of dubious significance (as Baxter, 1975; Edey, 1974; and Peasnell, 1978, all suggest), what can be the significance of an aggregate comprehensive income measure derived from the same valuation?

A paper by Bromwich (1977b) explored another aspect of value to the owner: its claim to be rooted in the economist's concept of opportunity cost. Bromwich demonstrated that this claim is valid only in closely defined circumstances, when the best alternative is that defined by the deprival situation, or when value to the owner is numerically equal to (and therefore a surrogate for) the value of the best alternative. Thus, the connection between value to the owner and the opportunity cost concept is not as strong as is sometimes suggested. Even if the connection were stronger, there would be a need to specify more clearly why the opportunity cost of individual assets should be relevant to financial reporting.

This flurry of academic papers reflected the general interest in deprival value in the 1970s when the 'current cost revolution' (Tweedie and Whittington, 1984) was taking place. Standards-setters and governments in this period expressed support for current cost accounting (CCA), which used or was consistent with a deprival value measurement base (Tweedie and Whittington, 1984). A particularly notable example of this was the Sandilands Report (Sandilands Committee, 1975) in the UK, which included a tabular presentation of the deprival value process similar to that in the preceding table.

In the 1980s, the CCA experiment in financial accounting failed (Tweedie and Whittington, 1997) and the academic debate on deprival value was less prolific. However, interest in CCA and deprival value was sustained in the public sector and in the increasingly privatised public utility sector, for regulatory purposes (Whittington, 1998a). The *Byatt Report* (Byatt, 1986), published by the UK Treasury proposed a detailed CCA accounting system for monitoring state-owned enterprises and determining their pricing policies, including a thorough discussion of the calculation of the replacement cost of fixed assets within a deprival value framework, although the system was not ultimately adopted, possibly because most of the relevant state enterprises, such as the public utilities, were soon privatised. However, DV continued to be used by the regulators of the privatised utilities in the UK and in Australia to establish the regulatory asset base used in price cap regulation (Clarke, 1998; Whittington, 1998b), although its use for this purpose has conceptual difficulties. A particular difficulty is that the process of setting a price cap directly affects the future cash flows of the business, so that PV, an important component of DV, cannot be measured independently as an input to the decision.[37]

In this period, a notable contribution to the theoretical literature of DV in relation to public policy was Edwards, Kay and Mayer (1987), three economists whose particular concern was with the *ex post* measurement of excess profits (monopoly rents) for the purpose of identifying the exercise of monopoly power and with the *ex ante* measurement of an accounting rate of return that can be compared with the cost of capital to establish whether additional investment by the entity is profitable. These are essentially the concerns of the industrial economist rather than the shareholder, who is more likely to be concerned with share valuation or stewardship, and that may explain the relative neglect of the work in the accounting literature. However, Edwards, Kay and Mayer do successfully and rigorously demonstrate the usefulness of an accounting rate of return based on deprival value for the specific purposes that they define. The analysis is based upon a segment of the entity's life, in which both opening and closing net worth are measured at deprival value, so that it is applicable to a continuing business. It therefore avoids a critical limitation of the earlier analysis of accounting profits by Kay (1976) and Peasnell (1982) which applied only to returns over the whole life of a business or project.

It is disappointing that no attempts have been made to explore the possible extension of the Edwards, Kay and Mayer analysis to share valuation models. For example, the valuation models derived from the work of Ohlson (1995), which have received great attention in the empirical and theoretical literature, assume that there are transitory profits which disappear over time until a normal rate of return is achieved. Presumably, this is the result of competition, so that the transitory profits are rents that are eliminated by competition. Hence, the analysis of Edwards, Kay and Mayer suggests that the long- run profits (those that are not transitory) should represent a normal rate of return on the deprival value of the entity's net worth (Walker, 1997). Thus, deprival value might be a more appropriate basis for determining the split between normal and transitory profit, rather than the undefined book value (typically taken to mean that value currently adopted by the firm) used in Ohlson's original model and in many subsequent empirical studies based upon it.

However, there has been some continuing interest in deprival value by academics in the past twenty years. Stark (1997) demonstrates how real options can be incorporated in the deprival value calculation. These are options for future investment which may be lost by current investment where that is irreversible, as is often the case of large infrastructure investments. Stark defines an option to wait, which should be deducted from PV when calculating DV. This complicates the calculation of DV by adding to its informational requirements. Stark demonstrates that his analysis is compatible with that of Edwards, Kay and Mayer but argues that the additional information required to incorporate real options can give rise to a more direct test of monopoly profits (essentially a comparison of his modified PV with RC) than that provided by their accounting rate of return.

Stark's analysis demonstrates the complexity involved in estimating the apparently simple components of DV. Another demonstration of this is Van Zijl and Whittington (2006), which discusses the 'redevelopment opportunity' which can exist when an asset can be sold for more than the replacement cost of its services because it is not optimally deployed in its present use. In such a case, replacement cost should include the cost of the redevelopment opportunity, and it is not appropriate to characterise the situation as one in which NRV > RC.

Baxter himself continued to contribute to the literature of deprival value, concluding with a very clear account of his view of the topic in Baxter (2003). He had a particular interest in its application to depreciation (Baxter, 1971, 1982, 2003), and this work was extended by Bell and Peasnell (1997). Baxter was the leader of the LSE school (Weetman, 2007), and the member of that school of thought who has been the most consistent advocate of deprival value in recent years has been Macve (2010). His particular interest has been in the application of deprival value to insurance liabilities and other performance obligations (Horton et al., 2011). The application of deprival value thinking to liabilities, to give a measure of 'relief value' tends to be counter-intuitive in the case of purely financial liabilities (i.e. ones with contractual obligations to pay pre-determined amounts of cash), possibly because, apart from transaction costs, the differences between entry, exit and holding values should be immaterial if capital markets are efficient (Whittington, 1975; Kulkarni, 1980; Baxter, 2003). However, when the liabilities reflect an obligation to perform a service, as in insurance or the fulfilment of warranties, then the various components of DV can plausibly be assumed to have wider differences and the possible relevance of the DV method becomes apparent. Lennard (2002) provides an interesting discussion of a number of practical examples of such liabilities, and Nobes (2011) provides a critique and some counter-examples which demonstrate some of the complexities of applying the concept of replacement to liabilities.

Deprival value has also remained on the agenda of accounting standard-setters, as they struggle to establish coherent principles for measurement. It received a thorough analysis from the Australian Accounting Research Foundation (1998) and was the UK ASB's preferred measure of 'fair value' or current value (FRS 7, Accounting Standards Board, 1994, and Statement of Principles, Accounting Standards Board, 1999), before that term was defined by the FASB (in SFAS 157, 2006) and the IASB (in a 2009 Exposure Draft, and subsequently in IFRS 13, 2011) to mean exit price. Although the IASB seemed to favour fair value as the measurement basis (e.g. in its issuance of the Discussion Paper on measurement on initial recognition, 2005, which was authored by staff of the Canadian Board), its subsequent deliberations (as of 2015) have favoured mixed measurement systems, of which DV is an example, providing a clear, logical framework for selecting between different 'pure' measures. Hence, DV seems likely to be considered in the future as a possible solution to the mixed measurement choice problem. DV is also under consideration in the International Public Sector Accounting Standards Board's development of its conceptual framework (IPSASB, 2010).

In conclusion, the 'value to the owner' concept has been advocated and explored by a number of academic writers. It has also had the distinction of being adopted as a basis for reforms of accounting practice, and there is no denying its intuitive appeal as a pragmatic compromise between competing valuation methods. However, its theoretical justification is confined to specific circumstances and uses (such as Edwards, Kay and Mayer's concern to identify monopoly profits), and even in those situations, its informational requirements may be difficult to meet with a satisfactory level of reliability. It is thus (as Edwards et al., 1987, p. 9, acknowledge) compatible with an *information* approach which emphasises the need to give the user a variety of relevant information rather than complete ideal measures, and it requires and deserves further analysis and development in this context. The aggregation problem is potentially serious (but not unique to DV), and the connection with opportunity cost is both tenuous and of questionable relevance. A particular area requiring further exploration is the application of DV to the measurement of liabilities as relief value. We have seen that this has posed difficulties in relation to financial liabilities and especially in relation to contractual liabilities. In both cases, it is the concept of replacement cost as applied to a liability (described by Baxter as the 'replacement loan') which has proved to be difficult to apply in some cases (Nobes, 2011).

However, as a practical technique, value to the owner has proved to be acceptable and has been applied in the UK as the valuation basis of the supplementary current cost accounts, required as a result of the publication of SSAP16 on 31 March 1980.[38] The subsequent withdrawal of support for that standard had more to do with macro-economic and political events than the practical difficulty of implementation. Looked at from a pragmatic standpoint, it is 'replacement cost or recoverable amount, whichever is the lower' (where 'recoverable amount' is the higher of market re-sale value or value in present use, i.e. Stamp's 'netback'). This avoids some of the potentially misleading valuations which might result from the universal application of replacement cost, even in situations in which replacement would not be worthwhile. By providing an acceptable means of introducing current values into accounts on a systematic basis, value to the owner might lead to the availability of data which provide a much more realistic picture of the current state of the business, as portrayed by the balance sheet, than is provided by historical cost data.[39] The depreciation and cost of sales adjustment, on the current cost basis, also provided valuable supplementary information in the income statement, although the capital maintenance concept embodied in SSAP16 (which has no necessary connection with value to the owner) was unsatisfactory and is discussed further in Chapter 6, as part of the section on the gearing adjustment.

### 4.3.5 Fair Value

Fair Value (FV)[40] is a concept with a long history in financial accounting, but it has achieved a particular prominence in the early years of the International Accounting Standards Board (IASB), from 2001 to the present time. The term was first used in regulatory and legal cases in the late nineteenth century. For example Boer traces its use in the regulation of railway charges in the US (Boer, 1966), at which time it was taken to imply replacement cost (particularly as a result of the case of *Smyth v Ames*, 1898). More generally, however, the term was used to describe a current market value, established between willing and well-informed parties. It was thus neutral as to whether it was an acquisition value (such as replacement cost) or a disposal value (such as net realisable value, so that the 'which market?' question (selling market or buying market?) was not addressed). Moreover, transaction costs were not discussed. These issues would not matter under idealised perfect market conditions in which there were no transaction costs and there was one perfect market available to all, so that the 'law of one price' would apply and there would be no differences between purchase costs and disposal values, both being equal to price.

In practice, transaction costs do exist, as do different prices in different markets, some of which the current holder of the asset or liability may not be able to access. Hence, the implementation of fair value encompassed a wide range of market prices and estimates based on market data, such as discounted cash flows ('marking to model'). As the use of fair value in accounting standards became more common (although still far from being prevalent) in the 1990s, it became apparent that a more precise definition was needed for standard-setting purposes. This was especially the case in measuring financial instruments, for which both the FASB (US) and the IASC (international standards) made extensive use of fair value but encountered some difficulty in, for example, the treatment of buying and selling costs. In response to this perceived need, the US standard-setter, the FASB, produced SFAS 157, Fair Value Measurement, in 2006. This defined fair value as a *selling price*. It thus rejected replacement cost, which had been out of favour with standard-setters since the current cost debates of the 1970s and 1980s, preferring a measure based on selling markets (exit value) rather than buying price (entry value). Selling price was to be the clear valuation objective, although where such prices were not observable in the market, estimates could be used, including, in the absence of better proxies, replacement cost. Equally important, SFAS 157 chose to use *price* rather than realisable value: transaction costs of sale were ignored.

As soon as SFAS 157 was issued, the IASB, as part of its convergence programme with the FASB, initiated a project to implement its provisions in international standards. This proved to be more difficult than had been expected, partly due to the opposition to fair value arising from the Global Financial Crisis (which started late in 2007) but eventually, it was substantially achieved in IFRS 13 (2011). The IASB argued that, in issuing IFRS 13, it was not extending the use of fair value, but merely defining it more clearly, and the new definition was specifically excluded from application to certain existing standards which included current values that might have been interpreted as fair value, such as those on share-based payments and impairment. However, by re-defining fair value, it was changing required practice in the remaining standards that used fair value. The most important of these related to financial instruments (IAS 39, which is currently being replaced by IFRS 9, and IFRS 7).

Accounting for financial instruments had seemed the most natural area in which fair value might be appropriate, at the time when IAS 39 (approved in December 1998 and effective from 1 January 2001) had been developed. Notably, a Discussion Paper published by the IASC in March 1997 proposed that all financial assets and liabilities should be measured at fair value, although IAS 39 stopped short of this. Financial instruments are often marketable at low cost and their prices relatively easily established. When prices are not directly available, it is often possible to 'mark to model' by estimating what the price would be on the basis of data such as interest rates which are directly observable in markets for similar instruments. Hence, the objection that fair value measurement is unreliable might have less weight in the case of financial instruments. Furthermore, fair value was not required universally in IAS 39: instruments held to maturity were to be measured at amortised cost.

Financial instruments, under IAS 39, have been the principal area of application of fair value measurement under IFRS[41] and this seems likely to remain the case under the new standard on financial instruments, IFRS 9, which is currently being introduced. The new standard is a response to the Global Financial Crisis (late 2007 onwards), which raised serious doubts about the role of fair value. Markets which had once appeared to be deep and liquid now evaporated, and the consequent lack of liquidity meant that fair values were no longer realisable. The consequence of this was substantial write-downs of financial assets from previous (possibly optimistic) high valuations to subsequent (possibly pessimistic) low valuations. Shin and various co-authors (such as Plantin et al., 2008) have demonstrated that the interaction of fair value with regulatory requirements could, in these circumstances, de-stabilise the banking system. Others, such as Laux and Leuz (2010) and Amel-Zadeh and Meeks (2013) have, through empirical studies, demonstrated that the quantitative impact of recording financial instruments at fair value was unlikely to have been a critical factor in the crisis.[42] However, whatever the merits of the case for fair value having an adverse impact on financial stability, a consequence of the crisis was increased distrust of fair value. The IASB instituted a Financial Crisis Advisory Group and a number of its recommendations have been adopted as part of the development of IFRS 9, although it is clear that these new developments are concerned with more effective application rather than entirely new principles and include a continuing significant role for fair value (as defined in IFRS 13) in accounting for financial instruments.

Fair Value also remains important in other areas of IFRS, particularly as the means of establishing the initial valuation of specific assets acquired and liabilities assumed in an historical cost framework. Notable examples of this arise in the application of the acquisition method of accounting for assets acquired in business combinations (IFRS 3). Fair value is used for regular re-measurement of assets for investment properties (IAS 40) and some agricultural assets (IAS 41). In other areas fair value has not recently increased its influence on IFRS in the manner that might have been expected before the Financial Crisis (Whittington, 2015). This is notably the case in the measurement of obligations, where recent developments in the projects on Insurance and on Revenue Recognition suggest a retreat from the IASB's earlier (as of about 2006) position of measuring obligations at fair value, with the possibility of 'Day 1' profits (gains on inception of a contract due to the fair value of cost of discharge being less than the consideration receivable), based on possibly dubious estimates of the market cost of discharging the obligation.

In summary, fair value is established as one of the valuation bases used in IFRS. Recent pronouncements on the Conceptual Framework project (International Accounting Standards Board, 2015) suggest that, for the future, the IASB is likely to favour a mixed valuation basis, selecting the basis for a particular standard on the perceived needs and circumstances (e.g. measurability) of the particular transaction involved. Thus, fair value (including such variants as fair value, less cost to sell) will continue to be used as one measurement basis amongst others. The definition of fair value for this purpose is that of FRS 13 (selling price in a competitive market). The more traditional view of fair value as a loosely defined current value could be taken to include all of the alternative values discussed in this chapter and is therefore too imprecise to provide a basis for the choice between them.

The *theoretical* justification for fair value is not as well explored as that for alternative current value measures. As we have seen, fair value has evolved as a practical method of measurement in appropriate circumstances, a process which culminated only recently with a precise definition of the concept (SFAS 157 and IFRS 13). Unlike the alternative current values, its application was not preceded by a body of academic literature which sought to refine and justify the concept. Rather, it was supported by a rather loose belief that freely bargained prices in competitive markets had a special significance.

More recently, that significance has been made more precise by the assertion that fair value represents the present value of the future economic benefits expected from the asset, as assessed by a fully informed market participant (Barth and Landsman, 1995). In an ideal world of perfectly competitive and complete markets, it might be expected that applying fair value to all of the assets and obligations of a business entity would yield a balance sheet which represented the market value of the business, so that no other information was required for valuation purposes. This extreme view has been characterised as 'the fair value view' (Whittington, 2008a), and it appeared to underlie the thinking of some accounting policy makers in the early years of the IASB. It represents what we earlier described as a *measurement perspective* on accounting: the idea that accounts can offer definitive measures of such aggregates as net worth or profit. However, some markets are demonstrably imperfect and incomplete (e.g. Whittington, 2010, cites the Grossman and Stiglitz, 1980, analysis of the innate imperfection of markets for information) and, as Beaver and Demski (1979) have argued, the existence of a demand for accounting information is inconsistent with a world of perfect and complete markets. Hence, the assumptions of the ideal 'fair value view' are not consistent with the market setting in which accounting operates; a view which seemed to be confirmed by the experience of illiquid markets during the Global Financial Crisis.

However, rejection of the 'fair value view' and its implication of full fair value measurement does not preclude alternative justifications which might imply more limited use of fair value. Such an alternative justification for using fair value might be derived from what was characterised earlier as the *information* perspective, which regards accounting data as inputs into the models of users, rather than definitive measures of the financial performance and condition of the reporting entity. Such an approach would select fair value as the measure of a particular item in the accounts when it appeared to be the most useful to users. Possible criteria foe usefulness might be relevance to the business model (fair value, as an exit value, is most obviously relevant to assets that are held for sale rather than consumption in operations) and reliability of measurement (are suitable market prices available as a basis for assessing fair value?). On a practical level, this is consistent with the mixed measurement approach adopted by the IASB in its recent statement on the future of the Conceptual Framework (International Accounting Standards Board, 2015). On a theoretical level, it is consistent with the approach of Nissim and Penman (2008), who regard cost measures as more appropriate for measuring inputs into operations but fair value measures as being more appropriate for measuring assets and liabilities whose fair value has a direct ('one-to-one') relationship to shareholder value. It is also consistent with the more informal proposals of economists such as Black (1993) and Scott (1976), who have sought to identify the measures of specific items which are most relevant to estimating their contribution to the value of the entity (where value is he economist's concept of discounted present value of future cash flows).

This approach does not aspire to yield direct aggregate measures of value or profitability, and it will not necessarily be associated with support for the narrow definition of fair value proposed in IFRS 13. For example, when selling costs are material and sale (rather than holding to maturity) is the most profitable means of realisation, the appropriate measure may be fair value less cost to sell, a measure which is used in some current IASB standards. This is the same concept as net realisable value (NRV), which was discussed earlier. It will be recalled that NRV is one measure used by the value to the owner algorithm. Hence, in some circumstances, value to the owner can be used to justify a measure based on fair value.[43]

## 4.4 SOME TENTATIVE CONCLUSIONS ON VALUATION

In Section 4.2, three basic methods of valuation (RC, NRV and PV) were discussed. Each was considered as a single valuation basis, to be applied to the exclusion of other values (except where other values could be used as surrogates for the preferred basis), because this is, for the most part, how their advocates have presented their cases. In Section 4.3 we considered value to the owner as the most popular eclectic valuation basis available, selecting one of the three bases according to the particular configuration of the three values. We also discussed fair value, a method of valuation which is closely related to NRV and has recently become prominent in discussions about international financial reporting standards.

In the discussion of single valuation bases, each was found to have some merits and some disadvantages. This is hardly surprising in view of the variety of uses to which accounting data are put and the variety of circumstances which can prevail. For example, it is not surprising that a valuation basis which produces a balance sheet which gives a useful description of the present financial resources and liabilities of a firm will not necessarily be equally effective in producing a profit and loss statement which gives a useful description of the firm's production and trading operations over a period of time. Equally, the type of asset valuation which we would use in appraising a firm's suitability for an 'asset-stripping' take-over bid would not necessarily serve equally well in appraising the profitability of its current productive operations with a view to making a synergistic take-over bid.

One possible means of overcoming this difficulty might be to select whichever of the alternative valuations was most relevant to the circumstances by means of some algorithm such as the 'value to the owner' rules. This particular set of rules does not appear to have a strong theoretical foundation as a method of pure *measurement* that is intended to provide *aggregate* measures of the entity's financial position and performance. However, it may be a useful pragmatic method within what we have characterised as an *informational* approach to financial reporting, especially if practical constraints dictate that if the choice is confined to reporting only one value for each individual asset or liability. It seems unlikely that any such algorithm is likely to prove entirely satisfactory, given the variety of uses to which a particular value is likely to be put, and value to the owner offers a transparent and logical framework that is consistent with the stewardship requirement of prudence (Replacement cost being an upper limit on value, whereas historical cost performed a similar function in the traditional accounting model) as well as with the economic logic of valuation from the perspective of the reporting entity. Value to the owner can discriminate according to the relative amounts of the different values but by no other criterion. Any alternative algorithm would face a similar problem: in making a choice of one value it is possible to satisfy only one choice criterion (as in the 'value to the owner' case) whereas in fact we might wish to have information which will satisfy several different criteria which will lead to alternative values. For example, many economic decisions involve the comparison of alternative values, such as a buying price, a value in use or a selling price, or a variant of these in alternative uses or markets.

In such a situation, the only approach which can provide the relevant information is the provision of multiple values for the same asset or transaction, sometimes referred to as 'multiple column reporting'. This has been the subject of a fierce debate, particularly between Chambers (1972) and Stamp (1972, 1979). Chambers claimed that multiple-column accounts, by communicating an excessive quantity of information, would lead to confusion in the minds of users. Stamp, on the other hand, stressed the relevance of alternative values. To some extent, this becomes an empirical argument about who are the users of reports, what are the uses to which the reports are put, what is the capacity of users to absorb information about alternative values, and what is the practical feasibility of producing alternative values. This is an important area for empirical research.

This issue also concerns accounting standard-setters. Although accounting standards usually avoid the recording of multiple valuations of the same item on the face of the accounts, there is a well-established practice of providing additional information, including alternative valuations, in the notes to the accounts. Sometimes (for example, in standards on pension obligations and financial instruments) this extends to providing further information which the user of accounts may wish to use in assessing the reliability of measures and estimating alternatives. However, this leads to greater complexity in financial accounts and standard-setters, such as the IASB, have recently been under some pressure to reduce the volume of footnote disclosures.[44] Thus, there is a practical trade-off between the benefit of additional information and its cost.

Although much empirical work remains to be done on the subject of current value accounting, a substantial amount has been achieved and Appendix A to this chapter provides a brief survey of this work. Finally, Appendix B provides simple numerical examples of one form of current value accounting, to supplement the algebraic exposition given earlier. In the following two chapters we shall deal with the controversial issue of the definition of capital for the measurement of income: this, in combination with the valuation basis, is fundamental to the design of any financial accounting system, and the existence of inflation renders the choice particularly important.

## APPENDIX A: SOME EMPIRICAL STUDIES OF CURRENT VALUE ACCOUNTING

There is a growing empirical literature on current value accounting.

The earliest and most common types of current value study were of the case study variety, seeking to estimate current values, typically concentrating on replacement cost estimates of depreciation and stock appreciation. Some early studies of this type, such as Dean's (1951, 1954) pioneering studies for the US and Baxter's (1959) study of British steel companies are summarised in Appendix E of American Institute of Certified Public Accountants (1963). An Australian case study of replacement cost accounting is Gress (1972). Similar studies were carried out to test Chambers' net realisable value-based system of continuously contemporaneous accounting, for example McKeown (1971) and Gray (1975, 1976). Manuals explaining how to prepare alternative forms of current value accounts were produced by the University of Waikato project (Hume 1976; Craswell 1976). Hope (1974) was a British study comparing six different systems for two companies. These studies served to demonstrate the technical feasibility of current value accounting systems and to demonstrate that they can yield results which are materially different from traditional, historical-cost-based accounts.

There also were a number of aggregative studies which attempted to estimate the quantitative effects of current value accounting. Usually these were concerned with adjusting conventional profit for replacement cost depreciation and stock appreciation. They were often the work of economists whose concern was with the adequacy of profits to finance replacement investment, and were related to the question of whether company taxation allows adequately for replacement costs. Early examples of this type of work are Harcourt (1958) for the UK and Mathews and Grant (1958) for Australia. There was a burgeoning of this type of work in the UK during the 'profits crisis' of the mid-1970s (immediately prior to the publication of the Sandilands Report and the granting of stock appreciation relief), good examples being Meeks (1974), King (1975), Flemming et al. (1976),[45] Merrett and Sykes (1974, 1980) and Moore (1980). A view of the implications for the reported profits of leading UK quoted companies of the various current cost accounting proposals was provided in a series of papers published by Philips and Drew under the direction of Martin Gibbs (listed in Gibbs and Seward, 1979). The results of these studies lent support to tax reforms, such as the introduction of stock appreciation relief, by demonstrating the importance of the divergence between replacement cost and historical cost in periods of rapid inflation.

Another type of research relating to the feasibility and materiality of current value accounting was the work on index numbers by Peasnell and Skerratt (1976a, 1977a, 1977b) and Bourn et al. (1976, 1977). Both of these teams of investigators set out to establish the materiality of divergences from general indices of special indices of fixed asset prices. The methodology of their approaches differs and there was controversy as to the correct interpretation of the results. However, both groups concluded that a single index can capture a significant amount, but by no means all, of the movements in special indices, i.e. there is some validity in using general indices as proxies for special indices, but this process introduces a degree of inaccuracy. There also seems to be agreement that indices specific to the type of plant capture information different from that captured by indices specific to the industry, i.e. if current cost accounts are to make use of specific indices as alternatives (or supplements in intermediate years) to direct valuations, different results will be obtained by using plant-specific indices rather than industry-specific indices.

A more sophisticated extension of the case studies, described earlier, is to assess the materiality of differences between accounting methods by statistical tests rather than by relying on the description of absolute differences in individual cases, whose general significance is difficult to assess. The statistical approach requires more data than the case study method, so that the scarcity of current value data has inhibited its development. A pioneering example of this type of study was Kratchman et al. (1974, 1975, 1976), who compared four alternative income measures (including current value income and current value adjusted to real terms) for real estate investment trusts in the US, finding high correlations (so that the measures were good surrogates for one another) in some cases.

Statistical studies can also be devised in order to assess the utility of accounting information. Early examples were the predictive ability studies by Frank (1969) and by Buckmaster et al. (1977), which assessed the self-predictive ability of alternative accounting income models, on the assumption that predictive ability gives rise to utility. A rich field for empirical research on the utility of accounting information is its impact on share prices: this has clearly been inhibited so far by lack of published current value data, but data have become more available in recent years as standard-setters have extended the reporting of current values and this type of research has become popular. An early study of this type was by Abdel-Khalik and McKeown (1978), which attempted to estimate the impact on share prices and risk measures of estimates of replacement cost holding gains. Another example was a symposium on the impact of the 1976 SEC '10-K' replacement cost disclosure requirements in the US (Watts and Zimmerman, 1980). The three studies in the symposium each had methodological limitations, but were designed and conducted independently, and it is therefore impressive that all three reached the common conclusion that the replacement cost disclosures had no incremental impact on share prices. This suggested either that replacement cost information was already available to the stock market or that it was not considered relevant.

Another approach to empirical research is the behavioural study based upon experiments. Tweedie's (1977) study was based on an experiment which used first-year accounting students as subjects and the results suggested that unsophisticated users of accounts tend intuitively to choose net realisable values as balance sheet measures and cash flows (with no accrual adjustment) as flow measures. This study is of particular interest because its author subsequently became chairman of the UK Accounting Standards Board (1990–2001) and then of the International Accounting Standards Board (2001–11). Another study, by Benston and Krasney (1978), used a set of 'sophisticated investors' (life assurance company investment officers) as subjects, and concluded that there was little demand for current value data, although the discussants of the study (Adkerson, 1978; Buzby and Falk, 1978) disagreed with the interpretation.

All of these types of research have been developed further in more recent times, partly because there have been proposals for greater use of current values in financial statements, making the research results policy-relevant, and partly because the consequent increase in current value disclosures has provided data for such studies.

The first big boost to empirical research on measurement came from the current cost accounting experiments of the late 1970s, particularly the supplementary current cost disclosures required in the US by the FASB's SFAS 33 and in the UK by the ASC's SSAP 16. In both countries, standard-setting bodies commissioned research programmes to evaluate the effectiveness of the new standards.

In the US, the FASB commissioned studies into the effects of SFAS 33. The most notable and influential output was the report by Beaver and Landsman (1983). This statistical study analysed the incremental effect on share prices of alternative measures of changes in earnings. It concluded that current cost earnings did not provide any information additional to that contained in historical cost earnings,[46] whereas historical cost earnings did contain information additional to that contained in current cost earnings. Hence it appeared that current cost disclosures added no useful information to that provided by traditional historical cost. This result was confirmed by using various alternative models, notably valuation models (looking at determinants of total share price rather than incremental changes in share price) and the relationship between balance sheet values of shareholders' interests and share price (using what is sometimes described as the Market to Book ratio). The authors suggested that measurement errors contributed to the apparently weak performance of the SFAS 33 disclosures. Also, they were careful to point out (p. 100) that their analysis was based on only three years of SFAS 33 disclosures, so that it was possible that a learning process would see greater use of the data in future years. This view was consistent with other studies in the FASB's programme (Berliner, 1983; Norby, 1983), which suggested that only a small proportion of financial analysts were making use of the new data at that time. However, the mood of preparers of financial statements, who bore the costs of the new disclosures, was strongly opposed to SFAS 33, and the lack of immediate benefit (combined with a declining rate of inflation, which made the problem of price changes seem less urgent) helped to persuade the FASB to abandon SFAS 33, replacing it with SFAS 89 (1986), which removed the mandatory nature of the requirements.[47] Subsequent empirical research, such as Murdoch (1986) and Bildersee and Ronen (1987), used alternative models which demonstrated possible value relevance of current cost earnings and suggested that Beaver and Landsman's initial conclusions should be qualified, but by then the policy debate had been decided and the current cost experiment had effectively ended.

In the UK, the ICAEW, which was one of the sponsoring bodies of the ASC, commissioned a programme of research into the effects of SSAP 16. The results were published as four volumes (edited by Carsberg and Page, 1984). The first volume, by Bryan Carsberg, provided an overview of the programme and attempted to derive some conclusions. The second volume contained studies of how current cost data were used by various different groups. and the third concentrated mainly on the effect of current cost data on stock market returns, one of the studies (by Appleyard and Strong) using the same statistical model as Beaver and Landsman's study for the US, and reaching very similar conclusions. The final volume was devoted to a single paper, by Archer and Steele, which reported the results of an extensive survey of preparers of SSAP 16 current cost data. This study revealed a significant degree of hostility by preparers to current cost, whereas the second and third volumes yielded varied and often indecisive results. For example, the Appleyard and Strong market-based study yielded no evidence that CCA data affected share prices, whereas a study by Skerratt and Thompson, using a different model, did provide some evidence in favour of CCA. Equally, the studies in volume 2 revealed some use of CCA data, but this was not extensive, and the production of the CCA data did incur costs, although these were not prohibitive and needed to be assessed in relation to benefits which were difficult to quantify.

Drawing conclusions from this varied array of studies was difficult, especially given the short time period for which SSAP 16 data were available and the novelty of CCA to practitioners. Bryan Carsberg's conclusion was that there was evidence of limited use of CCA data, which might grow over time, and that the costs were not prohibitive. Hence, the SSAP 16 experiment should continue, although modifications should be made to meet some of the criticisms revealed in the Archer and Steele survey. This optimistic interpretation of the consequences of SSAP 16 did not find favour with the policy makers, and, after an unsuccessful attempt to rescue the current cost experiment (ED 35, Accounting Standards Committee, 1985), SSAP 16 was subsequently withdrawn, ending the 'current cost revolution' in the UK.[48] However, the research programme summarised in Carsberg and Page should not be judged a failure. It was the first time that such a comprehensive academic research programme had been devised to inform the standard-setting process on a major issue. It did have an impact because the lack of compelling evidence supporting the CCA experiment enabled its opponents to argue that the costs exceeded the benefits. It is interesting, but fruitless, to speculate whether CCA would have survived if the supporting evidence had been stronger. Certainly, stronger evidence would have made the opponents' task more difficult, but certain fundamental forces, such as the declining rate of price change and the government's unwillingness to allow CCA adjustments as tax deductions would still have supported the opposition.

The retreat from CCA disclosures in the US, the UK and elsewhere[49] led to a reduced interest in CCA by researchers and less availability of data. However, empirical research on current value accounting did continue in the 1990s and the early years of the twenty-first century, concentrating mainly on fair value disclosures. This was a natural development because, as outlined earlier in this chapter, the requirement to report the fair value of certain items increased in both US and international standards from the 1990s onwards. Hence, fair value was a topic of policy interest and had an increasing body of data as a basis for research. Fair value was, in this period, more loosely defined than it became when SFAS 157 (2006) in the US and IFRS 13 (2011) made it clear that an exit (sale) measure was the objective. However, research based on this less restricted measure offers useful insights into the use of a form of current value accounting.

The research of this period is too voluminous to survey here. The evidence from capital market research, which is the most important strand in the work, is surveyed by Landsman (2007), but additional work continues to appear as standard-setters maintain and extend current value disclosures.[50] The capital market studies are mainly based on the US, the UK and Australia, which were leaders in adopting current value measurements. There are many studies of financial instruments that can be carried at fair value, especially in banks, which have particularly, large holdings of financial assets and liabilities (Barth et al., 1996). However, empirical studies of current values are not confined to banks and financial instruments. They also include studies of property, plant and equipment revaluations allowed by UK GAAP (Aboody et al., 1999), financial instruments, tangible and intangible asset revaluations in Australia (Barth and Clinch, 1998), and the valuation of employee stock options (Aboody et al., 2004; Landsman et al., 2006). The wide variation of populations, time periods and models used inevitably mean that it is impossible to draw sweeping conclusions. However, those studies that explicitly focus on market values tend to find that current value data do affect the price of shares. The relationship between *changes* in current value (revaluation) and *changes* in share prices (returns) is less clear cut: there is usually a positive association between the two but not as clear as that between value and share price. This weaker relationship between changes is often attributed to measurement error, the error having a greater proportionate effect on changes. This is supported by evidence of the greater volatility of current value earnings and the apparent lack of impact of the incremental volatility on share prices (Barth et al., 1995).

Other empirical studies have found evidence that current values have predictive value for future cash flows and earnings. There have also been studies of the consequences of using alternative methods to estimate current values and of the possible increase in credibility of revaluations when they are done by external appraisers rather than 'in house' (Muller and Riedl, 2002). Empirical research has also investigated the possibility that a requirement for regular revaluation reduces the use by management of opportunistic sales of assets as a means of hiding bad news (Black et al., 1998). A continuation of an earlier strand in the empirical literature has been the estimation of the quantitative significance of revaluation (Laux and Leuz, 2010). As discussed earlier, in the context of fair value, the Global Financial Crisis, starting in 2007, led to a number of studies of this type, designed to test the allegation that the measurement of financial instruments at fair value had made a significant contribution to causing the crisis.

In summary, empirical research has made a substantial and increasing contribution to our understanding of the properties of current value and their use by investors on stock markets. The lack of clearly substantial benefits from CCA gave support to ending the CCA experiments in the US and the UK in the early 1980s (although there were many other factors at work). Subsequently, the partial implementation of current values (loosely described as 'fair value') by the FASB and the IASB in a 'mixed measurement' model has enabled a variety of empirical studies which have, on the whole, provided evidence that these measures are used by investors. Standard-setting bodies, as part of their due process, are increasing their programmes of *ex post* appraisal of standards, so it is to be expected that the demand for empirical research will grow in importance in the future, as will the supply of data from the implementation of current value.

It is also the case that empirical studies and theoretical work are complementary: empirical studies without theory lapse into mere description and theoretical studies which have no empirically testable assumptions or implications give rise, at best, to unverifiable normative assertions and, at worst, are totally irrelevant to accounting as a practical activity. In the early days of accounting research (up to the late 1970s, when the inflation accounting debate was at its fiercest), much more attention was given to theory than to empirical testing, but subsequently this imbalance was redressed, perhaps even to the extent that theory is relatively neglected (as illustrated by the rise of fair value with relatively little theoretical analysis).

## APPENDIX B: A NUMERICAL ILLUSTRATION OF CURRENT VALUE ACCOUNTING

### B.I INTRODUCTION

In this appendix, the algebraic statements (4.1)–(4.7) are illustrated by a numerical example, based upon the facts of 'Old Fred's' business, used in the previous chapters. As indicated in Chapter 1, there is a

great variety of current valuation bases, of associated capital maintenance concepts (which will be discussed and illustrated in Chapter 6),
and of formats for presenting them. In the illustration which follows,
replacement cost is used as the valuation basis and two different capital maintenance concepts are employed: an 'entity' approach which
is used to strike the balance of operating profit, and a money capital
approach (a 'proprietary' approach) which is used in the calculation of
holding gains. This conforms with the current cost accounting model
expressed in equation (4.7) of the text.

It should be emphasised that this is a simplified example of a
specific form of current value accounting and does not conform even
with the current cost accounting model, as it was implemented in the
UK under SSAP16 (1980). Three particularly important divergences
are:

1. CCA, as required by SSAP16, had a different capital maintenance
   concept involving gearing and monetary working capital adjustments,
   which are discussed in Chapter 6. The present example is closer
   in spirit (but does not conform in precise detail) to the capital
   maintenance models of the Sandilands Committee (1975). The two
   main profit measures which it reports (current cost operating profit,
   based upon an entity capital maintenance concept, and total gains,
   based upon a proprietary concept) are summarised, and compared
   with historical cost profit, at the end of the numerical example.
2. The example uses only replacement cost valuation (RC), whereas
   SSAP16 (and the earlier Sandilands Report) required the use of value
   to the owner. We can, however, regard this example as being an
   application of value to the owner, if we assume that in every instance
   either NRV or PV or both exceed RC of the asset.
3. In practice, the application of CCA to complex businesses with many
   transactions involves a degree of estimation in the early stages of
   application, when CCA is a supplementary adjustment to traditional
   (HC) accounts. The SSAP16 proposals, for example, provided for an
   averaging method of calculating the current cost of goods sold. Our

numerical example is based upon very simple facts and it is assumed that precise information is available, so that no estimation methods are necessary.

A thorough exposition of the application of current cost accounting as embodied in SSAP16, will be found in Mallinson (1980). The Chambers method of CoCoA accounting is precisely defined in an appendix (in the form of the exposure draft of a proposed standard) to Chambers (1977) and in Hume (1976), which contains detailed worksheets and numerical examples. Lee (1985) contains clear numerical illustrations of a variety of forms of current value accounting.

## B.2 FACTS ASSUMED IN THE ILLUSTRATION

The facts assumed are those used in the appendix to Chapter 3. It is further assumed that the replacement cost of goods subsequently incurred when re-stocking was the replacement cost of goods at the time of sale, e.g. replacement cost of sales in period 1 is assumed to be the cost of purchases at the beginning of period 2. In periods 3 and 4, during which no re-stocking took place, we assume a replacement cost of £1.90 per stock unit. A further assumption is made with respect to the replacement cost of the cart: it is assumed that the cost of an equivalent cart rose by one half early in period 3, but that otherwise the depreciation rate chosen presented a realistic view of the decline in the cart's replacement cost over time.

### B.2.1 Current Cost Accounts

*Period 1*

Balance Sheet at *t*

| | £ | | £ |
|---|---|---|---|
| *Proprietor's Capital* | 150 | *Fixed Asset* | |
| *Loan* | 50 | Cart (at cost) | 100 |
| | | *Current Asset* | |
| | | Cash | 100 |
| | 200 | | 200 |

This is unchanged from the historical cost case (Chapter 3), since the fixed asset has only just been acquired, so that its historical cost represents its replacement cost, and the other assets and claims are of fixed monetary value.

Income Statement for period 1, $t$ to $t + 1$

|  |  | £ |
|---|---|---:|
| Sales |  | 120 |
| *Less* | Current cost of goods sold | 104 |
|  |  | 16 |
| *Less* | Depreciation | 10 |
|  | Current Cost Operating Profit | 6 |
| *Add* | Holding Gains on Stocks | 30 |
|  | Total Gains | £36 |

The current cost of goods sold is 80 items at £1.30 each, whereas historical cost was £1 each. The difference between the two, £24 (= £104 – £80), is the realised holding gain on stocks sold during the period. The gain on closing stocks, £6 (= £26 – £20), is calculated on the same basis, and this represents an unrealised holding gain. In this illustration, the two types of holding gain have been added together (£30 = £24 + £6), but, if realisation is considered important, they could be reported separately (as, for example, suggested by Edwards and Bell, 1961). Depreciation is unchanged from the historical cost case, because replacement cost is assumed to equal historical cost in this example.

The format adopted here is basically consistent with current cost accounting as advocated by the Sandilands Committee, although the Sandilands format would separate the income statement into two statements, a current cost profit and loss account (ending with current cost operating profit) and a Statement of Gains (which would end with the total gains figure). The Sandilands proposals would also ignore the unrealised holding gains on stocks. In terms of the algebraic notation used in the text, current cost operating profit shown here conforms with $Y_{CCA}$ in equation (4.7), measuring profit after maintaining the specific assets of the entity. Total Gains shown corresponds with $Y_{CVA}$ in equation (4.6), which maintains the capital of the entity in monetary terms.

### Balance Sheet at $t + 1$

| | £ | | £ | £ |
|---|---|---|---|---|
| *Proprietor's Capital* | | *Fixed Assets* | | |
| Opening balance | | Cart (at cost) | 100 | |
| (at $t$) | 150 | *Less* Accumulated | | |
| *Add* Total Gains | | Depreciation | 10 | |
| for the Period | 36 | | | 90 |
| | 186 | *Current Assets* | | |
| *Less* Drawings | 30 | Stock (at current | | |
| Closing balance | | cost) | 26 | |
| (at $t + 1$) | 156 | Cash | 90 | |
| *Loan* | 50 | | | 116 |
| | £206 | | | £206 |

The only difference between this balance sheet and the historical cost version given in the appendix to Chapter 3 is that the current cost value of stocks is £6 higher and this is reflected in a £6 increase in proprietor's capital (as a component of total gains). A further difference would arise if it were assumed that the replacement cost of the cart was different from its written-down historical cost. Total gains have been added to proprietor's capital: a more sophisticated system of reporting might distinguish between distributable profits and capital maintenance reserves to which would be credited gains due to asset appreciation (holding gains) which could not be withdrawn by the proprietor without eroding the physical substance of the business. In the preceding example, of the £36 total gains, £6 would be distributable profit and £30 (the holding gain) would be credited to the capital maintenance reserve.

*Period 2*

Income Statement for period 2, $t + 1$ to $t + 2$

|  |  | £ |
|---|---|---|
| Sales |  | 135 |
| *Less* | Current Cost of Goods Sold | 162 |
|  | Trading Loss | (27) |
| *Less* | Depreciation | 10 |
|  | Current Cost Operating Loss | (37) |
| *Add* | Holding gains on stocks | 50 |
|  | Total Gains | £13 |

Cost of goods sold is calculated at the replacement cost (£1.80 each) of the 90 items sold (£162). This represents a realised holding gain of £51 of which £6 had been recognised in the previous period as an unrealised gain on stock, and there is an unrealised holding gain of £5 (= £18 – £13) on stocks held at the end of the current period, bringing total holding gains on stocks to the £50 reported here. The detailed calculations are as follows:

*Realised Holding Gains:*

| | | |
|---|---|---|
| Current Cost of Goods Sold (charged to Profit and Loss) | | £162 |
| *Less* Historical Cost of Goods Sold (as in appendix to Chapter 3) | | £111 |
| Realised during the period | | £51 |
| *Unrealised Holding Gains:* | | |
| Current cost of closing stocks (10 at £1.80) | £18 | |
| *Less* Historical cost (10 at £1.30) | £13 | |
| Unrealised gain on closing stock (10 at £0.50) | 5 | |
| *Less* Unrealised gain on opening stock, realised during the period | 6 | |
| Net change in unrealised gains | | (1) |
| Total Holding Gains accruing in the period | | £50 |

### Balance Sheet at $t + 2$

|  | £ |  | £ | £ |
|---|---|---|---|---|
| *Proprietor's Capital* |  | *Fixed Assets* |  |  |
| Opening balance |  | Cart (at cost) | 100 |  |
| (at $t + 1$) | 156 | *Less* Accumulated |  |  |
| *Add* Total Gains for |  | depreciation | 20 |  |
| the period | 13 |  |  | 80 |
|  | 169 | *Current Assets* |  |  |
| *Less* Drawings | 106 | Stock (at current |  |  |
| Closing balance |  | cost) | 18 |  |
| (at $t + 2$) | 63 | Debtors | 15 |  |
| *Loan* | 50 | Cash | 52 |  |
| *Current Liabilities* |  |  |  | 85 |
| Creditors | 52 |  |  |  |
|  | £165 |  |  | £165 |

*Period 3*

### Income Statement for period 3, $t + 2$ to $t + 3$

|  |  |  | £ |
|---|---|---|---|
| Sales |  |  | 180 |
| *Less* | Current Cost of Goods Sold |  | 171 |
|  | Trading Profit |  | 9 |
| *Less* | Current Cost Depreciation |  | 15 |
|  | Current Cost Operating (Loss) |  | (6) |
| *Add* | Holding gains: On stocks | 11 |  |
|  | On fixed asset | 40 |  |
|  |  |  | 51 |
|  | Total Gains |  | £45 |

The calculation of cost of goods sold is based upon a current replacement cost of £1.90 each for 90 items. The holding gains on stocks are calculated as follows:

*Holding gains on stocks:*

|  | £ | £ |
|---|---|---|
| *Realised* gains: | | |
| Current cost, charged to Profit and Loss | 171 | |
| *Less* Historical cost | 157 | |
| Realised gain | | 14 |
| *Unrealised* gains: | | |
| Current cost of closing stock (20 at £1.90) | 38 | |
| *Less* Historical cost (20 at £1.80) | 36 | |
| Unrealised gain on closing stock (20 at £0.10) | 2 | |
| *Less* Unrealised gain on opening stock, | | |
| realised during the period | 5 | |
| | | (3) |
| Total holding gains on stocks accruing during the period | | £11 |

At the beginning of this period, a holding gain accrues on the fixed asset, the cart. It was assumed that the replacement cost of the cart rose by 50 per cent, and that the depreciation pattern is still appropriate. The revised values are therefore as follows:

|  | Opening value | Revised value | Increase |
|---|---|---|---|
| Cost | 100 | 150 | 50 |
| *Less* Accumulated depreciation | 20 | 30 | 10 |
| Written-down value | 80 | 120 | 40 |

The treatment adopted here is to show the revised values in the balance sheet (a net debit to the asset accounts of £40) and a corresponding net holding gain (a net credit of £40) in the final section of the profit and loss account. Some would argue that the net gain should be split into two components, a gross gain (on original cost) of £50, and an increased charge for accumulated depreciation, of £10. This latter charge is known as 'backlog depreciation' and it is some-times argued that it should be charged at an earlier stage in the profit calculation, rather than merely being offset against the gross holding gain on the cost of the fixed asset. This attitude (which is discussed further in Chapter 6) springs from an 'entity' view of the firm and from the view that the depreciation charge should somehow repre-sent an allocation of liquid funds for replacement, rather than merely being an indication for profit computation of the cost of using the asset during the period. This attitude has not been adopted here, and the depreciation charge against profit represents the current cost of using the asset during the period, where current cost is assumed to be one-tenth of the current replacement cost of the asset.

Balance Sheet at $t + 3$

| | £ | | | £ | £ |
|---|---|---|---|---|---|
| *Proprietor's Capital* | | *Fixed Assets* | | | |
| Opening balance | | Cart, at replacement | | | |
| (at $t + 2$) | 63 | cost | | 150 | |
| *Add* Total gains for | | *Less* Accumulated | | | |
| the period | 45 | depreciation | | 45 | |
| | 108 | | | | 105 |
| *Less* Drawings | 10 | *Current Assets* | | | |
| Closing balance | | Stocks, at current | | | |
| (at $t + 3$) | 98 | cost | | 38 | |
| *Loan* | 50 | Debtors | | 20 | |
| *Current Liabilities* | | Cash | | 165 | |
| Creditors | 180 | | | | 223 |
| | £328 | | | | £328 |

As compared with the historical cost balance sheet, shown in the appendix to Chapter 3, this current cost balance sheet shows the fixed asset and stocks at higher current cost values, and this is reflected in the proprietor's capital on the other side of the balance sheet.

*Period 4*

Income Statement for period 4, $t + 3$ to $t + 4$

|  |  | £ |
|---|---|---|
| Sales |  | 44 |
| *Less* | Current cost of goods sold | 38 |
|  | Trading profit | 6 |
| *Add* | Realised Holding Gain | 15 |
|  | Total Gains | £21 |

The current cost of goods sold is merely the current cost of opening stocks, no further price changes being assumed before realisation. The realised holding gain is the excess of the sale price of the cart (£120) over its written-down value (£105) at the start of the period: it is assumed that realisation took place before any further depreciation occurred.

Balance Sheet at $t + 4$

|  | £ |  | £ |
|---|---|---|---|
| *Proprietor's Capital* |  | Cash | 169 |
| Opening balance (at $t + 3$) | 98 |  |  |
| *Add* Total gains for the period | 21 |  |  |
| Closing balance (at $t + 4$) | 119 |  |  |
| *Loan* | 50 |  |  |
|  | £169 |  | £169 |

Apart from the division of proprietor's capital between the accrued balance and the gains for the period, this is identical with the historical cost closing balance sheet. This is because, as was demonstrated in Chapter 3, lifetime 'cash-to-cash' profit is the same, irrespective of the valuation method, which merely serves to shift profits between periods within the life cycle. However, this result holds only if a common capital maintenance concept is adopted, i.e. if the current value system uses a money capital concept identical to that used in the historical cost system. In the present case, this implies that we use total gains, rather than operating profit as our profit measure. This

is demonstrated in the following table. The choice of capital maintenance concept is discussed more thoroughly in Chapter 6.

B.3 LIFE CYCLE PROFITS

| | Current Cost | | | Historical Cost |
| | Operating | Holding | Total | |
| Period | Profit | Gains | Gains | Profit (Ch. 3) |
|---|---|---|---|---|
| 1 | 6 | 30 | 36 | 30 |
| 2 | (37) | 50 | 13 | 14 |
| 3 | (6) | 51 | 45 | 13 |
| 4 | 6 | 15 | 21 | 58 |
| Total | £(31) | £146 | £115 | £115 |

*Note*: Brackets indicate a loss.

NOTES

1 This does not mean that it is simple in practice to separate the effects
of inflation from valuation changes. For example, the Sandilands
Committee appointed by the UK government concluded that the
measurement of inflation was impractical and therefore recommended a
system of business accounting based solely on specific prices (i.e. values
of specific items rather than the purchasing power of money).

2 The Edwards and Bell system is discussed further in Whittington (2008)
and Peasnell and Whittington (2010).

3 Sandilands did not propose to recognise unrealised holding gains on
stocks and work-in-progress, which are recognised in (4.6), as part of
changes in $N''$. Sandilands proposed a specific form of current valuation,
value to the owner, which is discussed later in the chapter.

4 The detailed proposals for implementation deviate from the model in
some respects. For example, Sandilands did not propose the revaluation
of 'non-monetary' long-term loans, although it was accepted that this
would be desirable in principle. Also, Sandilands proposed certain
approximate methods of calculation, such as the use of periodic averages
and specific price indices.

5 Macdonald's specific suggestion is that exit values, such as NRV, are
most suitable for the balance sheet, which measures financial position,

but entry values, such as replacement cost, are more relevant to the profit and loss account, which measures the cost of maintaining the productive resources of the business.

6 Accounts in which the Income Statement and the Balance Sheet are part of the same double entry system, such that total income recorded in the former is consistent with changes in proprietors' interest in the latter.

7 *FAS33*, the final standard on the subject, was eclectic in its attitude to 'inflation accounting', which was taken to include replacement cost accounting as one element in the required disclosures, some CPP information also being required, and a 'real terms' combination of the two elements was also allowed.

8 Earlier UK proposals by the Association of Certified and Corporate Accountants (1952) and the Institute of Cost and Works Accountants (1952) advocated replacement cost systems.

9 Limperg also was a pioneer of proposals of the 'value to the owner' type and Sweeney's advocacy of replacement cost is based upon similar reasoning. See Mey (1966).

10 Although Bell (1971) subsequently favoured the service approach rather than reproduction.

11 Sweeney (1936) was an early advocate of reporting realised gains separately from realised gains: he also advocated measuring gains in real terms, i.e. a gain would be measured as the amount by which the current replacement cost of an asset exceeded its indexed historical cost.

12 Van Zijl and Whittington (2006) explore this issue in the context of value to the owner (deprival value).

13 The presentation of the income statement is an ongoing project of the IASB. The separate identification of meaningful sub-totals of comprehensive income, such as operating profit, is an important and difficult issue (Barker, 2004).

14 Factors leading to the decline in unit costs as the level of aggregation increases include bulk discounts (for materials), economies of scale and technical progress (replacement of a whole plant may enable a change of technique which is not possible in replacing one item which has to be compatible with the rest). Increases in unit costs as the level of aggregation increases could be due to inelastic supply, diseconomies of scale and loss of production due to the disturbance caused by a major reconstruction.

15 Drake and Dopuch (1965), Prakash and Sunder (1979), and Kay (1977).

16 The unrealised holding gains represent the difference between the historical cost and the replacement cost of assets appearing in the closing balance sheet. The uncertainty surrounding realisation is an important reason for segregating unrealised from realised holding gains in the income statement.

17 For longer accounts of Canning's work, see Chambers (1979) and Whittington (1980a). A laudatory contemporary review is Fisher (1930).

18 Market replacement costs would also avoid this problem, but in practice replacement cost systems usually involve the allocation of depreciation of fixed assets (Thomas, 1974, Chapter 7).

19 Which postulates that the stock market is efficient in the sense that the market instantaneously impounds all new information into the share price.

20 Fama (1970) and Beaver (1973, 1989) hold this view. This argument is, of course, based upon the view that investors are the primary users of accounting data, whereas, as was indicated in Chapters 1 and 2, the constituency of users is now considered to be much wider. Dyckman and Morse (1986) provide a critical review of evidence relating to market efficiency.

21 Goodwill being the excess of going concern value over the value of the aggregate net assets. The existence of goodwill can therefore be regarded as evidence of the extent of the aggregation problem, aggregate net assets being assessed on an individual basis.

22 In practice, many intangible assets which might have a market value are excluded from the balance sheet, unless they are acquired as part of a business combination.

23 Although, as stated earlier, where adequate second-hand markets are available, replacement cost depreciation could be assessed on second-hand values rather than on periodic allocations of the cost of new assets.

24 Including their covariance with returns to other investment, if we consider investment in a portfolio framework.

25 In particular, it was the starting point for the work of Wright (1964, 1970).

26 This problem is analysed by Peasnell (1978) in the context of using present values as part of the deprival value base, which is discussed later in this chapter.

27 This point was made by Gellein (1971) in his response to Staubus' (1971) paper.

28 For this reason, the Edwards and Bell description of net realisable value as 'opportunity cost' is an over-statement. It is an element of the *external* opportunity cost of assets *already held* by the firm, and *may* be an element of the opportunity cost in other cases. In any case, opportunity cost will not be full net realisable value, but the *difference* between net realisable value and the value in the alternative use being considered.

29 The 'value to the owner' rule can be defined as: 'choose the lower of "netback" or RC'. Another term for 'netback' is 'recoverable amount'.

30 Stamp later amended his rule to: 'The value to the firm of an asset is equal to its replacement cost except when it is clearly worth the owner's while to dispose of the asset immediately and not replace it. In the latter case, value to the firm is equal to net realisable value' (Stamp, 1979).

31 It will be recalled that this argument arose in the discussion of Staubus' present value surrogates, earlier in this chapter.

32 It is surprising that neither Chambers nor Wright referred directly (in these two papers) to Canning's contribution, as both were clearly influenced by Canning's ideas.

33 Accounting Standards Committee (1980).

34 Institute of Chartered Accountants in Australia and Australian Society of Accountants (1975).

35 It is notable that Barton (1975), whose paper was based upon a seminar given in Lancaster, also adopted the 'netback' approach to value to the owner, although he did not adopt the Gee and Peasnell extension.

36 In Edey's railway example, the replacement cost of each tunnel is justified by the cash flows of the whole railway, which would be lost entirely if any tunnel were closed.

37 A further conceptual difficulty created by any method of current value accounting is that, if the regulatory accounts are not prepared on a 'clean surplus' basis, capital gains due to revaluation will not be included in the *ex post* profit but will later be allowed to increase the depreciation charge against future profit and will be included in the capital base when calculating expected rates of return. Thus, past gains to shareholders

will be under-stated and the price cap will be set too high (Whittington, 1994).

38 The effects of CCA in the UK were assessed by the Carsberg Report, which is discussed in the appendix to this chapter.

39 Although, of course, current cost data were supplementary under SSAP16, and historical cost remained the basis of the main accounts.

40 A useful collection of papers on various aspects of fair value will be found in Walton (2007).

41 Strictly, this refers to re-measurement: the practice of up-dating the measurement regularly. Historical cost may be equal or approximate to the fair value of an asset at the time of acquisition, but under the historical cost convention, the measure will not be up-dated to reflect subsequent market price changes and thus will not subsequently reflect fair value.

42 Laux (2012) provides a useful survey of the evidence on the role of fair value in the Financial Crisis.

43 Van Zijl and Whittington (2006) discuss the relationship between value to the owner and fair value.

44 E.g. the UK Financial Reporting Council has instigated a 'Cutting Clutter' programme (FRC 2011).

45 The work by Flemming et al. (1976) was followed up in a number of articles in the *Bank of England Quarterly Bulletin*.

46 The other SFAS 33 disclosure, constant dollar earnings, was also tested and found to be as ineffective as current cost earnings. Constant dollar accounting is indexed historical cost, which is discussed in Chapter 5.

47 Tweedie and Whittington(1997) provide a more thorough account of the FASB's activities in this period.

48 The term 'current cost revolution' is used by Tweedie and Whittington (1984), who give an account of its history up to that date. Tweedie and Whittington (1997) discuss the events surrounding the withdrawal of current cost accounting in the UK, and Whittington (1985) reviews the Carsberg Report.

49 Several other countries had experimented with CCA (although none as comprehensively as the UK and the US) including the Netherlands, where replacement value accounting (which can be regarded as a specific form of CCA) had been allowed for many years. In the 1980s, this practice declined even in the Netherlands, where the flagship of the

replacement value movement, Philips, ceased to use replacement value as the basis of its main accounts in 1992 (Brink and Langendijk, 1995).

50 Some of these measures do not conform to the IFRS 13 definition of fair value. Examples specifically acknowledged in IFRS 13 included share-based payments, leasing transactions and pension fund assets.

# 5  Inflation and the General Price Level

## 5.1 INFLATION

In this chapter, we consider the problems created when the measuring unit of accounting, money, changes in value, in terms of its general command over other assets and services. Historically, this has typically been a process of inflation: a decline in the purchasing power of money. However, there have been periods of deflation, when the relative value of money has increased, a notable recent case being Japan during the past two decades. In either situation, some form of price-level-adjusted accounting may be appropriate. Such forms of accounting are popularly described as inflation accounting, and they have typically been called for in inflationary conditions. Hence, we shall focus our illustrations on the more common situation of inflation, although the systems that we discuss are equally relevant to correcting the distortions created by deflation.

## 5.2 THE INFLATIONARY PROCESS

Inflation may be loosely defined as a decline in the purchasing power of money, due to an increase in the general level of prices. It has been experienced throughout history, e.g. as a result of currency debasement, or, as in the late sixteenth century, when gold and silver from America was imported into Europe, increasing the currency supply. Inflation has been a particularly acute problem in the twentieth century, when the reliance on fiat money has combined with increasing demands on government expenditure, often financed by borrowing rather than taxation, to make inflation the typical condition in many economies. In some countries, such as Germany after the First World War and certain Latin American countries in more recent years, inflation has reached extremely high levels which amounted to a collapse

Table 5.1 *World Market Economies: Rates of Change in Consumer Prices, 1971–79*

| Country Groups (Averages) | Annual Average 1971–78 | Annual Rates | | |
|---|---|---|---|---|
| | | 1977 | 1978 | 1979 |
| Developed market economies | 8.1 | 8.4 | 7.5 | 9.9 |
| Major industrial countries | 7.7 | 7.7 | 6.8 | 9.4 |
| Other industrial countries | 7.9 | 7.3 | 5.5 | 5.3 |
| Primary producing countries | 13.5 | 18.1 | 17.3 | 20.3 |
| Developing market economies | 15.0 | 21.5 | 20.7 | 32.6 |
| Oil-exporting countries | 12.1 | 15.8 | 11.0 | 14.3 |
| Non-oil-exporting countries | 15.9 | 23.3 | 23.4 | 36.5 |

*Source:* United Nations, *World Economic Survey 1979–1980*, Table III-1. The numbers are annual percentage point increases.

in the value of the currency and has followed or been followed by serious political problems. For example, at the height of the German hyper-inflation, the value of the paper mark in December 1923 (expressed in gold equivalent) had fallen to one millionth of its value in August of the same year (Sweeney, 1927, p. 182). More often, inflation has been at more moderate rates which nevertheless have important economic consequences (e.g. at average annual percentage rates of 10 per cent or less). During the 1970s, particularly following the oil crisis of 1973, inflation increased on a worldwide scale and many countries, including the UK, experienced sustained inflation at levels (typically greater than 10 per cent per annum) previously unknown in times of peace.[1] Evidence of inflation rates in market economies (as opposed to centrally planned economies) during this period is given in Table 5.1. In the UK the price level approximately quadrupled between 1969 and 1981.

The relatively high inflation rates experienced in the 1970s stimulated great activity in the debate on inflation accounting, culminating in the publication of the first American and British accounting standards on the subject (FAS 33, Financial Accounting Standards Board, 1979a; SSAP16, Accounting Standards Committee, 1980).

It is beyond the scope of the present book to review the historical evolution of the inflationary process or economists' efforts to explain it. Accessible reviews of the latter, dating from the high inflation period of the 1970s, will be found in the books by Flemming (1976) and Trevithick (1977) and the history of inflation in the UK is surveyed in Deane (1979) and by MacFarlane and Mortimer-Lee (1994).

The inflationary crisis of the 1970s led to tighter monetary policies, associated, for example, with the Thatcher government (1979 onwards) in the UK and the Reagan administration (1981 onwards) in the US. After experiments with various monetary targets, inflation targeting by the central bank, which was free to use such monetary policy instruments as it wished in order to meet the target inflation rate (set by government) became common practice in a number of leading economies, including the US and the UK. The first country to adopt inflation targeting was New Zealand (1989). Inflation targeting in the UK started in 1992, initially as the responsibility of the Treasury, but in 1997 the implementation role was handed over to the independent Bank of England Monetary Policy Committee, whose most visible role is the setting of the central bank lending rate. The inflation target set by the government in 1997 was 2.5 per cent above RPIX, the Retail Price Index excluding mortgage interest costs (Allen, 1999). Subsequently, in 2003, this was changed to 2 per cent above CPI (the Consumer Price Index) and it has remained at this level subsequently (McCafferty, 2013). Table 5.2 shows that the target has been substantially met, even through the Global Financial Crisis of 2007 onwards.

This period of relative stability in inflation rates led to the end of the public policy debate on inflation accounting, or, as it was more correctly described, price-change accounting[2] (Tweedie and Whittington, 1997). However, governments invariably have set positive inflation targets, even in a deep recession, and many economists argue that mild inflation is beneficial for economic growth, so it seems that

Table 5.2 *Price Indices for the UK, 1988–2015*

| Year | Retail Price Index (RPI): Annual Average | | Consumer Price Index (CPI):[a] Annual Average | | RPI/CPI |
|---|---|---|---|---|---|
| | Index | % Change | Index | % Change | |
| 2015 | 134.6 | 1.0 | 128.0 | 0.0 | 105.2 |
| 2014 | 133.3 | 2.4 | 128.0 | 1.5 | 104.2 |
| 2013 | 130.3 | 3.0 | 126.1 | 2.6 | 103.3 |
| 2012 | 126.4 | 3.2 | 123.0 | 2.8 | 102.8 |
| 2011 | 122.5 | 5.2 | 119.6 | 4.5 | 102.4 |
| 2010 | 116.5 | 4.6 | 114.5 | 3.3 | 101.7 |
| 2009 | 111.3 | -0.5 | 110.8 | 2.2 | 100.5 |
| 2008 | 111.9 | 4.0 | 108.5 | 3.6 | 103.1 |
| 2007 | 107.6 | 4.3 | 104.7 | 2.3 | 102.8 |
| 2006 | 103.2 | 3.2 | 102.3 | 2.3 | 100.9 |
| 2005 | 100.0 | 2.8 | 100.0 | 2.1 | 100.0 |
| 2004 | 97.2 | 3.0 | 98.0 | 1.3 | 99.2 |
| 2003 | 94.4 | 2.9 | 96.7 | 1.4 | 97.6 |
| 2002 | 91.8 | 1.7 | 95.4 | 1.3 | 96.2 |
| 2001 | 90.3 | 1.8 | 94.2 | 1.2 | 95.8 |
| 2000 | 88.6 | 3.0 | 93.1 | 0.8 | 95.2 |
| 1999 | 86.1 | 1.5 | 92.3 | 1.3 | 93.3 |
| 1998 | 84.8 | 3.4 | 91.1 | 1.6 | 93.1 |
| 1997 | 82.0 | 3.1 | 89.7 | 1.8 | 91.5 |
| 1996 | 79.5 | 2.4 | 88.1 | 2.5 | 90.3 |
| 1995 | 77.7 | 3.5 | 86.0 | 2.6 | 90.3 |
| 1994 | 75.1 | 2.4 | 83.8 | 2.0 | 89.6 |
| 1993 | 73.3 | 1.6 | 82.1 | 2.5 | 89.3 |
| 1992 | 72.1 | 3.7 | 80.1 | 4.3 | 90.1 |
| 1991 | 69.5 | 5.9 | 76.8 | 7.5 | 90.5 |
| 1990 | 65.7 | 9.5 | 71.5 | 7.0 | 91.9 |
| 1989 | 60.0 | 7.8 | 66.8 | 5.2 | 89.8 |
| 1988 | 55.7 | 4.9 | 63.5 | – | 87.7 |

[a] The CPI was started in 1996, but it was estimated retrospectively to 1988 by the ONS. Estimates are not available before 1988, so it is not possible to calculate a change between that year and 1987. The RPI has been rebased to 2005 to facilitate comparison with the CPI.

*Source:* UK Office for National Statistics.

inflation is unlikely to disappear within the foreseeable future, although it might be hoped that well targeted monetary policies will avoid the excessive inflation rates experienced in the 1970s. Even a 2 per cent per annum inflation rate can create material distortions in accounting measurement, particularly over longer periods, because the compounding effect of an annual rate implies exponential growth of the price level. Moreover, higher inflation rates are often experienced by individual countries.[3] Thus, despite the lack of current public interest in the subject, accountants need to be aware of the problems which inflation poses for them, and the most fundamental of these is that money is the measuring unit commonly used by accountants and that inflation implies that this measuring unit fluctuates in value through time. The remainder of this chapter is devoted to analysing these problems and their possible solution by index adjustment. This will also involve discussion of the properties of the index numbers that are used to measure inflation.

## 5.3 IMPLICATIONS OF INFLATION FOR ACCOUNTS AND CONTRACTS

We have implicitly made the assumption that inflation is approximately measured by changes in a broadly based consumer price index, which reflects the general level of prices. However, such an index represents the cost of living (and its inverse, the purchasing power of money) strictly only for an individual who buys commodities in proportion to their weighting in the index. For others, the index is an approximation whose accuracy will be reduced to the extent to which their expenditure pattern diverges from that assumed by the index and the prices of the divergent expenditures change out of proportion with the index. For example, a non-smoking, teetotal vegetarian might consider inappropriate to his or her needs a consumer price index which includes tobacco, alcohol and meat, in periods when this group of commodities varies in price relative to the other commodities which are in the index. A comparison of the two consumer price indices, the CPI and the RPI, reported in Table 5.2, illustrates the importance of index selection. This shows material differences between the percentage changes in the two indices (their measure of inflation) in most years. Moreover, the cumulative effect of these differences, captured by the ratio of the two indices (given in the final column), shows that the RPI has risen more rapidly than the CPI over the long term, i.e. the indices have tended to drift apart rather than merely deviating randomly over the long term. This effect has serious implications for pensioners and others whose contracts are adjusted for 'inflation' on the basis of one of these indices: the choice of index will have a significant influence on their returns.

This type of objection assumes less importance at higher rates of inflation, at which most prices tend to move upwards and, for all but the most perverse of consumers, a 'nominal' money unit (such as the $ or the £) tends to be a less satisfactory comparative measure of purchasing power than a 'real' unit calculated by reference to a broadly based index of current prices. Thus, it is not a coincidence that it has been in countries with persistently high rates of inflation, such as Brazil, that the use of general indices to alleviate the distortionary measurement effects of inflation has been most extensive. In countries with lower inflation rates, there has been more controversy about the usefulness of measuring inflation by the use of general indices. In Britain, for example, the Report of the Sandilands Committee (1975), an official government committee of enquiry into inflation accounting, came to the conclusion that 'inflation is not a phenomenon capable of objective measurement affecting all individuals and entities equally' (para. 48) and used this as an argument to justify the complete rejection of the use of general indices in the system which it proposed, this system being based solely on specific price changes.

The index number problem will be discussed further in Section 5.3. If we can, for the present, ignore the difficulties of measuring the general price level, we can make important conceptual distinctions between the general price level, specific prices and relative prices. The general price level is a measure of the purchasing power of money, as represented by some general index. Specific prices are the observable prices of specific goods and services. These specific prices may change relative to one another and to the general price level. If a specific price changes over a period, we may divide the change into two components, that which is due to changes in the purchasing power of money in general (provided we can measure it), and that due to the change in the price of the specific commodity relative to that of other commodities, the 'real' increase in the price of the specific commodity. Thus, if the price of a specific commodity rose from £10 to £15 in a period in which the general price level rose by 20 per cent (the rate of inflation), we might attribute £2 of the increase to inflation and £3 to a relative price change.[4] These distinctions are important components of some systems of inflation accounting.

Since accounts are concerned with the measurement of economic activity and inflation affects the value of the conventional currency unit of measurement, inflation can clearly have an important effect on accounts. This is especially so in the case of accounts prepared on the traditional historical cost (HC) principle, in which assets and liabilities are recorded at their nominal values at the time of acquisition rather than their current values. In times of inflation, current monetary values are likely to exceed historical values by considerable amounts. Equally, when measuring income, the monetary value of the capital which must be maintained by a business before recognising a profit (i.e. the amount of capital which will maintain the business, or its proprietors, as 'well off' at the end of a period as it was at the beginning) will also need to reflect inflation and does not do so on the traditional historical cost convention.

It is these problems which are at the root of the fierce debates which have taken place in the past over such issues as whether the increase in the nominal (i.e. monetary rather than real) value of stocks held by companies ('stock appreciation') should be regarded as profit, and whether firms which are financed by borrowing have made a 'gain on borrowing' as a result of inflation, because they are able to repay their loans in currency units whose purchasing power has depreciated.

These issues will be taken up in more detail in later chapters.[5] Section 5.3 gives an introduction to the index number problem; later sections explain the techniques of inflation accounting, by means of a simple numerical illustration, and offer some quantitative evidence as to the practical importance of the choice between alternative methods. Both the numerical illustration and the quantitative evidence will show that our assessment of the profitability of an individual business, and of business in general, can be changed radically by our choice of accounting method.

This problem is not, of course, confined to the accounts of businesses. For example, the measurement of national income is also affected by inflation, and economists have long been accustomed to use specific indices to estimate stock appreciation and replacement cost depreciation ('capital consumption') in the calculation of Net National Product, or 'national income' (Stone and Stone, 1977). Thus, the national income statistician's approach to measuring national income is similar to that used by current cost accounting in measuring business income. However, the national income statistics go further than this, using broadly based price indices to re-state the annual national income figures in 'real' terms, as an aid to inter-year comparison. These 'real' national income figures have much in common with what we described earlier as 'real terms accounting'.

Nor is the inflation problem merely one of *ex post* measurement. The vagaries of unanticipated inflation lead to arbitrary re-allocation of resources between parties who have contracted in money terms. For example, the more rapid is inflation, the more will those who have borrowed money on fixed terms gain at the expense of those who have lent to them. Equally, if the wage bargain has been set in money terms at an annual pay-round, the more rapid is subsequent inflation, the more will employers gain at the expense of employees. The result of this type of problem in relation to fixed money contracts is not only possible inequity, due to the arbitrary impact of unanticipated inflation, but also inefficiency, due to the creation of unnecessary uncertainty by linking real contractual rewards to an uncertain inflation rate. Thus, lenders and borrowers will have to make *ex ante* estimates of the likely inflation rate before they can fix an appropriate interest rate, and wage negotiations will also involve taking a view as to the probable inflation rate during the period of the agreement.

In order to deal with the latter problem, a number of economists have proposed indexation, i.e. adjusting the terms of contracts by a price index to allow for inflation. This would enable the terms of contracts to be fixed in 'real' rather than money terms, insofar as it is possible to construct an appropriate price index. Irving Fisher (1920) was an early advocate of indexation and was also a pioneer in the construction of index numbers. Subsequently, the case for indexation has been associated with Friedman (1974), who advocated it as a means of speeding the stabilisation effects of controlling the money supply, although this argument depends crucially upon stabilising effects occurring: otherwise indexation might speed de-stabilisation. British advocates of indexation in the 1970s, when inflation was at its peak, were Jackman and Klappholz (1975) and Fane (1975), and the case for indexation was explored thoroughly in Liesner and King (1975) and Carsberg et al. (1974), although neither book provided a thorough exploration of the contrary case. A review of this work will be found in Whittington (1976).

Apart from academic discussion, indexation has been adopted in practice in a number of countries, notably in Latin America, especially in Brazil and later in Chile, although the range of contracts that were indexed was never as comprehensive as that contemplated in the theoretical literature. In these countries, the indexation of accounts on a CPP basis was also adopted as part of the policy of indexation. In Britain, an experiment in the partial indexation of wage rates, the so-called threshold agreement of 1973–74[6] was abandoned, presumably in the belief that it was strengthening, rather than weakening, the inflationary spiral. This experience may have been instrumental in motivating the government effectively to reject the accounting profession's proposals for CPP, which can be regarded as a form of indexation of accounts, by setting up the Sandilands Committee in 1974. The terms of reference of the Sandilands Committee required it to examine the wider economic implications of inflation accounting and parts of its Report[7] suggested some anxiety that the indexation of accounts might lead to the indexation of taxes, wages and other transactions and that this in turn might lead to further inflation. The only forms of indexation existing in Britain at the present time (as of 2016) are public-sector pensions, a decreasing number of private-sector 'defined benefit' pension schemes, index-linked National Savings Certificates, a restricted amount of government stock issue and a small number of index-linked bond issues by private companies (such as utilities) whose prospective cash flow profiles are particularly appropriate (e.g. regulated firms whose prices are set on an 'RPI minus x' indexed basis). Some insurance companies offer index-linked annuities but, because of the limited volume of index-linked investments available to back them, they are regarded by the providers as risky and the consequent risk premium makes them expensive. The indexation of pensions[8] is currently being challenged on grounds of cost, and the decline in the number of indexed private pension schemes is, like the high cost of index-linked annuities, attributable partly to the shortage of indexed stock for investment by pension funds. Thus, there is currently a widespread reluctance to enter into index-linked obligations.

## 5.4 INDEX NUMBERS AND THE MEASUREMENT OF INFLATION

Implicit in the preceding discussion of inflation and indexation has been the assumption that it is possible to construct a price index which is a useful measure of the changing values of money relative to goods. The type of indices most widely advocated for this purpose are broadly based indices of retail prices (such as the UK Retail Price Index or the Consumer Price Index, shown in Table 5.2) or the indices used to obtain 'real' national income figures (such as the GNP deflator in the UK, which measures the price level of all the components of

Gross National Product, or 'national income'). It must be admitted that, for a variety of reasons, no index is likely to be an ideal measure, but, in considering the deficiencies of indices, we must be prepared to balance the deficiencies of indexation against the deficiencies of data which are completely unadjusted for changes in the purchasing power of money.

The literature of index numbers is very large and no attempt will be made to survey it here. We shall concentrate on a brief statement of the elementary principles of index numbers, which are essential for an appreciation of their use in accounting, and a broad outline of their theoretical limitations, which are stated more fully elsewhere in the literature.[9]

A price index is used to measure how the purchasing power of money over goods differs at different times or at different locations. In the context of inflation, we are concerned with the comparison of different times. If there were only one good in the world, traded in a single market, the construction of a price index would be very simple: the index at any time would merely be the ratio of the current unit price of the good to its price at the constant reference time chosen as the base of the index. Thus, if time 0 is the base, time 1 is when we wish to measure the index, and $p_0$ and $p_1$ represent the unit prices ruling at these times, the index at time 1 is $p_1/p_0$. However, in this simple situation, we do not really require a price index, because, in a single-commodity world, we can measure wealth, income or whatever other economic attribute is being assessed, in terms of physical units of the good. Measurement in monetary terms becomes essential only when we have more than one good. Monetary measurement is then a device for translating heterogeneous physical measures into a common unit of measurement, the monetary unit.

In this more complicated but realistic situation, we are faced with a set of prices $p_i$, where $i$ indicates the $i$th commodity. If these prices change, we may wish to use a price index to reduce such monetary aggregates as income or expenditure over different periods of time to a common 'real' basis of measurement, by eliminating the illusory upward trend caused by the declining purchasing power of money in a period of inflation (or the corresponding downward trend caused by deflation). The problem of reducing the changes in many prices, $p_i$, to a single index is the essence of index number construction, and it poses difficulties in all but the simplest case, when all prices increase in the same proportion. In the latter case, we can derive the appropriate index by choosing arbitrarily any particular commodity, $i$, and calculating the ratio of the current price (at time 1) to that of the base period (time 0), $p_{i1}/p_{i0}$. This ratio is known as a *price relative*. Alternatively, we could take an average of price relatives for different commodities (weighted or unweighted) and we would, by definition, obtain the same ratio. However, in the realistic situation in which there are differences in the rate of price change of different commodities, the selection of commodities to be included in the index and the relative weights attached to them in the averaging process are likely to affect the value of the index, and this is the central issue in the debate on index numbers amongst both economists and accountants. However, it should be remembered that, in practice, there is often a great deal of correlation between different index numbers and between contemporaneous changes in index numbers (as demonstrated, in an accounting context, by the work of Peasnell and Skerratt, 1976a) and, in discussing the problem of relative price changes, which is central to the specification of index numbers, we should not lose sight of the fact that, in many situations, even an imperfect index number may be of practical use, by pointing in the right direction even when it cannot be regarded as precisely accurate. It is notable that the adjustment of accounts by using broadly based general indices has been widely practiced, and the precise estimation of specific price changes has commonly been ignored, in those countries such as Brazil which have experienced very high rates of general inflation (Baxter, 1976). In this situation, any broadly based index is likely to capture a large proportion of the change in most prices.

There are two basic approaches to the index number problem. Frisch (1936) in a classic survey of index number theory, classified these as the 'atomistic' and the 'functional' approaches. The *atomistic*' approach is essentially statistical. It assumes that there is a general price level from which individual prices may diverge in a random fashion, so that the purpose of the index number is to average prices across commodities in such a way that the random element is minimised, so that we have the best possible estimate of the general price level. This approach is associated with Edgeworth, the pioneer of index number theory, and with Irving Fisher, who reinforced the approach by specifying a number of tests of mathematical properties which an index number should possess.

Fisher's allegiance to this approach is particularly important, because his book, *The Purchasing Power of Money* (1911), is referred to by both the first English writer (Fells, 1919) and the first American writer (Middleditch, 1918) on inflation accounting, and his writings are extensively referred to by Sweeney (1936) who can be regarded as the seminal writer on CPP accounting in the English language. Sweeney's work was the model for the American Institute of Certified Public Accountants' (1963) research study ARS6, 'Reporting the Financial Effects of Price-Level Changes', which subsequently became a model for CPP proposals in both the US (by the Accounting Principles Board in 1969, and by the Financial Accounting Standards Board, FASB, in 1974, 1978 and 1979a), and in the UK (in the Accounting Standards Steering Committee's ED8, 1973, and PSSAP7, 1974). It is notable that Appendix A of ARS6, on the index number problem, takes an overtly statistical (or, in Frisch's terminology, 'atomistic') view of the index number problem, and it therefore advocates the GNP implicit price deflator (a price index covering all of the components of Gross National Product) as the most appropriate index, on the ground that this has the widest coverage and is therefore presumably the best indicator of 'the general price level'.[10] Subsequent advocates of CPP accounting have accepted this argument, sometimes accepting a consumer price index on practical grounds (consumer indices being more frequently published), but always retaining the broader GNP deflator as an ideal. For example, a pronouncement of the US

Financial Accounting Standards Board (FASB) on the subject (*Constant Dollar Accounting*, March 1979) stated:

> The index to be used in Constant Dollar Accounting in the United
> States shall be the Consumer Price Index for All Urban Consumers
> (CPI-U).... The Board has designated the CPI-U instead of the
> Gross National Product Implicit Price Deflator because the CPI-U
> has the practical advantages of being calculated more frequently
> (monthly instead of quarterly) and not being revised after its
> initial publication. Also, the rates of change in the CPI-U and the
> GNP Implicit Price Deflator tend to be similar and, therefore, use
> of the CPI-U will tend to produce a comparable result. *(p. 2)*

This 'atomistic' approach was described as such by Frisch because it
ignores the relationship between prices of commodities $(p_i)$ and the
quantities consumed $(q_i)$ regarding them as two sets of independent
variables. The other approach, labelled by Frisch as the *'functional'*
approach, is that adopted by economists and regards the relationship
between prices and quantities as being one of interdependence. This
approach is grounded in the concept of welfare, regarding goods as a
means of creating utility for the individual consumer. The economist
does not, therefore, attempt to measure the change in 'the general
level of prices' as a uniquely defined objective concept but attempts
to measure the change in 'the cost of living' defined by reference
to the utility function which expresses the subjective preferences
of the individual consumer. Thus, the basic approach used by the
economist is to define a certain standard of living for the individual
consumer (a 'reference indifference curve') and to calculate the cost
of attaining this standard under different sets of prices. The ratio
of this cost measured at various points in time to its level in the
base period provides us with a cost of living index, reflecting how
all price changes have affected the cost of living of the individual
consumer.

The strength of the economist's approach is that it provides
a precise rationale for and definition of 'the cost of living'. It thus
provides a framework within which the problems of index number

construction can be identified precisely, which is a necessary prelude to understanding them. In particular, the problem of weighting different commodities is clarified: the appropriate weighting is the quantity of each commodity which would be consumed at the set of relative prices existing at the particular times being considered, at the reference standard of living. Thus, where $n$ commodities are consumed, the ideal economic index is

$$\frac{\sum_{i=1}^{n} p_{i1} \cdot q_{i1}}{\sum_{i=1}^{n} p_{i0} \cdot q_{i0}}$$

where the $q_i$ are those quantities necessary to achieve the reference standard of living at the prices reigning at the relevant time (1 or 0). The quantities depend on relative prices because a rational, welfare maximising consumer seeks to achieve the maximum benefit from a given budget (and therefore will achieve the reference standard of living at minimum cost), and this will imply that as relative prices change, the consumer substitutes those commodities which have become relatively cheap for those which have become relatively more expensive (except in the extreme case of commodities which have a zero elasticity of substitution, i.e. demand for them is invariant to their relative price).

However, the greater precision of the economist's welfare-based concept of 'the cost of living' as opposed to the statistical concept of 'the general price level' is purchased at the cost of a number of restrictions on its applicability. The more important of these restrictions are as follows:

1. The measurement of the 'true' economic cost of living index strictly requires full knowledge of the individual's preferences, i.e. the relative rankings of all possible bundles of goods. In practice, this is not available, so we have to infer preferences from actual behaviour.
2. When, as is usual in accounting applications, the index refers to a group (such as shareholders or proprietors), we have the problem of aggregation. In order to avoid this, we have to make the assumption

that preferences of individuals within the group are represented by a group preference map.[11] This requires the restrictive assumptions that all members of the group have identical preferences such that, at any set of relative prices, they have the same expenditure allocations irrespective of income ('homothetic preferences'). This is unlikely to be the case in practice.

3. Even when constructing an index at the individual level, unless the individual's utility function assumes a very restrictive, and highly unlikely, form,[12] the classic 'index number problem' arises, i.e. in measuring a *change* in the cost of living, defined as a change in the expenditure necessary to maintain a given standard of living, do we take as our point of reference for the price index the relative weights (relative quantities consumed) at the closing prices or at the opening prices? If we take the base-weighted approach of using the quantities consumed at the opening prices for the comparison of the cost of living (known as the Laspeyres index), we ignore the likelihood that the consumer will substitute goods that are now relatively cheap for those that are now relatively expensive, thus over-stating the current cost of maintaining the initial standard of living. If, on the other hand, we take the current-weighted approach of using the current quantities consumed as determined by current prices (known as the Paasche index), we over-state the initial cost of living by imposing the consumption pattern of the later period rather than the more efficient pattern implied by the prices of the first period. Thus, one index (Laspeyres) provides an upper limit to what it is intended to measure whilst the other (Paasche) provides a lower limit to what it is intended to measure. Moreover, because the two bases are different, it is not the case that they are measuring exactly the same thing, so we cannot argue that they provide upper and lower bounds on the 'true' index. Hence, under realistic conditions where relative prices change, it is not possible to define a unique price index that measures 'the cost of living'.[13] In practice, official indices are usually calculated on the Laspeyres (base weighted) method because of its relative convenience, the weights being available from the start of the period.

4. The economist's approach starts from an individual with stable preferences. In practice, individual preferences can vary through time. This is potentially a serious problem, because the use of indices in practical situations often involves comparisons over significant periods of time (e.g. in the case of financial accounting, the periods will be years rather than months). This difficulty can be dealt with by making appropriate assumptions, such as stability of preferences through time, or by techniques such as 'chaining' (changing the weights for different periods to reflect changing tastes). The validity of the resulting index will then be dependent upon the empirical accuracy of the assumptions and the precision of the techniques upon which it is based.

5. The nature and quality of the goods consumed changes over time. The appearance of new goods, or disappearance of old ones, is an extreme form of the weighting problem (non-existence implying a zero 'q'). Quality changes imply a redefinition of individual goods and an assessment of the relative values of the services provided by the new and the old, achieved empirically by the use of hedonic techniques (Deaton and Muellbauer, 1980, Chapter 10). In practice, these assessments are incorporated in the process of periodically rebasing and chaining indices.

The use to which the price index is put will often be to devise a measure of 'real income' or 'real capital' by applying the index to unadjusted data measured in monetary units recorded at different times. It is important to note the limitations of the resulting 'real' measure as a reflection of the satisfaction which an individual might derive from the income or capital being measured. The 'real' measure will be a positive *function* of utility but not necessarily a cardinal *measure* of it: a person whose income rises from £15,000 a year to 20,000 a year is not necessarily ⅓ better off than before, although he or she will be better off to some extent (i.e. 'real' income will be an ordinal measure, giving correct rankings of the individual's preferences for different income streams). The 'real' measure tells us that the individual is better off, but not by how much. Thus, the individual is left to translate the measure into something which has a more precise but subjective meaning in terms of a personal feeling of well-offness.[14] 'Real' accounting measures, based upon the use of indices, cannot therefore provide a direct measure of the utility of an income stream or capital sum to the proprietor of a business, but they can potentially provide useful measures of command over goods and services which will assist the individual proprietor in assessing the significance of income in terms of personal utility. However, in the context of financial accounting, the assessment of individual utility is not a primary concern: many users of the information are not individual proprietors but institutions, such as investment companies or state bodies (such as revenue authorities) whose primary interest is in maximising financial returns (in real, inflation adjusted, as well as nominal monetary form).

Economists and statisticians have devised a number of ingenious techniques for overcoming the difficulties of estimating price indices. As we have seen, these techniques typically make assumptions which restrict the theoretical applicability of the resulting indices, but the importance of the restrictions is not necessarily such as to rule out the use of the indices: for practical purposes, we must recognise that perfect measures do not exist and we must select the imperfect but feasible measure whose restrictions seem least important for the particular purpose which we have in mind.[15] The two indices listed in Table 5.2 serve to illustrate this point.[16]

The older of the two indices, the RPI, was originally established after the Second World War as a 'compensation index', designed to calculate the compensation for the adverse effects of inflation on various incomes and benefits. It therefore excluded very high and low income households (who were not likely to be recipients of relevant benefits) but it did have a wide coverage of expenditure, including housing costs. The CPI was introduced much later, in 1996, as a response to a European Union requirement to provide a measure of inflation that was comparable across member states, for macro-economic purposes.

Thus, the original purpose of the CPI was more closely related to the statistician's 'atomistic' approach, whereas the RPI was intended to mirror the welfare effects of inflation on a target population, which is closer to the economist's 'functional' approach. Hence, the CPI covered all of the population present in the UK, irrespective of income and including overseas visitors. The CPI also had a different commodity coverage; notably it did not include housing costs, but that was for practical reasons (data being unavailable in some comparator countries) rather than for sound conceptual reasons. A third difference between the two indices, which is important in its quantitative effect, is the way in which observed prices are averaged at the lowest level of aggregation in order to obtain an average for each commodity group. The RPI uses an arithmetic average whereas the CPI uses a geometric average.[17] The geometric average moderates the price change by allowing for the substitution effect, whereby items that increase more in price will be consumed less. This reflects the economist's approach rather than the statistician's, as characterised earlier (allowing no inter-dependence of price and quantity), although the precise extent of substitution assumed by geometric averaging does not necessarily reflect the reality of consumer behaviour. Hence, neither the RPI nor the CPI can be regarded as indices that are uniquely suited to a particular purpose or approach. As a result of this, the national statisticians have devised a number of variants of both of these indices to focus them more clearly on particular policy targets.

Thus, whether we approach index number construction from the statistical or the economic standpoints, we reach a common area of middle ground. The statistical approach requires some additional theoretical underpinnings to give a precise meaning to the concept of 'the general price level' and to justify the relative weighting attached to different prices, so that the implementation of this approach naturally draws us towards economic theory. The economic approach, on the other hand, inevitably encounters difficulties in the empirical implementation of measurements based upon so subjective a concept as welfare, so that it necessarily relies on a number of assumptions and

approximations which lead it towards measures which can be justified by the statistical approach. The outcome is that neither approach
would claim to lead to an index number which is a perfect representation of the effect of price changes on the cost of living of an individual
with a fixed sum of money to spend, but both would hope to give a
better representation of this than would be obtained by making no
correction at all. In deciding which index is the best for some particular purpose, we would resort, on a theoretical level, to economic
theory, but on a practical level we would also need to know whether
the use of alternative indices led to a material difference.

Perhaps the difference of emphasis between the economic and
statistical approaches is not made clear enough in the accounting
literature. The statistical approach, at least in the form in which it
is employed in arguments for CPP accounting, seems to be arguing
for replacing the nominal £ by a unit which has more stable general
purchasing power, e.g. the practical origins of CPP were in the German
and French stabilisations in terms of gold currency (Sweeney, 1936).
This approach does not claim to reflect the consumption pattern of
an individual in any particular manner (e.g. it would be an unusual
individual indeed who consumed only gold): it is designed to construct
a unit of measurement representing constant (or more constant than
money) command over those goods and services which are traded in
the economy. It thus assumes that it is necessary for the individual
to make a subjective translation from this CPP unit into personal
welfare, and it may well be that the rate of exchange of CPP units
into welfare will be different not only for different individuals but
also for the same individual at different times.

The economic approach, on the other hand, starts from the
much more ambitious position that an ideal measure should reflect
individual welfare. In its most extreme form, as expressed, for example, by the Sandilands Committee (1975), it rejects entirely any concept of the general price level. In its more moderate and realistic
form, it recognises that the practical problems of measuring individual welfare are such that any index is bound to be an approximation.

Furthermore, in the case of the accounts of a company, it would be impracticable to supply a separate set of accounts to each shareholder, adjusted by an individual price index, or, alternatively, to construct an index based upon some concept of the social welfare of shareholders as a group.[18] However, in adapting to practical constraints, the economic approach retains the essential assumption that the index should ideally reflect the effect of price changes on the individual. Thus, although the statistical and the economic approach may, in practice, occupy a common middle ground, they are, in their aspirations, facing in different directions.

This difference may perhaps be discerned in the advocacy of alternative indices for use in CPP accounting. As stated earlier, professional pronouncements on the subject have traditionally preferred a statistical approach and have advocated the use of as broadly based an index as possible, such as the GNP implicit deflator, with the aim of identifying a reliable estimate of 'the general price level'. Economists, however, tend to prefer a consumer price index (e.g. Scott, 1976), on the ground that command over goods and services should be confined to items which will, potentially at least, be consumed by shareholders. This implies that 'the general price level' should be defined in terms of 'the cost of living' of shareholders, which is perhaps more consistent with what we earlier described as the proprietary approach to financial accounting.[19]

Later in this chapter, we shall return to the issue of index number selection for CPP accounting and discuss, in a pragmatic and practical manner, some considerations which might lead us to accept the use of a general index, despite the unavoidable ambiguities surrounding the interpretation of any particular index.

## 5.5 CONSTANT PURCHASING POWER ACCOUNTING

Constant Purchasing Power Accounting (CPP) is a consistent method of indexing accounts by means of a general index which reflects changes in the purchasing power of money. It therefore attempts to deal with the inflation problem in the sense in which this is popularly understood, as a decline in the value of the currency. It attempts to deal with this problem by converting all of the currency unit measurements in accounts into units at a common date by means of the index. We shall concentrate on the *current* purchasing power variety of CPP, i.e. one which uses the current currency as the CPP unit.

Two common criticisms of CPP are, firstly, that general price indices are inappropriate for up-dating the historical costs of specific assets and, secondly, that general price indices cannot reflect the consumption patterns of individual shareholders and are therefore inappropriate for up-dating the amount of proprietors' capital to be maintained intact. We shall return to the second issue later, but the first must be dealt with here, because it indicates a misunderstanding of CPP accounting. CPP is concerned with the measurement unit, not with the techniques used to value assets and liabilities. It is possible to apply CPP methods to any valuation base, whether it be historical cost, replacement cost, net realisable value, or some eclectic combination (as in the Sandilands version of current cost accounting). The 'real terms' approach, illustrated in Chapter 1, combined CPP methods with current values. Some important pioneers of CPP, such as Sweeney (1936) and Accounting Research Study No. 6 (American Institute of Certified Public Accountants, 1963) and PSSAP7 (Accounting Standards Steering Committee, 1974) in the UK have been at pains to point out the fact that CPP can be applied to a current value base, although, as a matter of practical expediency, CPP has typically been proposed (e.g. in Accounting Research Study No. 6 in the US and PSSAP7 in the UK) as a means of amending traditional historical cost accounting.

A brief illustration of the CPP approach and its applicability to alternative valuation bases is as follows. Suppose a firm has a single asset, £100 in cash, which it holds in a period of 10 per cent inflation. If the sole source of finance is equity, the CPP approach would show a loss of £10 due to the fact that the asset had not risen in monetary value to match inflation: at the end of the period 110 devalued £s would be required to maintain the equity interest in terms of general purchasing power, but the asset would be only worth £100 in the devalued currency. This is an example of 'the loss on holding money' in a period of inflation. Suppose now that the firm was partly financed by an interest-free loan of £40. In this case only 40 devalued pounds would be required to pay the loan, so there would be a 'gain on borrowing' of £4 (10 per cent of £40) to offset against the loss on holding money, the net loss being £6 (which is the loss on money holding financed by the equity stake, 10 per cent of £60). These calculations are common to all CPP systems because it is assumed that the money holding and the loan do not fluctuate in nominal money value, i.e. for these items, historical cost and current value are equal in terms of monetary units, although the value of the monetary unit itself fluctuates. A simple numerical example of CPP, based on the 'Old Fred example of Chapter 3, will be found in Appendix B to this chapter.

Assume now that, instead of holding money, the firm has held shares which are quoted on the stock exchange and that these rose in market value to £150 at the end of the period. If we revert to the 'all equity' finance assumption, CPP applied to historical cost (HC) would show neither a profit nor a loss. The re-stated closing value of the shares would be £110, their HC in 'opening £s' translated into 'closing £s' to allow for inflation, because shares are a 'real' asset not denominated in fixed monetary units. The equity interest would similarly be re-stated, by applying the general index, to be £110, leaving no net gain or loss.

If, on the other hand, CPP were applied to a current value base in a 'real terms' system, the closing value of the asset (the share investments) would be £150.[20] This is, by definition, in terms of current (closing) £s, so no further re-statement is required. The equity stake, on the other hand, will need to be re-stated as before: it was £100 in 'old £s' at the start of the period, and this is equivalent to £110 'new £s' at the end. Thus, our closing balance sheet, expressed in 'new £s', shows an asset of £150, equity capital of £110 and a surplus, attributable to equity, of £40.

If we now reintroduce the assumption of loan finance, so that opening capital is £60 equity and £40 loan, the 'gain on borrowing' of £4 will reappear. This will add £4 to the surplus attributable to equity, irrespective of the valuation basis of the non-monetary (or 'real' asset), bringing the total to £4 in the case of HC valuation and £44 in the case of current value.

For the purpose of this chapter, we shall confine the discussion to CPP as a means of amending historical cost accounting, but CPP adjustments will re-emerge in the next chapter as a means of amending current value accounts to produce 'real terms' accounting.

## 5.6 A BRIEF HISTORY OF CPP

The CPP technique owes its origins to the inflation which followed the First World War, particularly in France and Germany. In both of these countries, the paper currency was extremely unstable in value and it became customary to draw up financial accounts in terms of the equivalent gold currency (the gold franc and the gold mark) which was much more stable in value. Thus, in the early days, the parallel which is frequently drawn between currency translation and CPP accounting[21] was an exact one. The European experience was studied by a number of American scholars, such as Wasserman (1931) and Sweeney (1927, 1928), and there was a significant American literature on the subject in the period 1918–35, much of which is gathered together and reviewed by Zeff (1976). Outstanding amongst the American writers was H. W. Sweeney, whose book *Stabilized Accounting* (Sweeney, 1936) is the classic statement of the case for and the techniques of CPP accounting.[22]

Interest in CPP accounting naturally declined during the depression years of the 1930s, but it revived during the inflationary period following the Second World War. During this period, the American Accounting Association published two influential empirical studies by R. C. Jones (1955, 1956) which examined the quantitative effect of CPP adjustment, and a brief manual by Perry Mason (1956) on the technique of CPP adjustment, using an HC valuation basis. This work, together with the earlier work by Sweeney, was clearly a powerful influence on *Accounting Research Study No. 6*, published by the American Institute of Certified Public Accountants in 1963. This, in turn, was the basis of the Accounting Principles Board's[23] *Statement No. 3* of June 1969, which recommended a supplementary statement showing the effects of CPP adjustment to traditional (HC based) accounts. Subsequent American proposals by the FASB in 1974 and 1978 were also of this type.[24] In the UK, the professional proposals for CPP accounting, *Exposure Draft 8* (1973) and *Provisional Statement of Standard Accounting Practice No. 7* (1974) resembled *APB3*, and were clearly influenced by the earlier publication, *Accounting for Stewardship in a Period of Inflation* (1968), which, in turn, was influenced by the earlier American work.[25]

Thus, by the early 1970s, CPP adjustment of historical cost had emerged as the inflation accounting technique favoured by professional bodies in both the UK and the US. Professional bodies in Australia, Canada, New Zealand and South Africa followed this trend. CPP was also in use in practice in certain Latin American countries which had experienced high rates of inflation (Baxter, 1976). However, it has failed to be adopted as the only approved technique in any country outside Latin America: in the UK it was supplanted by current cost accounting, and in the US the principal pronouncement by the Financial Accounting Standards Board in the inflation accounting debate (FAS33, FASB, 1979) was eclectic, requiring both CCA and CPP information.

One possible reason for this failure is that the professional proposals for CPP have always been based on its application to a traditional, historical cost valuation base. This was presumably done to portray CPP as an evolutionary reform, growing naturally out of traditional accounting and avoiding the subjectivity involved in estimating the current values of specific assets, but it had the effect also of putting CPP in apparent competition with other reforms, such as CCA, although it was potentially compatible with them.[26] When inflation is not at very high levels, so that relative price changes are more important than changes in the general price level, current values may be seen as a more urgent reform of traditional accounting, especially from the point of view of the users of accounts. They are likely to be concerned with the specific current values of the assets of the entity in which they have an interest, rather than with the CPP adjustment of historical costs which are of doubtful relevance to current circumstances.

Another reason for the widespread rejection of the professional proposals for CPP may have been fear of its possible economic consequences. CPP could be seen as a step towards indexation, and there may have been anxiety in government circles that indexation could institutionalise inflation, possibly even reinforcing inflationary spirals by leading to automatic inflation adjustment of wages, tax reliefs and the national debt. Certainly, the move to current cost accounting (CCA) in the mid-1970s was initiated by a series of government reports and interventions such as the requirement of the US Securities and Exchange Commission (SEC) for replacement cost accounting disclosure, announced in 1975, the UK's Sandilands Report (Sandilands Committee, 1975), the Mathews Report on Taxation in Australia (Mathews, 1975), and the Richardson Committee Report (1976) in New Zealand. This 'current cost revolution' initiated by government intervention is described and discussed more fully in *The Debate on Inflation Accounting* (Tweedie and Whittington, 1984).

## 5.7 THE TECHNIQUE OF CPP

The basic technique of CPP is extremely simple. In practice, of course, complications arise, and it is not proposed to explore these here. Many admirable textbooks, manuals and case studies have been published which deal with these problems, and some of these are listed in Appendix A at the end of this chapter. A numerical illustration is provided in Appendix B.

As stated earlier, the essence of CPP is to translate all measurements in currency units into units at a common date by using a general price-level index as an indication of the purchasing power of currency at different points in time. Thus, the proportionate change in the price index represents the 'exchange rate' between currency units of different dates. The justification for making such an adjustment is that accounting requires a stable measuring unit and an 'unstabilised' (i.e. not indexed) currency unit fails to provide this.

A simple illustration of CPP adjustment is to use the notation of earlier chapters and apply a general price index to the accounts of a period. It will be recalled that the opening balance sheet was defined as

$$N_t + M_t \equiv L_t + P_t \qquad (5.1)$$

where　　$N$ represents non-monetary assets

　　　　　$M$ represents monetary assets

　　　　　$L$ represents liabilities (assumed to be fixed in

　　　　　　　monetary terms)

　　　　　$P$ represents the proprietor's net worth.

The closing balance sheet, rearranged to show proprietor's interest on the left hand side is

$$P_{t+1} = N_{t+1} + M_{t+1} - L_{t+1} \qquad (5.2)$$

If we assume that the valuation of $N_t$ is in £s of that date, either because the assets were acquired on that date or because previous indexation exercises have up-dated historical cost to that date, we can translate the opening balance sheet from £s of $t$ into £s of $t + 1$ by the following adjustment. If the general price index increases by $p$ per cent between $t$ and $t + 1$ the re-stated opening balance sheet becomes[27]

$$P_t(1 + p) = N_t(1 + p) + M_t(1 + p) - L_t(1 + p) \qquad (5.3)$$

In order to assess total gains to the proprietor (sometimes known as 'comprehensive income'), we need to compare this with the closing balance sheet, which also has to be re-stated in £s of $t + 1$. Assume for simplicity that the balance sheet structure of the firm has been undisturbed during the period, i.e. there have been no transactions.[28] In order to re-state the closing balance sheet, we can increase the valuation of the non-monetary asset to compensate for the decline in the value of the £, one historic £ (at $t$) being equivalent to $(1 + p)$ current £s (at $t + 1$).[29] We cannot, however, alter the valuations of $M$ or $L$, because they are fixed in monetary units, irrespective of the fluctuations in purchasing power of those units. Thus, a £1 liability at $t$ is still a £1 liability at $t + 1$, albeit the £ has depreciated in value. The closing balance sheet, in $t + 1$ £s is now

$$P_{t+1} = N_t(1 + p) + M_t - L_t \tag{5.4}$$

Subtracting the price-level-stabilised opening balance sheet, (4.3), from the equivalent closing balance sheet, (5.4), gives us CPP total gains:

$$Y_{CPP} = \Delta P = L_t p - M_t p \tag{5.5}$$

$L_t p$ is the 'gain on borrowing', i.e. the gain to the firm due to the facts that the loan is fixed in money terms and the purchasing power of money has declined. $M_t p$ is the 'loss on holding money' (or assets denominated in monetary units), which is the mirror-image of the gain on borrowing: it represents the loss of purchasing power of the monetary units held. Thus, CPP accounting, applied in this manner as a modification of historical cost, recognises only two methods of valuation: re-statement of HC to allow for the fluctuating purchasing power of money, which applies to non-monetary assets and to proprietors' net worth (the capital to be maintained before income is recognised), and the fixed value in terms of the monetary units, which applies to 'monetary' assets and liabilities. Clearly when, as in 'real terms' accounting, the valuation base of the accounts being stabilised is some form of current value, there is no need to apply the general index to 'non-monetary' balance sheet items which are stated at current values, as these are, by definition, already expressed in current £s. However, a current value income statement will be stated in terms of values current at the time of transactions *within* the year, and this will require CPP re-statement into *end of year* units if transactions are to be recorded in monetary units of constant value.

This conclusion should be qualified, in that it assumes that CPP takes on the current purchasing power form, rather than using some other unit of constant purchasing power, based at a past date. It is also important to note that the preceding example deals with CPP accounting *within a particular year*, whereas a particularly important use of CPP is for the *comparison of different years*, or series of years: the longer the period, the more important are changes in the purchasing power of money likely to be. In the case of such comparisons, it is necessary to ensure that the same CPP unit is used for all the years being compared, although, if the figures within individual years are based upon consistent CPP units, translation between units is a simple matter, merely involving multiplication of the numbers in the accounts by the appropriate 'rate of exchange'. Thus, if the accounts are expressed in current purchasing power units as of the end of each individual year, in order to make figures for earlier years comparable with those for the current year, we need to calculate the rates of exchange between the £ at the end of the current year and the £ at the end of each preceding year: this rate of exchange is simply the ratio of the current price index to that of the earlier years. We then re-state the accounts for each earlier year by multiplying each item by the rate of exchange relevant to the year. This is a purely mechanical process, analogous to the translation of £s into $s at a given exchange rate.

Although, for simplicity and precision, the algebraic illustration in equations (5.1)–(5.5) was confined to the 'no transactions' situation, it can easily be extended to the more realistic situation in which transactions take place. In general, we can define current purchasing power comprehensive income (total gains), by deducting the opening balance sheet, stabilised in closing £s, from the closing balance sheet, similarly stabilised, as[30]

$$Y_{CPP} = P'_{t+1} - P'_t(1 + p) = [N'_{t+1} - N'_t(1 + p)]$$
$$+ [M_{t+1} - M_t] - [L_{t+1} - L_t] - M_t \cdot p + L_t \cdot p \qquad (5.6)$$

where the valuation basis of $N_t'$ and $N_{t+1}'$ is historical cost re-stated to the relevant date by application of a general price index. The primes indicate variables which differ from historical cost data because they are indexed to date. If a current value base were used, the primed variables would represent current values as of the respective dates, and these would, by definition, be expressed in currency units as of the valuation date.

This formulation brings out clearly the essential feature of CPP: the use of the general index $p$ to adjust all items in the accounts so that they are expressed in currency units as of a constant date, and therefore of constant value. Opening capital is measured in real, rather than in monetary terms, where real terms is defined in general purchasing power $[P_t'(1 + p)]$. Real, or 'non-monetary', assets $(N)$ are assumed to fluctuate in value in terms of monetary units: in this case, using a historical cost valuation basis, they are assumed to retain their real historical values, so that, if the same assets were held throughout the period, there would be no change in the real value of these assets, because $N_{t+1}'$ would be equal to $N_t'(1 + p)$. 'Monetary' assets and liabilities $(M$ and $L)$, on the other hand, are assumed to have values fixed in monetary units, resulting, in a period of inflation, in the gain on borrowing $(L_t.\ p)$ and the loss of holding money $(M_t.\ p)$ which are separated out on the right-hand side of equation (4.6). However, this is a correct expression of these two factors only when $M$ and $L$ have remained constant throughout the period (as in our earlier transactionless example). In other circumstances, the only strictly accurate method of calculating the gain on $L$ or the loss on $M$ is to stabilise each transaction individually: examples of this will be found in Sweeney (1935, 1936) and Ijiri (1976). Strictly, this method requires the availability of an index for each time at which transactions took place. A simpler method, which is quicker and cheaper but less precise, averages transactions over the whole period and assumes that they occurred linearly through time, so that the mid-year index can be taken as the average at which transactions took place. Examples of this approach will be found in *Accounting Research*

*Study No. 6* and *Provisional Statement of Standard Accounting Practice No. 7*. A simple numerical example of CPP adjustment will be found in Appendix B to this chapter, and another will be found in Lee (1985).

The balance sheet formulation of equation (5.6) provides a definition of profit but does not identify the flows of which profit is the net result, and which are reported in the income statement. A fully stabilised CPP accounting system includes an income statement restated in units of constant purchasing power. The following simple example should serve to illustrate the principles involved in stabilising the income statement, and the relationship between the Income Statement and the Balance Sheet.

Assume that a business starts the accounting year with a single asset, £1,000 of stock, which has just been acquired, so that it is expressed in 'beginning of year £s', and which is financed by the proprietor's capital. At the beginning of the year, the general price index stands at 100 and at the end it stands at 120. During the year, with the index standing at 105, the stock is sold for £1,200, which is received in cash, and held in this form to the end of the year.

The historical cost (HC) and constant purchasing power (CPP) accounts are as follows:

Income Statement for the year:

| | HC (Opening £) | CPP Adjustment | CPP (end of year £) |
|---|---|---|---|
| Sales | 1,200 | $\times \dfrac{120}{105}$ | 1,371 |
| *Less* Cost of Sales | 1,000 | $\times \dfrac{120}{100}$ | 1,200 |
| Operating Profit | £200 | | 171 |
| *Less* Loss on holding money | | $1,200 \times \left( \dfrac{120}{105} - 1 \right)$ | 171 |
| Net CPP Profit | | | £0 |

Closing Balance Sheet at end of year:

|  | HC (£) | CPP Adjustment | CPP (end of year £) |
|---|---|---|---|
| *Asset* |  |  |  |
| Cash (Fixed monetary value) | £1,200 |  | £1,200 |
| *Financed by* |  |  |  |
| Opening capital | 1,000 | $\times \dfrac{120}{100}$ | 1,200 |
| *Add* Profit for the year | 200 |  | 0 |
| Closing capital | £1,200 |  | £1,200 |

Each HC item is translated into CPP by applying the change in the general index between the date at which the HC value is established and the date of the CPP unit (the end of the year). Sales and cost of sales (and any other revenue and expense items) are therefore re-stated in CPP units. In this particular example, the loss on holding money entirely wipes out the CPP operating profit, but this is not a general result: a net CPP profit would have remained had the selling price been higher, or had the sales proceeds been reinvested in a non-monetary asset, such as replacement stock, which would be assumed to maintain its real value and would therefore have avoided the loss on holding money. This example uses a precise 'transaction by transaction' indexing method, which is made possible by there being only one transaction. If the sales and general purchasing power changes were spread evenly over the year, the averaging method would suggest using the mid-year index (rather than 105, which is specific to a single transaction) for adjusting the sales and for estimating the loss on holding money.

There are inevitably a number of variations on the CPP method. Sweeney (1936), for example, did not recognise gains or losses on holding money as part of the income statement (although they did affect the reserves in his balance sheet): this is discussed critically in Baxter (1975). There are also a number of variations on the actual technique. Apart from the choice between the stabilisation of individual transactions and the averaging method, discussed earlier, and the choice of price index discussed in Section 5.4 and in the following section, there is the question of the date of the currency unit used for stabilisation. As was noted earlier, *Current* Purchasing Power presumes that the latest (closing balance sheet) date will be the date at which the standard currency unit will be measured, but this is a special case of *constant* purchasing power, which allows stabilisation in any currency unit, provided that the stabilisation is carried through consistently. Sweeney (1936) recommends that, for record-keeping purposes, accounts should be stabilised on a standard unit of a past date, which remains constant from year to year. It is then possible to stabilise transactions before the closing index value is known, and it is a simple matter to translate constant purchasing power figures stabilised on a past date into current purchasing power: this is done by multiplying the constant purchasing power figures by the ratio of the current price index to the index at the base date.

One other technical problem of CPP accounting is the definition of 'monetary' assets and liabilities. Conceptually, this may seem straightforward, 'monetary' implying fixed in value in terms of nominal monetary units, and therefore declining in real value as the real value of the monetary unit declines. In practice, the wide variety of financial assets and claims means that there are 'grey areas' such as holdings of foreign currency and various forms of interest-bearing deposits, which might be classified as either 'monetary' or 'non-monetary' depending upon the precise definition used. The difficulty arises because such items may entail a fixed nominal monetary obligation but may also have a market value which is different. This issue is explored thoroughly at a conceptual level by Heath (1972), who compares the definitions used by various writers and professional pronouncements on the subject. A useful case study by Wanless (1976) has demonstrated that this issue is of practical importance. In a case study, applying the provisions of the British provisional accounting standard (Accounting Standards Steering Committee, 1974) to the accounts of the Scottish Wholesale Co-operative Society, she demonstrates that a material increase in reported profit (or reductions in the 'loss on holding money') can be obtained by deliberately interpreting the definition of 'non-monetary' assets as liberally as possible. This problem is, of course, avoided if a comprehensive current value system is adopted, which re-states all assets and liabilities at their current values. However, we then face the problem of choosing between alternative current values, which was discussed in the previous chapter.

However, it is not our central purpose to expound the technicalities of CPP accounting: this has already been done elsewhere. We now turn to the important question of the merits and deficiencies of CPP.

### 5.8 CRITICISMS OF CPP

The case for CPP adjustment rests primarily on the variability of the value of the currency, which renders it inappropriate as a unit of measurement. CPP claims to produce a stable (or at least a relatively stable) currency unit for measurement purposes. Two broad lines of attack have been mounted against this case: firstly, that general index adjustment of historical cost is an inappropriate method of valuing assets and liabilities, and, secondly, that the general index adjustment does not reflect accurately the change in the cost of living of the individual shareholder, or the cost of the goods which the firm will need to buy in order to maintain its assets intact.

With regard to the first line of criticism, that CPP applied to historical cost produces poor current valuations, we have already seen that this relates only to a limited range of applications of the CPP technique, since CPP can also be applied to current value bases. The discussion in Chapter 3 makes it clear that the case for historical cost accounting as a representation of the current position is rather weak. It is therefore clear that translating historical cost into 'real' terms by means of a general index is not likely to produce figures which are of great utility, despite the fact that this may be a consistent way of dealing with the effects of inflation on historical cost accounts. In particular, this type of adjustment will not produce current market values of assets and liabilities, which are also expressed in current £s, and which are probably of greater relevance to many potential users and uses of accounts. The case for current values was discussed in the preceding chapter. This line of criticism is, of course, aimed at the historical cost base rather than CPP itself, and it must be reiterated that the proponents of CPP have typically seen it as complementary to, rather than competitive with, current values. The association of CPP with historical cost has been due to its proposal as an evolutionary reform of traditional accounting, although it must be admitted that not all of its supporters have recognised this, and that its attractions to the accounting profession may have been enhanced by the prospect that its implementation would postpone the day when accountants would have to deal in such subjective matters as the estimation of replacement costs, or, more recently, fair values.[31] The possibility of combining some form of current value accounting with CPP adjustment in a system of 'real terms' accounting will be discussed further in Chapter 6.

The second line of attack on CPP rests on the inappropriateness of a general index adjustment as a measure of the loss in purchasing power of money. If we accept the argument of the previous paragraph, that the issue of valuation is (or can be) separate from that of measuring the effects of inflation, then this second line of attack becomes a matter of questioning the appropriateness of using general purchasing power adjustments to measure the capital which is to be maintained intact. This can be demonstrated, in terms of our earlier notation, as follows. Assume that non-monetary assets are valued at some acceptable form of current value, indicated by a double prime $(N'')$. For simplicity, maintain the assumption that all liabilities, $L$, are 'monetary' and therefore, like 'monetary' assets $M$, have a current value equal to their face value. The proprietors' interest, at current value, will now be

$$P_t'' = N_t'' + M_t - L_t$$

and

$$P''_{t+1} = N''_{t+1} + M_{t+1} - L_{t+1} \tag{5.7}$$

If we now wish to apply an adjustment for general price-level changes to bring all items into current purchasing power units, no further adjustment is necessary to the closing balance sheet, as all items are expressed in current currency equivalents. In measuring profit, however, we shall need to bring the opening balance sheets, now expressed in £s at $t$, up to date, into £s at $t + 1$, to produce a 'real terms' profit measure:

$$Y_{RT} = P''_{t+1} - P''_t(1 + p) \tag{5.8}$$

In the case in which there are no transactions, this can be applied to individual assets and liabilities to separate 'real' gains and losses (in constant £s) from 'fictitious' gains and losses (those due to changes in the value of the £) as follows:

$$P''_{t+1} - [P''_t(1 + p)] = [N''_{t+1} - N''_t(1 + p)] + [M_{t+1} - M_t(1 + p)]$$
$$- [L_{t+1} - L_t(1 + p)] \tag{5.9}$$

or, treating the rise in the value of $N''$ as being due to a rise of $s$ per cent in the specific index of the firm's non-monetary asset values (i.e. $[N''_{t+1}/N''_t = (1 + s)]$) and separating out the loss on holding money and the gain on borrowing:

$$Y_{RT} = N''_t(s - p) - M_t.p + L_t.p \tag{5.10}$$

where the first term on the right-hand side is the real gain (if $s > p$) or loss (if $s < p$) on holding non-monetary assets, the second term is the loss on holding money (a gain if $p < 0$) and the third term is the gain on borrowing (a loss if $p < 0$).

Thus, the general price-level adjustment $(1 + p)$ is applied to the opening capital figure to define the real capital to be maintained intact before recognising real income over the period. This adjustment can also be applied to individual assets and liabilities to separate 'real' gains and losses (due to $s > p$ for gains, or $s < p$ for losses) from those which merely reflect a maintenance of 'real' value when the value of the monetary unit is changing (at a rate $p$). This approach can be attacked from two rather different standpoints.

Firstly, the general index approach embodies a 'proprietary' view of capital maintenance, i.e. the real value of shareholders' funds in terms of their general command over goods and services is assumed to be the central concern. The alternative 'entity' capital maintenance approach, discussed further in the next chapter, holds that it is the maintenance of the assets specific to the firm which is the object of capital maintenance: this clearly leads to the rejection of a general index for the adjustment of capital, in favour of a specific index, representing the changes in price of the specific assets held by the firm. This can be characterised as a *physical* concept of capital maintenance, in contrast to the *financial* concept embodied in the proprietary approach.

Secondly, even if it is accepted that the general purchasing power of the proprietors is that which should be maintained intact before a gain in money value is recognised as income, it can be argued, following the discussion of index numbers earlier in this chapter, that a general index does not adequately capture changes in the purchasing power of any particular individual shareholder. This line of argument is particularly associated with Gynther (1966, 1974) and with the Sandilands Report (Sandilands Committee, 1975). Some of the counter-arguments to Gynther were aired by Bromwich (1975b) and a critique of the Sandilands position is provided by Chambers (1976, pp. 5–12). The attitude of the Sandilands Committee (1975) is summarised as follows:

> The term inflation describes a situation where the movement in
> the average price level of goods and services in a period is upward.
> However, the average movement of prices and the rate of inflation
> will vary for different individuals and entities in the country
> according to the selection of goods and services which they buy. It
> is incorrect to assume that a wide-ranging index such as the Retail

> Price Index can be a measure of the rate of inflation equally
> appropriate to all individuals and entities. *(para. 28)*

This argument clearly adopts the 'economic' rather than the 'statistical' view of index numbers, and claims that a general index fails to meet the criteria for measuring the cost of living of individual shareholders. The following counter-arguments can be made to the Sandilands view:

1. The fact that 'inflation' is not precisely quantifiable is not necessarily a reason for ignoring it. We must compare the value of 'inflation-adjusted' information with that of information which is unadjusted, not with some ideal measurement standard which might be possible if no prices changed. This argument is often supported by quoting Keynes' proverbial epigram 'It is better to be approximately right than precisely wrong'. As we saw in the earlier discussion of index numbers, it is impossible in practice to obtain a 'true' index which directly measures the effects of price changes on individual welfare, so some degree of approximation is inevitable, particularly in accounts which are intended for the general use of a wide range of individuals.

2. Although it is clearly possible that individual prices will change in a different manner, and even in a different direction, from a general index, it is reasonable to assume that the typical consumer purchases a variety of commodities. It is therefore possible that the averaging effect of purchasing a variety of commodities will mean that changes in the cost of the individual's basket of goods will not differ greatly from changes in a general index, this being the result of a process analogous to the averaging out of unsystematic investment risk by holding a portfolio of investments rather than a single investment. Moreover, it is likely that there will be a considerable overlap between most individual consumption patterns and the composition of a general index, since certain basic needs, such as food, clothing and housing are common to all (although of course there may be differences within these broad commodity classes).

These a priori arguments were supported by empirical testing by Peasnell and Skerratt (1978), who concluded, on the basis of UK experience, that 'the impact of inflation is remarkably constant across income groups, suggesting that the concept of inflation is meaningful to different individuals'. It should be noted that Peasnell and Skerratt studied income groups rather than individuals. However, their results are encouraging for those who support the use of general price-level indices.

3. In the earlier discussion of index numbers, it was argued that it is not possible to measure directly the welfare of the individual. We can merely hope to measure a person's command over goods and services. It is arguable that the use of a general index, preferably as broadly based as possible, such as the RPI or the GNP implicit deflator,[32] will best reflect this, by giving a measure of potential consumption which individuals may be able to translate into their own consumption patterns and welfare. This is essentially a 'statistical' approach and, of course, by restricting ourselves to measuring potential consumption in this general sense, we are forgoing the right to say anything directly about any specific individual's welfare, i.e. because 'real' income (in the sense of general command over goods and services) has gone up, the individual is not necessarily better off in the welfare economist's sense (i.e. not necessarily on a higher indifference curve, because the weighting of items in the general index may not match individual preferences). Moreover, if we accept that a person's utility function can change over time, the individual is not necessarily better off even with a greater command over the specific basket of goods which he or she chooses to buy at a particular point in time.[33] More generally, as we saw in the earlier discussion of index numbers, the precise measurement of welfare is essentially a subjective process, and economic magnitudes, adjusted by index numbers, should be judged as useful inputs into that process, rather than as direct measures of welfare. In assessing alternative forms of information, it should be stressed that some form of monetary measurement underlies all of the alternatives. If we abandon money we are left with heterogeneous

quantities of physical assets, but expressing these quantities in money terms overcomes the heterogeneity problem only if the weighting scheme has some significance for the individual in assessing potential welfare.

Thus it is arguable that we can hope, by means of a general index adjustment, to produce a useful (but not exact) measure of command over goods and services in general which is of use to individuals in assessing their potential welfare, but we cannot hope to measure the utility which the individual derives from exercising that power, unless we are prepared to tread the difficult, tortuous, and (for accountants) practically infeasible path of exploring individual utility functions. It is up to individuals, who presumably do have knowledge of their own past and present preferences, to establish what their current purchasing power means in terms of utility. It was suggested earlier that one issue for behavioural research is whether individuals find it easier to use unadjusted monetary data or 'real' CPP data to establish whether they, individually, feel that they are better or worse off. It is possible that unadjusted data do have an advantage in this respect, because they do represent prices which actually prevailed at particular points in time, whereas a constant general purchasing power unit is an abstract construct which might be more difficult for the individual to relate to personal consumption patterns. On the other hand, memory of past prices may be short and confused, and the general index adjustment does at least give the individual some indication of how prices have moved, although not a perfect one from the point of view of the assessment of personal welfare.

We can summarise the present state of knowledge as follows. Financial accounts are intended to report the economic performance of the firm to the individual shareholder or proprietor. In times of rapid inflation it seems likely that such a report should remind the proprietor of the effects of the change in the purchasing power of the monetary unit. For comparability between firms and consistency in reporting to many individual shareholders it seems likely that a general index adjustment will perform this task at least as well as any feasible alternative. In terms of the problem originally stated, that of defining capital to be maintained, general index adjustment implies recognising a profit only when the proprietors' interest, P, has been maintained in terms of command over a basket of goods broadly representative of that purchased by the average consumer. In terms of splitting the holding gains into 'real' and 'fictitious', general index adjustment compares movements in the price of the specific assets with movements in the price of a portfolio of commodities contained in the general index. We shall return to this subject in Chapter 6.

The relevance and feasibility of CPP accounting cannot be determined purely by theoretical argument. This has to be augmented by empirical evidence. A considerable body of empirical work on the subject has accumulated over the past century, and this is summarised in Appendix C.

## 5.9 SUMMARY

In this chapter we have described briefly the history and the method of CPP accounting. Attention has been focused on the CPP method defined narrowly as general index adjustment of historical cost accounts, but it was pointed out that the CPP method can equally well be applied to current value accounts, in which case a current purchasing power balance sheet for a particular year can be obtained by adjusting only the measurement of opening capital, the assets and liabilities already being recorded in current £s. However, the flows of the period recorded in the profit and loss account will have to be restated in current (end-of-period) £s. This type of 'real terms' accounting system will be discussed further in Chapter 6. CPP applied to historical cost deals only with the problem of the changing value of the currency and does not, therefore, provide a general solution to the deficiencies of historical cost relative to current values, discussed in the previous chapter.

The CPP adjustment of the capital to be maintained intact is controversial but has strong arguments in its favour. The main criticisms of this approach are, firstly, that it does not lead to the maintenance of the specific capital of the firm, and, secondly, that it does not maintain the purchasing power of any particular individual proprietor or shareholder. The first criticism comes from 'entity' theorists, who reject the 'proprietary' capital maintenance concept upon which CPP is based: this will be discussed further in the next chapter. The second criticism leads us into somewhat pragmatic arguments. If accounts are intended for the use of a whole community of shareholders and others, it is not possible to provide different individual index adjustments for each user, yet, if inflation exists at a significant rate, it seems likely to be useful to remind users of the possible order of magnitude of its effects on accounting measurements, and general index adjustment may be the best practical method of doing this. Furthermore, it is possible that the divergences of the impact of inflation on the cost of living of different individuals are not very great. Finally, the argument for constructing individual indices is suspect, since it is not possible to measure individual utility without imposing severe restrictions on the assumed form of the individual's utility function. If all that we can do is to measure general command over goods and services, a general index may be as good, or better, than a specific index.

Finally, in Appendix C a brief survey is made of the empirical literature relating to CPP accounting. The 'case study' approach has established that CPP adjustments can lead to material changes and has shown that such adjustments are practically feasible, as well as highlighting the technical aspects which require close definition. The more recent trend in research is towards establishing the usefulness of CPP data, e.g. by considering its actual or potential impact on stock market prices, or by assessing its value in predicting the future. This type of research has yet to yield decisive results and has been inhibited in recent years by scarcity of empirical data, due to the fact that CPP has not been used in practice outside a limited range of hyper-inflationary economies.

The other two appendices to this chapter provide, respectively, a select bibliography of books describing and illustrating the CPP technique (Appendix A) and a worked example of the CPP technique applied to a historical cost basis (Appendix B), based on the example used in earlier chapters.

## APPENDIX A: SELECT BIBLIOGRAPHY ON CONSTANT PURCHASING POWER ACCOUNTING

### A.I ORIGINAL SOURCES

The classic monograph on this subject is:

*Stabilized Accounting*, by H. W. Sweeney, Harper, New York, 1936. Reprinted by Arno Press, 1978.

Sweeney's book contains detailed case studies and worked examples, including CPP adjustment applied to a replacement cost (RC) valuation base.

In the mid-1950s, the American Accounting Association published three monographs on the subject, which were very influential in subsequent developments:

*Effects of Price Level Changes on Business Income, Capital and Taxes*, by R. C. Jones, American Accounting Association, 1956.

This examines the distortionary effect of inflation on accounts in theoretical terms, and advocates CPP adjustment, whilst accepting the usefulness of replacement cost rather than historical cost as a valuation basis, as in Sweeney's system.

*Price Level Changes and Financial Statements – Case Studies of Four Companies*, by R. C. Jones, American Accounting Association, 1955.

This companion volume provides case studies of four real companies, adjusting their published (historical cost) accounts by the Consumer Price Index to provide CPP re-statement in December 1951 dollars. It serves as an illustration of the CPP technique and demonstrates its materiality.

*Price-Level Changes and Financial Statements, Basic Concepts and Methods*, by Perry Mason, American Accounting Association, 1956.

This is a concise 'how-to-do-it' manual of the CPP technique, illustrated with clear numerical examples.

Much of this earlier work is surveyed and incorporated in:

*Reporting the Financial Effects of Price-Level Changes*, Accounting Research Study No. 6 ('ARS6'), by the Staff of the Accounting Research Division, American Institute of Certified Public Accountants, 1963.

This became the model for subsequent professional proposals for supplementary CPP adjustment of published (historical cost) accounts, in both the US and the UK.

The model for subsequent British proposals was:

*Accounting for Stewardship in a Period of Inflation*, The Research Foundation of The Institute of Chartered Accountants in England and Wales, 1968.

The anonymous author of this pamphlet was W. E. Parker. It provides a concise 'how-to-do-it' blueprint for supplementary CPP adjustment of traditional historical cost accounts, similar in many respects to the Perry Mason pamphlet, listed earlier. It became the model for the subsequent CPP proposals of the Accounting Standards Steering Committee.

## A.2 PUBLICATIONS OF STANDARD-SETTING BODIES IN THE US, THE UK AND INTERNATIONAL STANDARDS

The first recommendation for supplementary disclosure of CPP-adjusted accounts in the US came from the Accounting Principles Board (APB):

*Statement No. 3, Financial Statements Re-stated for General Price-Level Changes*, Accounting Principles Board (APB3), June 1969.

This recommended supplementary statements based on CPP adjustment of the main accounts, following the proposals of ARS6. It was a recommendation rather than a requirement and was widely ignored. The statement contains a useful exposition of the technique, with numerical illustrations.

In 1974, the Financial Accounting Standards Board (FASB) which had replaced the APB, issued an exposure draft which largely reiterated the contents of APB3:

*Financial Reporting in Units of General Purchasing Power*, Exposure Draft, Financial Accounting Standards Board, 31 December 1974.

The FASB also initiated a field study, which provided evidence on problems of application:

*Field Tests of Financial Reporting in Units of General Purchasing Power*, Research Report, Financial Accounting Standards Board, 1977.

A further FASB exposure draft, published in December 1978, proposed a choice between supplementary CPP and current cost disclosure, but concentrated on expounding the current cost technique. The CPP technique associated with this model was a slightly modified form of that proposed in the 1974 exposure draft (e.g. the choice of index and the definitions of 'monetary' items were modified) and was expounded in another exposure draft (strictly a supplement to the 1974 exposure draft):

*Constant Dollar Accounting*, Financial Accounting Standards Board, March 1979.

Finally, a standard was issued in September 1979, which proposed certain supplementary CPP restatements (of profit and loss account items and holding gains and losses on assets), some of which were applied to a current cost, rather than a historical cost, valuation basis (notably in measuring real holding gains on certain assets):

*Statement of Financial Accounting Standards No. 33: Financial Reporting and Changing Prices*, Financial Accounting Standards Board, September 1979.

This represented the high point of CPP in the US. Subsequent standards marked the progressive withdrawal of FAS33, without replacement.

In the UK, the first pronouncement on the subject by the Accounting Standards Steering Committee (ASSC) was a 'Discussion Paper and Fact Sheet':

*Inflation and Accounts*, published by Accountancy on behalf of the Accounting Standards Steering Committee, 1971.

This largely followed the argument of the earlier *Accounting for Stewardship in a Period of Inflation*, proposing supplementary CPP adjustment of traditional accounts. It provided a worked example, together with brief details of inflation rates, empirical studies of the effects of inflation on accounts, and accounting practice in the UK and abroad. The design of its cover led to its popular title, 'the Tombstone'. It was mainly drafted by Christopher Westwick, who has provided a useful first-hand account of the development of inflation accounting standards in the UK (Westwick, 1980).

In 1973, the ASSC produced an exposure draft, which followed the proposals of 'the Tombstone':

*Accounting for Changes in the Purchasing Power of Money*, Exposure Draft 8 (*ED8*), Accounting Standards Steering Committee, January 1973.

This was supplemented by a two-volume working guide:

*Accounting for Inflation, a working guide to the accounting procedures, Part 1: Text and Part 2: Tables*, Institute of Chartered Accountants in England and Wales, General Educational Trust, 1973.

This provides a very helpful guide, with many worked examples, to the detailed application of the proposed system.

The provisional accounting standard (PSSAP7) published in the following year did not differ substantially from ED8:

*Provisional Statement of Standard Accounting Practice No. 7 (PSSAP7), Accounting for Changes in the Purchasing Power of Money*, Accounting Standards Steering Committee, May 1974.

This statement was provisional, because, by the time it was issued, the Sandilands Committee had already been appointed by the government. This committee recommended current cost accounting in its Report, published in 1975, and since then none of the exposure drafts or standards of the Accounting Standards Steering Committee or its successors has recommended the use of CPP methods.

In international standards, the International Accounting Standards Committee struggled, in its early years, to reconcile the advocates of current cost (notably the Dutch) with those of CPP (mainly the US and the UK)[34] and its first standards on accounting for changing prices, IAS6 (1977) and IAS 15 (1981) were non-specific as to the preferred method and offered no detailed implementation guidance. Faced with the problem of hyper-inflation in some of its member countries, notably in Latin America, it issued IAS 29, *Financial Reporting in Hyper-inflationary Economies*, in 1989. This did explicitly recommend the re-statement of accounts (whether on a historical cost or a current cost basis) in units of current purchasing power (i.e. closing balance sheet purchasing power units), thus explicitly embracing a specific form of CPP, although it lacked implementation guidance. This standard was subsequently adopted by the IASB and remains in force (although it is not compulsory and the definition of hyper-inflation is elastic).

This survey has been confined to three standard-setters. Others have also contributed to the development of CPP methods, particularly those in countries such as Brazil which have used CPP accounting in practice.

## A.3 TEXTBOOKS
There are many textbook treatments of the CPP method. Amongst those which can be recommended are:

*Inflation Accounting*, by W. T. Baxter, Philip Allan, 1984.
*Inflation Accounting. A Guide for the Accountant and the Financial Analyst*, by S. Davidson, C. P. Stickney and R. L. Weil, McGraw-Hill, 1976.
*Accounting for Changing Prices*, by J. A. Largay III and J. L. Livingstone, Wiley, 1976.
*Income and Value Measurement: Theory and Practice*, by T. A. Lee, Van Nostrand Reinhold, 1985 (3rd edition).

All of these books deal with the application of CPP techniques to current value bases ('real terms accounting'), as well as to the historical cost valuation basis. Davidson, Stickney and Weil gives the most comprehensive account of the detailed computational techniques of CPP, within the framework of the 1974 American Exposure

Draft, and Largay and Livingstone also provide a thorough, but more concise, treatment of this aspect of the subject.

## APPENDIX B: A NUMERICAL EXAMPLE OF CONSTANT PURCHASING POWER ACCOUNTING

This illustration is based upon the example of 'Old Fred', using the facts as stated in the appendix to Chapter 3. CPP re-statement is applied to the historical cost figures, as used in the earlier illustration. The appendix to Chapter 6 describes the CPP re-statement of current value figures to yield what is described as 'real terms accounting'. CPP will be applied here by translating the accounts for each period into £s as of the end of the relevant period, i.e. we shall use the *current* purchasing power variety of CPP, which is that most commonly advocated for practical use. A wide variety of CPP techniques has been developed and, whilst this illustration indicates the more important alternatives which are available, it does not purport to be a comprehensive demonstration of the available techniques: those requiring such a demonstration should refer to the works listed in Appendix A.

### B.1 THE INDEX

The levels of the general price index, and the corresponding periodic increases, assumed in the appendix to Chapter 3, are as follows:

| Time | Index level | Period | Percentage increase |
|------|-------------|--------|---------------------|
| $T$ | 100 | | |
| | | 1 | 10 |
| $t+1$ | 110 | | |
| | | 2 | 20 |
| $t+2$ | 132 | | |
| | | 3 | 10 |
| $t+3$ | 145.2 | | |
| | | 4 | 5 |
| $t+4$ | 152.46 | | |

### B.2.1 Period 1

The first stage of CPP re-statement in end-of-period £s is to re-state the opening balance sheet in end-of-period £s for comparison with the closing balance sheet. This involves increasing each figure in the opening balance sheet in proportion to the rise in the general index during the period, as the opening balance is, in this example, expressed consistently in beginning-of-period pounds. The appropriate rise in the general index is 10 per cent for each item (i.e. multiply by 1.1).

Opening Balance Sheet at $t$, re-stated in £s of $t + 1$

| | £ | | | £ |
|---|---|---|---|---|
| *Proprietor's Capital* | | *Fixed Assets* | | |
| [150 × 1.1] | 165 | Cart (at cost) | | |
| *Loan* (Aunt Mabel) | | [100 × 1.1] | 110 | |
| [50 × 1.1] | 55 | *Current Assets* | | |
| | | Cash [100 × 1.1] | 110 | |
| | 220 | | 220 | |

Figures in square brackets show the calculations necessary to re-state the historical figures at $t$, given in the appendix to Chapter 3, into £s as of $t + 1$ [historical figure × proportionate rise in the general index].

The income statement may be re-stated as follows:

Income Statement for Period 1, $t$ to $t + 1$ re-stated in £s of $t + 1$

| | | £ |
|---|---|---|
| Sales [120 × 1] | | 120 |
| *Less* | Cost of goods sold [80 × 1.1] | 88 |
| | Trading profit | 32 |
| *Less* | Depreciation [10 × 1.1] | 11 |
| | Net Profit | 21 |
| *Add* | Gain on borrowing [50 × (1.1 − 1)] | 5 |
| | Total Income | 26 |

The explanation for the income statement adjustments is as follows:

1. *Sales* were assumed in this example to take place at the end of the period, so that they are already stated in current £s. If they had occurred at the beginning of the period, they would have been increased by 10 per cent, to £132, but this increase of £12 would have been offset by a corresponding 'loss on holding money' (£120 × 0.1) due to the fact that the cash received from the sales had deteriorated in purchasing power during the period. Thus, the total profit figure would be unchanged. Large firms with many transactions might find it impractical to make adjustments on the basis of a precise dating of each transaction, and an approximate adjustment which is often proposed is to assume an even flow of transactions throughout the period and adjust by reference to an average index. In this example, if we assume that the rise in the index was linear through time, the appropriate index value would be 105, sales would be re-stated as £126 [= 120 × 1.05], and the corresponding 'loss on holding money' would be £6.

2. *Goods sold* were assumed in this example to be purchased at the beginning of the period. Cost of goods sold is therefore increased by the full 10 per cent rise in the index to £88. If the goods had been bought at the end of the period, no re-statement of their cost would have been necessary (as in the case of sales) but there would have been a corresponding 'loss on holding money' of £8, due to the fact that the £80 used to purchase the goods had declined in general purchasing power whilst it was held during the period. As in the case of sales, precise dating of purchases may not be possible in practice and averaging devices may be used to give an approximate adjustment.

3. *Depreciation* is adjusted by the rise in the general price level since the asset was acquired (10 per cent), so that the depreciation charge

represents an appropriate proportion of the cost of the asset expressed in end-of-period £s (i.e. the charge can be calculated either as [10 × 1.1] or as a proportion of re-stated cost [110 × 1/10], the two bases being equivalent).

4. *The gain on borrowing* is one of the most controversial features of CPP accounting. It represents the decline in purchasing power of the loan, which, as explained in the text of the chapter, implies a lightening of the real burden of debt on the firm (Fred) at the expense of the creditor (Aunt Mabel). There has been a great deal of controversy as to whether the gain on borrowing (and the corresponding loss on holding money) should be regarded as part of profit or merely credited to a reserve, especially when the borrowing is long term, so that the gain might be regarded as not realisable in the immediate future. When interest is paid on loans, there is a strong case for offsetting the gain on borrowing against the interest payment, as the interest payment should include compensation for any inflationary loss which was anticipated by the lender at the time when the loan was made.

One general aspect of the income statement is that some proposals for CPP accounting advocate re-statement in average-for-the-year prices. This has the advantage that sales figures require no adjustment, so that there is a direct correspondence between the figure reported in the income statement and the amount actually realised and, if a replacement cost valuation basis is used, there is a correspondence between the reported cost of goods sold and replacement cost at the time when the goods were disposed of. However, if the closing balance sheet is expressed in end-of-period £s, an income statement in average-for-the-period £s means that the two statements are not expressed in strictly comparable units. This issue is discussed by Edwards and Bell (1961, p. 253).

This re-stated closing balance sheet is as follows:

Closing Balance Sheet, at $t + 1$, re-stated in £s of $t + 1$

| | £ | | | £ |
|---|---|---|---|---|
| *Proprietor's Capital* | | | | |
| Opening balance | | Cart (at cost) | | |
| (at $t$) [150 × 1.1] | 165 | [100 × 1.1] | | 110 |
| *Add* Income for the | | *Less* depreciation | | |
| period (as in | | [10 × 1.1] | | 11 |
| re-stated Income | | | | 99 |
| Statement) | 26 | *Current Assets* | | |
| | 191 | Stock (at cost) | | |
| *Less* Drawings | 30 | [20 × 1.1] | 22 | |
| Closing balance | | Cash | 90 | |
| (at $t + 1$) | 161 | | | 112 |
| *Loan* | 50 | | | |
| | 211 | | | 211 |

The re-statement is different from that of the opening balance sheet because it distinguishes between monetary and non-monetary items. The monetary items, cash and the loan, are fixed in monetary value, so that it would be unrealistic to state them at the amounts which they ought to assume in order to maintain constant real value (£55 in the case of the loan, but no adjustment necessary in this example for cash, since it is assumed to have been received only at the end of the period). Thus, the closing balance sheet assesses monetary items at their fixed nominal money value, and non-monetary items at their real historical cost, i.e. original cost revised by reference to a general price index. The role of the re-stated opening balance sheet is different: it does not purport to state year-end values, but merely provides a benchmark for comparative purposes, showing the period-end equivalent of the opening position. Thus, the re-stated opening proprietor's capital in the closing balance sheet (£165) is the same as that in the re-stated opening balance sheet, and the comparison of the two balance sheets lies behind the calculation of the gain on borrowing (£55–£50).

The non-monetary assets in the closing balance sheet are valued at historical cost adjusted by the change in the general index since acquisition. In the present example, both assets are assumed to have been acquired at time $t$, so that they are both subject to a 10 per cent adjustment. It should be noted that, in most practical proposals for CPP, an upper limit on re-statement of non-monetary assets is imposed by the requirement that they should appear at re-stated historical cost or current market value, whichever is the lower: this is intended to ensure prudent valuation.

The proprietor's capital, as already noted, starts with the beginning-of-period balance, re-stated in end-of-period £s. To this is added the profit from the re-stated income statement, which is already expressed in end-of-period £s. The proprietor's drawings are deducted and do not require re-statement in this case because they were assumed to take place at the end of the period. If the transaction had taken place at the beginning of the period, drawings would have been re-stated as £33 [= 30 × 1.1] and there would have been a corresponding reduction in the loss on holding money, had there been a money balance out of which drawings could have been paid.

### B.2.2 Period 2

The same basic procedures are adopted for period 2, and for subsequent periods, although certain details assumed in the example for these periods, but not for period 1, make it worthwhile following the example through to the end of Fred's career $(t + 4)$.

Firstly, the closing balance sheet for Period 1, expressed in £s of $t + 1$, becomes the opening balance sheet for Period 2 and is re-stated, for comparative purposes, in £s of $t + 2$:

Opening Balance Sheet, at $t + 1$ re-stated in £s of $t + 2$

|  | £ |  | £ |
|---|---|---|---|
| *Proprietor's Capital* |  | *Fixed Assets* |  |
| Closing balance (at |  | Cart (at cost) |  |
| $t + 1$) [161 × 1.2] | 193.20 | [110 × 1.2] | 132.00 |
| *Loan* [50 × 1.2] | 60.00 | *Less* accumulated |  |
|  |  | depreciation |  |
|  |  | [11 × 1.2] | 13.20 |
|  |  |  | 118.80 |
|  |  | *Current Assets* |  |
|  |  | Stock [22 × 1.2]  26.40 |  |
|  |  | Cash [90 × 1.2]  108.00 |  |
|  |  |  | 134.40 |
|  | 253.20 |  | 253.20 |

Inflation in period 2 is at a 20 per cent rate, so that the pro-portionate increase in the various items is 1.2, but otherwise the procedure is identical to that adopted in period 1.

The income statement is then re-stated, again using the same basic technique as for period 1:

Income Statement for period 2, $t + 1$ to $t + 2$ re-stated in £s of $t + 2$

|  |  | £ |
|---|---|---|
| Sales |  | 135.00 |
| *Less* | Cost of goods sold [(22 × 1.2) + (91 × 1.2)] | 135.60 |
|  | Trading Loss | .60 |
| *Add* | Depreciation [10 × 1.32] | 13.20 |
|  | Net Loss | 13.80 |
| *Less* | Gain on net monetary items [64 × 0.2] | 12.80 |
|  | Total Loss | 1.00 |

The individual components of the income statement are subject to the same assumptions and limitations as were described for period 1. The following additional features should be noted:

1. Cost of goods sold now has two components: opening stocks and purchases during the period (less closing stocks, adopting the First-in-First-out convention). Each of these components should be adjusted separately, as they will, in practice, typically involve different time lags and therefore different adjustment factors. In the present example, both elements are subject to the same adjustment factor (1.2) because opening stocks have already been re-stated in beginning-of-period pounds and it is (artificially) assumed that purchases were made at the very beginning of the period and are therefore also denominated in £s of this date.

2. The depreciation charge has been expressed as the historical cost written off (£10), adjusted proportionately to the rise in the general price index since the date at which the historical cost occurred (1.32). It could equivalently be expressed as an appropriate proportion (1/10) of the historical cost of the asset expressed in end-of-period £s in the balance sheet (£132).

3. The gain on net monetary assets is the gain on borrowing (calculated on the same basis as for period 1), less the loss on holding monetary assets, which is the mirror-image of the gain on borrowing. The borrowings which give rise to the gain are the long-term loan (from Aunt Mabel) of £50, and the £52 credit given by the supplier of purchases, both of which existed throughout the period and therefore gave rise to gains of £10 [= 50 × 0.2] and £10.40 [= 52 × 0.2] respectively. The loss on holding money is on the £38 [the £90 opening cash balances, less £52 paid for purchases at the beginning of the period] which was held throughout the period: the loss of purchasing power is £7.60 [= 38 × 0.2]. Since all of the monetary items were held for the full period and therefore have a common inflation factor applied to them, we can calculate the net gain of £12.80 [= £10.00 + £10.40 – £7.60] more simply by applying the inflation factor to their net amount, a net loan of £64 [= £50 + £52 – £38].

The adjusted closing balance sheet for period 2 is as follows:

Closing Balance Sheet at $t + 2$ re-stated in £s of $t + 2$

| | £ | | | £ |
|---|---|---|---|---|
| *Proprietor s Capital* | | *Fixed Assets* | | |
| Opening balance | | Cart (at cost) | | |
| (at $t + 1$) | 193.20 | [110 × 1.32] | | 132.00 |
| *Less* Total loss for | | *Less* | | |
| Period | 1.00 | accumulated | | |
| | 192.20 | depreciation | | |
| *Less* Drawings | 106.00 | [20 × 1.32] | | 26.40 |
| Closing balance | | | | 105.60 |
| (at $t + 2$) | 86.20 | *Current Assets* | | |
| Loan | 50.00 | Stock [13 × 1.2] | 15.60 | |
| *Current Liabilities* | | Debtors | 15.00 | |
| Creditors | 52.00 | Cash | 52.00 | 82.60 |
| | 188.20 | | | 188.20 |

The proprietor's capital in the balance sheet starts with the opening balance in £s of $t + 2$, as shown in the re-stated opening balance sheet. The loss which is deducted is taken from the re-stated income statement and the drawings are assumed to be made at $t + 2$, so that no re-statement is required. The 'monetary' items (the loan, creditors, debtors and cash) all appear at their fixed monetary amounts and do not require re-statement. The non-monetary items, stock and the cart, are re-stated by reference to the change in the general price index since their date of acquisition: in the case of the cart, this is equivalent to cost, less depreciation, in the re-stated opening balance sheet, less the additional depreciation for the period, charged in the re-stated income statement.

One point of general interest is that, if comparison is required with earlier periods, the figures for earlier periods should be re-stated in current £s. When the earlier figures are expressed consistently in

£s of a given date, this is merely a matter of multiplying all the figures by the proportionate rise in the general index from that date to the present, as was done with the $t + 1$ balance sheet when it was re-stated in $t + 2$ £s. For example, this procedure could be adopted for the re-stated period 1 income statement, all of the figures being multiplied by 1.2, in order to express it in £s of $t + 2$.

### B.2.3 Period 3

The closing balance sheet for period 2, at $t + 2$, is the opening balance sheet for period 3, and is re-stated in £s of $t + 3$ for comparative purposes, and the income statement and closing balance sheet for period 3 are derived on the basis of the same techniques as were used in periods 1 and 2.

Opening Balance Sheet, at $t + 2$ re-stated in £s of $t + 3$

| | £ | | | £ |
|---|---|---|---|---|
| *Proprietor's Capital* | | *Fixed Assets* | | |
| Closing balance (at | | Cart (at cost) | | |
| $t + 2$) [86.2 × 1.1] | 94.82 | [132 × 1.1] | | 145.20 |
| *Loan* [50 × 1.1] | 55.00 | *Less* | | |
| *Current Liabilities* | | accumulated | | |
| Creditors [52 × 1.1] | 57.20 | depreciation | | |
| | | [26.40 × 1.1] | | 29.04 |
| | | | | 116.16 |
| | | *Current Assets* | | |
| | | Stock [15.60 × | | |
| | | 1.1] | 17.16 | |
| | | Debtors [15 × | | |
| | | 1.1] | 16.50 | |
| | | Cash [52 × 1.1] | 57.20 | |
| | | | | 90.86 |
| | 207.02 | | | 207.02 |

Income Statement for period 3, $t + 2$ to $t + 3$ re-stated in £s of $t + 3$

| | | £ |
|---|---|---|
| Sales | | 180.00 |
| Less | Cost of goods sold [(15.6 + 144) × 1.1] | 175.56 |
| | Trading Profit | 4.44 |
| Less | Depreciation [10 × 1.452] | 14.52 |
| | Net Loss | 10.08 |
| Add | Gain on net monetary items [215 × 0.1] | 21.50 |
| | Total Income | 11.42 |

*Note:* Net monetary items held during the period were creditors £180, plus loan £50, less cash £15, a net borrowing of £215. With 10 per cent inflation, this gives rise to a net gain on borrowing of £21.50.

Closing Balance Sheet, at $t + 3$ re-stated in £s of $t + 3$

| | £ | | £ |
|---|---|---|---|
| *Proprietor's Capital* | | *Fixed Assets* | |
| Opening balance | | Cart (at cost) | |
| (at $t + 2$) | 94.82 | [100 × 1.452] | 145.20 |
| *Add* Total income | | *Less* accumulated | |
| for the period | 11.42 | depreciation | |
| | 106.24 | [£29.04 + £14.52] | 43.56 |
| *Less* Drawings | 10.00 | | 101.64 |
| Closing balance | | *Current Assets* | |
| (at $t + 3$) | 96.24 | Stock [36 × 1.1]  39.60 | |
| *Loan* | 50.00 | Debtors  20.00 | |
| *Current Liabilities* | | Cash  165.00 | |
| Creditors | 180.00 | | 224.60 |
| | 326.24 | | 326.24 |

## B.2.4 Period 4

Opening Balance Sheet, at $t + 3$ re-stated in £s of $t + 4$

| | £ | | £ |
|---|---|---|---|
| Proprietor's Capital | | Fixed Assets | |
| Closing balance (at | | Cart (at cost) | |
| $t + 3$) [96.24 × | | [145.20 × 1.05] | 152.46 |
| 1.05] | 101.05 | Less accumulated | |
| Loan [50 × 1.05] | 52.50 | depreciation | |
| Current Liabilities | | [43.56 × 1.05] | 45.74 |
| Creditors [180 × | | | 106.72 |
| 1.05] | 189.00 | Current Assets | |
| | | Stock [39.60 × | |
| | | 1.05] | 41.58 |
| | | Debtors [20 × | |
| | | 1.05] | 21.00 |
| | | Cash [165 × 1.05] 173.25 | |
| | | | 235.83 |
| | 342.55 | | 342.55 |

Note: All figures are rounded to the nearest penny.


Income statement for period 4, $t + 3$ to $t + 4$ re-stated in £s of $t + 4$

| | | £ |
|---|---|---|
| Sales | | 44.00 |
| Less | Cost of goods sold [39.60 × 1.05] | 41.58 |
| | Trading Profit | 2.42 |
| Add | Gain on net monetary items | |
| | [(50 + 180 – 20 – 165) × 0.05] | 2.25 |
| | | 4.67 |
| Add | Realised holding gain | 13.28 |
| | Total Income | 17.95 |

*Note*: The realised real holding gain arises on disposal of the cart. Its written-down value at the beginning of the period (in $t + 4$ £s) was £106.72 and it was sold for £120, the difference being the gain, expressed in $t + 4$ £s (i.e. it is a 'real' gain).

Closing Balance Sheet, at $t + 4$ re-stated in £s of $t + 4$

| | £ | | £ |
|---|---|---|---|
| *Proprietor's Capital* | | *Current Assets* | |
| Opening balance | | Cash | 169.00 |
| (at $t + 3$) | 101.05 | | |
| *Add* Total income for | | | |
| the period | 17.95 | | |
| | 119.00 | | |
| *Loan* | 50.00 | | |
| | 169.00 | | 169.00 |

*Note:* This balance sheet is drawn up after the liquidation of the assets but prior to the repayment of the loan and the final withdrawal of the proprietor's funds.

## B.3 LIFE CYCLE INCOME

The total income of the business over its lifetime, on three different bases, is reported in what follows. Firstly, we show historical cost income, as reported in the appendix to Chapter 3. Secondly, we report total CPP income, expressed in £s of the end of each individual period, as reported previously, and thirdly we re-state the CPP profits in terms of constant £s of $t + 4$. The comparison of the totals of the three columns shows that the different methods yield different aggregate income, and comparison of the figures for different years shows that the different methods give a different view of the relative profitability of operations in different periods.

| Period | Historical Cost Income, in £ | CPP income in end-of-period £s | Adjustment factor | CPP income in £s of $t+4$ |
|---|---|---|---|---|
| 1 | 30 | 26.00 | (1.2) (1.1) (1.05) | 36.04 |
| 2 | 14 | (1.00) | (1.1) (1.05) | (1.15) |
| 3 | 13 | 11.42 | (1.05) | 11.99 |
| 4 | 58 | 17.95 | 1.0 | 17.95 |
| Total | 115 | 54.37 | | 64.83 |

*Note:* Bracketed income figures indicate loss.

## APPENDIX C: SOME EMPIRICAL STUDIES

A considerable number of empirical studies of CPP accounting has been carried out in the past century. The object of this brief survey is to convey the broad thrust of this work and to refer the interested reader to some of the main sources. It will not be possible to do full justice to these empirical studies by providing a comprehensive survey.

Early empirical studies, such as those by Sweeney (1936) and Jones (1949, 1955) in the US and by Baxter (1959) in the UK tended to be of the case study type. A useful survey of the earlier work will be found in ARS6 (American Institute of Certified Public Accountants, 1963, Appendix E). This type of work applies CPP adjustments to the accounts of real firms with two broad objectives: to establish the materiality of CPP adjustments and to establish problems of interpretation and application. As an example of the first type of result, Sweeney (1936) has a case in which a significant unadjusted loss becomes an adjusted (i.e. Sweeney version of CPP) gain. As an example of the second type, Wanless' (1976) study of a co-operative society demonstrates some of the difficulties of defining 'monetary' assets and the materiality of the differences which arise from using alternative definitions. This type of research continued to be pursued until the early 1980s, when the practical debate on inflation accounting waned, some examples being the work of Petersen (1973, 1975, 1978), Davidson and Weil (1975) and Parker (1977)[35] and the FASB's own Field Tests (1977), in the US, Cutler and Westwick (1973) and Hope (1974) in the UK and the University of Waikato project in New Zealand (Emanuel, 1976). This type of research has, in general, shown that CPP does in practice lead to materially different results from those of traditional accounting. It has also shown that CPP adjustment is feasible in practice and has served to highlight some of the practical issues which arise in its implementation. An alternative to the case study method is the simulation approach, used by Arnold and El-Azma (1978) which assesses how alternative accounting income measures (including CPP-adjusted ones) reflect alternative economic conditions.

Other lines of research have been developed which hope to identify the utility as well as the materiality, of price-level adjustments. One such approach is the behavioural approach, based upon confronting users of accounts with a choice between traditional accounting data and CPP. Dyckman (1969) carried out such a study using investment analysts as subjects and found that CPP data did lead to different decisions. Subsequent studies by Heintz (1975) and McIntyre (1975), using students as subjects, failed to establish such differences.[36] An alternative approach is to look at the predictive power of alternative accounting measures, and there were a number of studies of this type. For example, Buckmaster et al. (1977) studied the relative self-predictive ability (i.e. the extent to which the past value of a variable can be used to predict its future value) of historical cost, replacement cost and CPP income measures across 42 US companies, and found that historical cost produced the best self-prediction, and CPP the worst. However, the criterion of self-predictability is appropriate only if the future value of the variable has some intrinsic value to a user of accounting information, e.g. as an indication of future dividend potential for the shareholder: prediction for its own sake is of no use. A more obviously useful criterion is the ability to predict directly an event which is relevant to the user's needs. For example, Ketz (1978b) and Norton and Smith (1979) considered the question of whether traditional historical cost or CPP data produced the best prediction of corporate bankruptcy in the US. CPP data appeared to perform as well as historical cost in this respect, but not significantly better (Patell, 1978).

Finally, there is a group of studies which have attempted to assess the impact of CPP data on share prices. Basu (1977) is a study, based on the COMPUSTAT file of accounting data of North American firms to obtain estimated CPP data. Basu used an efficient markets framework, assuming that all relevant information is reflected in share prices as soon as it becomes available. He failed to find a significant advantage in using CPP rather than conventional data to explain 'unsystematic' returns.[37] He concluded that 'GPL re-stated measures' (i.e. CPP) 'of risk and return, by and large, do not convey information beyond that transmitted by the basic historical cost alternative' (p. 32). An alternative view could be that sophisticated investors already have access to such measures. Basu's conclusion is based upon studying the possible benefits of CPP reporting at a time when it was not provided. A UK study by Morris (1975), which also used an efficient markets framework, attempts to assess the market response to the release of estimated CPP data for 132 listed companies by a firm of stockbrokers in 1971. He was unable to detect a significant response and concludes that there is no evidence that the CPP data had any additional value. A later American study by Hillison (1979), which, like Basu's study, used COMPUSTAT data and an efficient markets framework (although the detailed methodology is different) also failed to find any superior returns by using CPP data. A study by Short (1978) found some evidence that CPP adjustment improves the ability of accounting data to explain market risk, but the conclusions are qualified by serious statistical problems. Another American study, by Devon and Kolodny (1978) claimed that CPP earnings were more closely related to stock price changes than historical cost earnings, but this study, unlike the others, did not allow for risk.

The issuance of a new standard, FAS33, in 1979, which required CPP disclosures as well as current cost disclosures, gave rise to a flurry of empirical work. The influential study by Beaver and Landsman (1983) concluded that the FAS33 disclosures had little incremental effect (i.e. incremental to that which was predicted by historical cost data) on changes in or levels of share price. The main focus of their study was on the current cost disclosures required by FAS33, but they also included the price-level-adjusted (CPP) disclosures. Over the next decade, several papers modified this view. Murdoch (1986) showed that the gain or loss on monetary items, a CPP adjustment not separated out in the Beaver and Landsman study, did appear to affect share prices. Bublitz et al. (1985) extended and refined the Beaver and Landsman analysis and were able to detect incremental information content in the CPP ('constant dollar') disclosures. Lobo and Song (1989), using a different model, also concluded that constant dollar earnings information did affect share prices. However, the CPP disclosures were no longer required after 1984 (when FAS82 was issued) and lack of new data, lower inflation rates, and the much lower interest of standard-setters led to a premature cessation of this empirical debate in the US.

Elsewhere, CPP accounting, or supplementary disclosure of CPP data, were still required in some countries that suffered from very high rates of inflation, and there were occasional empirical studies of the experience of CPP in these countries. An example is Mexico. Davis-Friday and Rivera (2000) found, in the case of Mexican firms, that the market prices of their American Deposit Receipts were affected by the CPP disclosures required by Mexican GAAP. Another example relates to Turkey, another economy that suffered high levels of inflation. Whittington et al. (1997) estimated the CPP profits of large Turkish companies (using a methodology similar to that applied in Brazil), at a time when inflation accounting was not required, and the results provided much more plausible measures of metrics such as rate of return and growth than appeared from the unadjusted accounts. Later (in 2003) when inflation was very high, CPP accounting was required in Turkey, and Kirkulak and Balsari (2009) and Bilgic and Ibis (2013) have carried out studies which demonstrate that this improved the value relevance of Turkish accounts. A third example is Israel, which required inflation-adjusted accounts as a result of hyper-inflation in the 1980s. Barniv (1999) studies the value relevance of inflation-adjusted accounting earnings in the period 1984–88 and concludes that inflation adjustment did yield relevant information. Thus, the limited empirical evidence that is available supports the view that inflation adjustment produces useful information in hyper-inflationary environments.

In summary, it may be said that empirical work in this field has been limited by the lack of use of CPP methods in recent years outside hyper-inflationary economies. This has obviously limited the availability of empirical data, but it has also reduced the motivation of researchers, because CPP accounting is no longer seen as an urgent policy issue. Past research has shown that CPP adjustment does produce material changes in reported figures in certain individual cases, e.g. companies which are highly geared show large gains on borrowing, but it is also clear that there is a large common information content in CPP and traditional accounting. It has not been demonstrated conclusively that the additional information content of CPP is not already taken account of by investors, who obtain the information from other sources or from their own estimates when it is not produced by the company, or that there simply is little information content in CPP. However, the variety of approach, the statistical limitations and the relatively narrow data coverage of the studies referred to is such that they do not provide a firm foundation for forming an opinion as to the merits of published financial accounts incorporating CPP adjustments to traditional historical cost information. Even if investors do take account of CPP adjustments already, by making them for themselves, it could be argued that the company should supply such information as a 'public good' made freely available to all users of the accounts to eliminate the excessive cost of such calculations having to be duplicated by different users of accounts.

NOTES

1 An analysis of worldwide inflation during this period will be found in United Nations (1980, Chapter 3), from which Table 5.1 is extracted.

2 The CCA systems widely discussed at the time emphasised individual price changes, although the US standard, SFAS 33 (1979), did also include general price level adjustments.

3 The IASB currently has a standard (IAS 29) on financial reporting in hyper-inflationary economies, but this gives very loose and unsatisfactory guidance.

4 If we wanted to express the relative price change as a real gain in terms of the opening currency unit, the gain would be £2.50p (= [£15/1.2] – £10).

5 And in the companion volume, *The Debate on Inflation Accounting* (Tweedie and Whittington, 1984), which offers a broader historical perspective. These matters involve important political issues, such as whether oil companies should be taxed on their stock appreciation, so that the course of events cannot be understood purely in terms of the rational evaluation of theoretical models.

6 Phase 3 of the counter-inflation policy. The retail price index in October 1973 was the base line and rises of 40p per week for those subject to threshold agreements were 'triggered' by each percentage point rise in the index from 7 per cent onwards. The 7 per cent 'trigger' was reached in May 1974 and ten further rises were triggered before the policy was abandoned in November 1974. I am grateful to Frank Wilkinson of the Department of Applied Economics, Cambridge, for this information.

7 *Sandilands Report* (Sandilands Committee, 1975, Chapters 18 and 20, particularly paras. 795–96). The latter chapter denies that inflation accounting is a form of indexation, because the form of reporting does not directly affect the money amount of contractual payments. This is a somewhat narrow interpretation of indexation.

8 The traditional convention of basing 'defined benefit' pensions on final salary contains an element of inflation adjustment even when the subsequent pension is not adjusted for future inflation. This is because the final salary reflects inflation that occurred during the working life of

the employee. The diminishing number of direct benefit schemes that survive are tending to switch to an average salary basis in order to reduce this effect.

9  Allen (1975) provides an accessible survey of the subject and Afriat (1977) a more advanced treatise. Sen (1979) provides a lucid survey of the whole problem of making real income comparisons, at both the personal and the national levels. Deaton and Muellbauer (1980, Chapter 7) provide a concise account of the economic theory of index numbers, and Deaton (1980) provides an extended treatment of the subject, with special emphasis on the assumptions necessary for the practical use of index numbers in the measurement of welfare.

10  Although it should be noted that GNP only covers transactions which give rise to new value added and excludes transactions in second-hand assets, such as land and buildings.

11  Allen (1975, p. 48).

12  See Deaton and Muellbauer (1980, p. 173).

13  Deaton and Muellbauer (1980, pp. 171–73).

14  This limitation of 'money-metric utility' measures is stressed by Sen (1979).

15  Deaton (1980) provides a good illustration of this approach.

16  The following discussion of the RPI and the CPI draws upon a detailed analysis by the Office for National Statistics (2011).

17  An arithmetic average sums the $n$ observations and divides by $n$. A geometric average multiplies the $n$ observations together and takes the $n$th root: this is equivalent to taking the antilog of the arithmetic average of the logarithms of the observations.

18  Although it might be possible to justify some of the 'entity' capital maintenance concepts in this manner, such as the maintenance of operating capacity as advocated by the Sandilands Report, because they focus on the need to maintain the capacity of the single entity rather than the purchasing power of a community of proprietors.

19  This does not imply that the 'statistical' view of price indices is more compatible with the entity approach to accounting. The latter requires indices such as those used in current cost accounting which reflect the purchasing pattern of business entities rather than their proprietors, but the change of focus does not eliminate the problems of the statistical approach.

20 Here we ignore the choice between alternative current values, which was discussed in the previous chapter. The choice is not material in the case of quoted securities because buying price, selling price and net present value (at least as estimated by participants in the market) should not differ widely.

21 See e.g. *Accounting for Stewardship in a Period of Inflation* (Institute of Chartered Accountants in England and Wales, Research Committee, 1968, pp. 6–8).

22 It should be noted that Sweeney preferred replacement cost to historical cost as a valuation basis, although his case studies, based on real-world examples, necessarily involved the CPP adjustment of traditional historical cost data.

23 The Accounting Principles Board (APB) preceded the Financial Accounting Standards Board as the voluntary, private-sector standard-setting body in the US.

24 Although the 1979 proposals contained in the first American standard on the subject (FAS33) also require some current cost disclosure and an element of 'real terms' reconciliation of current cost values with CPP re-statement.

25 The author of *Accounting for Stewardship in a Period of Inflation* was Mr (later Sir) W. E. Parker, who, at the time, was president of the ICAEW. In conversation with the present writer, he acknowledged his debt to the American work, specifically mentioning Perry Mason's monograph and his personal association with George O. May, an active member of the Study Group on Business Income, which was at the centre of the debate on inflation accounting in the US in the late 1940s.

26 Parker (1975) provides a lucid exposition of this. As W. E. Parker was instrumental in introducing CPP to the British profession (as author of *Accounting for Stewardship in a Period of Inflation*), this paper is a particularly interesting indication of the thinking which lay behind CPP.

27 Note that it is legitimate to re-state $M$ and $L$ in this case, because we are merely re-stating the *opening* balance sheet in closing currency units, for comparison with the closing balance sheet. We are not attempting to measure the closing position in the opening balance sheet.

28 A similar illustration will be found on pp. 12–13 of Accounting Research Study No. 6 (American Institute of Certified Public Accountants, 1963).

29 In practice, professional pronouncements such as the British PSSAP7 (Accounting Standards Steering Committee, 1974), have applied the conservative principle of 're-stated historical cost or current value, whichever is the lower'.

30 A similar formulation will be found in Barton (1975).

31 This view is consistent with the arguments for an objective historical cost base in PSSAP7 (Accounting Standards Steering Committee, 1973) and in *Accounting for Stewardship in a Period of Inflation* (Institute of Chartered Accountants in England and Wales, 1968).

32 This is preferred by Moonitz (1973), who uses a similar argument to that advanced here.

33 If we allow a person's consumption pattern to change as income and relative prices change, even when tastes are constant, we face the traditional base-weighted versus current-weighted problem of index number construction. For practical reasons (the closing basket of commodities cannot be known until the end of the period) consumer price indices are usually of the base-weighted (Laspeyres) type. The basket is reassessed at the end of each period (usually a year) and the new weights used to calculate the index over the following period.

34 Camfferman and Zeff (2007), pp. 106–110.

35 These studies are surveyed by Ketz (1978a).

36 Dyckman (1975) criticises these later studies.

37 'Systematic' returns to holding a share are those which are correlated with returns on other shares ('the market portfolio'), and can be attributed to common factors such as changes in interest rates. 'Unsystematic' returns are the residual returns and are the result of factors unique to the individual company, such as the effect of new accounting information. This separation of systematic and unsystematic risk is obtained by using the Capital Asset Pricing Model.

# 6 Current Value Accounting 2: Capital Maintenance Concepts and Real Terms Accounting

## 6.1 INTRODUCTION

In this chapter, we return to the discussion of current value accounting, which incorporates specific price changes in financial accounts, although, as we shall see, there is scope for 'real terms' systems (introduced and illustrated in Chapter 1) that combine specific valuation of assets and liabilities with general price-level indexation of proprietors' capital.

Chapter 4 concentrated on the question of the choice of basis for valuing assets and liabilities, but, as indicated in Chapters 1 and 2, there is another important question to be discussed, the definition and measurement of the capital which is to be maintained intact before a profit is recognised. This question is of the greatest importance for the definition of profit in the profit and loss account, but it also affects the division between capital and retained profits in the section of the balance sheet which describes the proprietor's interest. The questions of valuation and capital maintenance are separate but not entirely independent, as they are both essential ingredients of an income measure, and the choice of a particular income measure will therefore require answers to both questions.

The choice of capital maintenance concept hinges on whether we wish to take a 'proprietary' or an 'entity' view of the firm. The former approach regards the equity interest as being central to the purpose of financial reporting, so that it is the value of the firm to the proprietor which must be maintained intact. It is assumed that this implies some measure of the proprietor's command over goods and services in general, rather than over the type of asset which the firm holds. The proprietary approach is therefore consistent with maintaining the money amount of proprietor's capital, or, when money is changing in value, with maintaining the real value of proprietor's capital, as defined by applying a general purchasing power index to the historical money amount. The entity approach, on the other hand, regards the maintenance of the substance of the business entity as being the central assumption of the capital maintenance concept. It therefore requires that the amount of capital to be maintained should equal the current cost of the net assets of the firm, i.e. money capital, as recorded in the opening balance sheet should be adjusted to allow for changes in the prices of the specific assets held by the firm. Such an adjustment will be necessary whenever the relevant specific price changes, and irrespective of changes in the general price level. In times of changing prices (which will introduce economic obsolescence) or technical change (which will introduce technical obsolescence), replication of the physical assets held at the beginning of a period may not be an appropriate assumption, so that the entity approach should be modified to maintenance of operating capability in the most economic manner. For this reason, we prefer to characterise this approach as an entity approach, rather than as a physical capital maintenance approach.[1]

The proprietary and entity approaches represent two self-consistent alternative systems of capital maintenance. An eclectic approach, which combines elements of both, is the so-called gearing adjustment. This was adopted briefly as the basis of standard accounting practice in the UK (SSAP16, Accounting Standards Committee, 1980), and was debated vigorously at that time, so it will be discussed after the two 'pure' bases.

In Chapter 4, multiple-column reporting was discussed as a possible solution to the dilemma posed by the fact that more than one valuation basis may be relevant for the same asset. In the case of capital maintenance also, there may be a case for reporting the results of applying more than one concept. In this case, however, it is necessary to have only a multi-row income statement rather than a multi-column set of accounts, the different rows representing different measures of income resulting from applying different concepts of capital maintenance. This possibility will be discussed and illustrated in a later section of this chapter.

Before embarking upon a more detailed discussion of capital maintenance concepts, it is important to recall some of the fundamental principles discussed in Chapter 2. In particular, it is important to remember that only one of Hicks' definitions of income (Hicks No. 1) was based directly on capital maintenance, in the sense of maintaining a fixed value of capital. The others (Hicks No. 2 and Hicks No. 3) involved *ex ante* consumption maintenance, which may involve maintaining a variable amount of capital. An obvious illustration of the difference between the two approaches is when an entity holds a fixed-interest bond and the market interest rate rises. The interest rate rise will reduce the market value of the bond but not its prospective returns (fixed interest) which will be available for consumption. Hence, if the entity is concerned to maintain the value of capital (Hicks No. 1), it will record a loss equal to the decline in value of the bond, but if it is concerned with future consumption (Hicks No. 2 and 3), it will record no gain or loss, because future returns are unchanged. If future consumption prospects were to change, the maintenance deduction made from receipts in the Hicks No. 2 and 3 definitions would be that amount considered necessary to maintain expected future consumption levels and would therefore depend upon expected future prices, costs and rates of return. Where there is certainty and interest rates are not expected to change, this approach could be described as net present value maintenance, i.e. the preservation of the economic value of the equity.[2] In more realistic conditions of uncertainty, however, consumption maintenance will have no obvious capital maintenance counterpart. The subjective nature of this approach, involving as it does the estimation of future returns, has led to a preference for a capital maintenance approach by practical accounting reformers (e.g. the Sandilands Committee), the only explicit exploration of consumption maintenance being that by Scott (1976). However, the idea of consumption maintenance did seem to be implicit in some of the arguments of those who advocated current cost accounting with an entity base (e.g. Merrett and Sykes, 1974, 1980) and the gearing adjustment, particularly in its split-level form (Gibbs and Seward, 1979). It is also apparent in the later theoretical contributions of Fischer Black (1980, 1993), and in the attempts of practising accountants and standard-setters to separate 'windfall' gains and losses (which are assumed to be non-recurrent) from profits (which are assumed to be a sustainable feature of the entity).

## 6.2 PROPRIETARY CAPITAL

Perhaps the simplest and most obvious concept of capital is a sum fixed in historical money units. It will be recalled that this was the basis of historical cost accounting (Chapter 3), in which it had an obvious rationale, representing the amount contributed by the proprietor, either in the form of capital subscriptions or retained profits.

In the context of current value accounting, as described in Chapter 4, the maintenance of money capital implies the recognition of the nominal amount of holding gains as part of profits. In terms of the Sandilands current cost proposals, this implies that the profit would be the total gains, derived from the Statement of Gains. This has already been defined in Chapter 4 (equations (4.2), (4.3), (4.4) and (4.6)). It will be recalled that, in the case of a transactionless period, current value income was defined as

$$Y_{CVA} = P''_{t+1} - P''_t = N''_t.s \qquad (6.1)$$

where $N''_t.s$ represents the nominal holding gain on (i.e. rise in money value of) the 'non-monetary' assets held during the period. In the more general case, where there are transactions, current value income additionally has to reflect changes in the amount of assets and liabilities during the period and becomes

$$Y_{CVA} = P''_{t+1} - P''_t$$
$$= (N''_{t+1} - N''_t) + (M_{t+1} - M_t) - (L_{t+1} - L_t) \qquad (6.2)$$

This gives a correct aggregate income figure for the period, but its balance sheet approach (deriving income from the net comparison of opening with closing balance sheet of the period) does not provide an analysis of the components of income, such as operating profit, and realised and unrealised holding gains. This would require that the income calculation is made on a transaction by transaction basis, to reflect the effects of individual transactions and events within the period.

In times when inflation does not exist, i.e. when the general price level is stable, the definition of capital in money terms is an adequate description of proprietors' past capital contributions (including retained profits and deducting amounts withdrawn) which they would wish to maintain intact before recognising income. In times of inflation, however, the general price-level adjustment (CPP) described in Chapter 5 might be more appropriate, on the ground that proprietors will wish to maintain the real value of their capital, where 'real' is taken to imply measurement in terms of general command over goods and services rather than a monetary unit which fluctuates in value. It will be recalled that 'real terms' income was defined in Chapter 5 (equations (5.8)–(5.10)), in the transactionless case, as

$$
\begin{aligned}
Y_{RT} &= P''_{t+1} - P''_t(1 + p) \\
&= [N''_{t+1} - N''_t(1 + p)] + [M_{t+1} - M_t(1 + p)] \\
&\quad - [L_{t+1} - L_t(1 + p)] \\
&= N''_t(s - p) - M_t.p + L_t.p
\end{aligned}
\tag{6.3}
$$

In the more general case, in which transactions do take place, this formulation is still adequate as a definition of total income, subject to the reservation expressed earlier in relation to equation (6.2) concerning the components of income. The definition in the first line is solely concerned with the definition of total income and is therefore not subject to this reservation.

The final definition in equation (6.3) is the most revealing in the sense that it shows the nature of the gains recognised by a real terms system. The first term $[N_t''(s - p)]$ is the real holding gain on non-monetary assets. Thus, the nominal holding gain $N_t''.s$ is no longer recognised in full, as was the case when money capital was maintained, but is instead reduced by the rise in the general index, $p$. When the rise in price of the specific assets $(s)$ fails to keep pace with inflation $(p)$, a real holding loss is deducted from profit $(p > s$, so that $N_t''(s - p) < 0)$. The second term is the loss on holding monetary assets in a period of general inflation, and the third is the gain on having loans which are of fixed monetary amounts. The explanations of the latter two items are the same as those given in their explanation in the context of CPP accounting in Section 5.7: this is hardly surprising, in view of the fact that the 'real terms' approach is the application of CPP adjustment to a current value base rather than the historical cost base.

Although the 'real terms' approach has the possible merit of providing an income measure which is expressed consistently in current pounds,[3] and which is unaffected by the rate of inflation during the reporting period, this property is not always desirable. Indexation is relatively uncommon, outside certain hyper-inflationary countries, so that accounting income numbers will often be evaluated by comparison with un-indexed data. Hence, Edwards and Bell (1961, Chapter 8) regard the real terms adjustment of capital as less important than the current valuation of assets. In particular, rates of interest observed in markets are money rates rather than real rates. Thus, if we wish to value a company's shares by discounting its prospective returns to shareholders, or by some related procedure such as the application of a Price/Earnings ratio to its current earnings, we require money returns or earnings, with no 'real terms' adjustment. This has been demonstrated elegantly by Kennedy (1976). Because of the difficulty of estimating the expected inflation rate, which is necessary in order to derive the real interest rate from observed market rates, it will generally be preferable to compare nominal rates of interest (as observed in the market) with expected money rates of return, rather than comparing estimated real rates of interest with expected real rates of return.

However, financial accounts are typically used for *ex post* appraisal, and the real interest rate is known *ex post* and can be compared with 'real terms' rates of return. Furthermore, the calculation of 'real terms' rates of return and profit figures might be relevant to inferring the future performance of a firm in an inflationary environment, when the firm's market position and pricing policy make maintenance of its real rate of return or income the likely course of future events. Thus, there are potential uses for proprietary income measures based on both money capital maintenance and real capital maintenance. There is no conflict between these requirements, as it is quite possible to draw up a profit and loss account which reports the 'real terms' adjustments (the $p$ adjustments in equation (6.3)) separately, so that both monetary and real profit measures can be derived from the same statement. This will be discussed in a later section of this chapter.

An important modification of the 'pure' proprietary real income measure, which is made by a number of leading writers on the subject, is to distinguish between realised and unrealised gains. Edwards and Bell (1961) for example, propose a measure of 'realised profit' which includes realised holding gains (those on fixed assets consumed in use, by depreciation, and stocks realised by re-sale) and a measure of 'business profit' which includes, in addition, unrealised holding gains (gains on fixed assets not yet consumed and stocks not yet sold).[4] This distinction is consistent with the objective of providing a useful set of information about the economic progress of the firm: it has already been emphasised that unrealised holding gains are of a different quality from those which have been realised, especially when gains are assessed at replacement cost, because their ultimate realisation will depend upon the future course of costs and prices. Sweeney (1936, Chapter 1), in his pioneering work on real terms accounting, insisted on the strict division of the profit and loss account into realised and unrealised sections. His system 'consists, first, in using a realised-income section the contents of which are identical with those in the ordinary profit and loss statement. Second, an unrealised income section is added because of the helpful information that it contains. Finally, at the very bottom of the profit and loss statement the total of the realised and unrealised income is shown. This total is called "final net income for the period"' (Sweeney, 1936, p. 21).

Sweeney's approach is adopted notably by Baxter (1975) amongst later writers, although Baxter rejects Sweeney's somewhat strict view of realisation, which is carried to the extent of not recognising gains or losses on any monetary liabilities or assets, including cash, until they are exchanged in a transaction (Baxter, 1975, p. 47). Baxter is, however, more cautious than Sweeney in that, whereas Sweeney reported total income in his profit and loss statement, merely using the realisation criterion to segregate different types of gain, Baxter's income statement (Baxter, 1975, Chapter 15, appendix) excludes unrealised gains, confining their reporting to the proprietors' equity interest in the balance sheet.[5] Thus, Baxter's income measure is not based on current values, as it excludes the unrealised real holding gains (or losses), which are implicit in the closing balance sheet values. The result of this is that Baxter's income measure yields an identical total to that of CPP-adjusted historical cost income, although his method of arriving at the total is more informative than CPP, isolating the realised real holding gains (Baxter, 1975, pp. 190–91).[6]

Thus, adherents of the 'real terms' approach to accounting have proposed several income measures which are not on a pure proprietary capital maintenance basis, i.e. maintenance of capital in terms of real purchasing power. Following the realisation principle, unrealised holding gains sometimes appear 'below the line' and are not included in the initial income number, but are added to the calculation of alternative income measures (Sweeney, 1936; Edwards and Bell, 1961) or to capital reserves in the balance sheet (Baxter, 1975). In the latter case, the capital maintenance principle being applied in the profit and loss account is the real purchasing power of opening capital, plus the unrealised real holding gains of the period, and less unrealised real holding losses of the period. This is an important modification of the capital maintenance basis of real terms accounting, if we attach particular weight to a single number measuring real income. If we adopt the broader approach of regarding real terms accounting as producing a set of useful information, we shall be less concerned about the precise format in which the information is presented, provided that it is all accessible. In this case, both the capital maintenance concept and the method of reporting unrealised gains and losses will be less important, although we might prefer a statement such as Sweeney's profit and loss statement, which reports unrealised and realised gains separately, rather than Baxter's system, which forces us to search the balance sheet to discover unrealised gains.

## 6.3 ENTITY CAPITAL

The entity view of capital maintenance is invariably linked with the advocacy of some form of replacement cost accounting.[7] The reason for this is that the entity approach assumes the continuity of the business entity as the basis of financial reporting. Replacement cost is a particularly appropriate valuation basis if we contemplate continuity, which implies the replacement of assets which are used up. An early pioneer of the entity approach was Schmidt (1930, 1931).[8] Later advocates of this approach were Gynther (1966), Mathews (1968) and Merrett and Sykes (1974, 1980). Professional recommendations incorporating this view were made by the Institute of Cost and Works Accountants (1952) and by the Association of Certified and Corporate Accountants (1952), and an entity approach has been applied in practice in the Netherlands, notably by Philips N. V. (Goudeket, 1960). There are, of course, a number of detailed variations on the basic entity principle, but all approaches have in common a capital maintenance concept which is designed to compensate for the price changes of the specific assets of the firm (a 'special index' approach), rather than for changes in the value of money (a 'general index' approach).

The consequence of this approach is that holding gains on assets are never recognised as part of profit, whether they are real (i.e. due to the price of the asset appreciating more rapidly than the general price level) or merely nominal (i.e. due to asset price rises which merely compensate for changes in the general price level). Instead, the holding gain is regarded as an accretion of the firm's capital. In double entry terms, the asset is debited with the appreciation in value, and capital (e.g. in the form of a revaluation reserve) is credited, whereas, in a system which recognised appreciation as profit, the profit and loss account would be credited. The reason for this, given by Schmidt (1931), is as follows:

> Some theoretical explanation of the reasons why appreciation cannot be profit is needed at this point. For this purpose we must consider the enterprise as a part of the national production machine. It will then be clear that a maintenance of total productivity as of a certain moment will only be possible, if the productive instrumentalities of all individual enterprises concerned are preserved intact. The maintenance of productive power as a whole is not possible if accounting is based on an original value basis. The reason is that pure appreciation would then appear as profit whenever a change of value has taken place between the purchase and selling dates for the materials and wages that compose a product. (p. 289)

Gynther defends this point of view from the standpoint of the individual shareholder, as follows:

> if it is believed that the whole or prime purpose is to assist the entity (the firm) in its daily struggles (and that only in this way will the interests of shareholders be looked after in the long term), then it is almost certain that the use of specific indexes will be favoured, i.e. so that the physical assets of the business will be maintained during the period of changing prices. (p. 45)

This plea for maintaining the specific assets of the business intact is intuitively appealing, but further analysis suggests weaknesses in the argument. If the concept is to be useful in accounting it must lead to a measurable and justifiable capital maintenance concept. Schmidt's 'productive power as a whole' is difficult to define clearly or measure precisely. If it implies a physical quantity of output, we meet the problem that output may have a different value per unit (in either real or nominal terms) at different times, so that the maintenance of physical output might not be in the interests of the shareholders, the entity, or the community (e.g. when the product is becoming obsolete). If we resort instead to maintaining the total value of output, irrespective of its composition, we meet the difficulty that varying profit margins might mean that different types of output are of different value to the entity and its shareholders: in the extreme, maintenance of sales of a product which makes a loss is clearly undesirable. We might then resort to maintenance of the profit stream earned by the entity, but this takes us away from notions of capital maintenance and into the area of standard stream income (Hicks No. 2 and No. 3), which is essentially a proprietary approach (maintaining consumption of shareholders or proprietors), although it might be consistent with the entity approach under certain circumstances, e.g. when the profitability of a certain physical output was expected to remain constant in the future.

Gynther's proposal for maintaining physical assets can be criticised on similar grounds. If there is technical progress, relative factor price changes or product price changes, the value of the physical assets of the firm will change, and the optimal replacement policy will not involve identical replacement of the assets currently held. If we overcome this difficulty by resorting to the maintenance of the value of the assets rather than a physical quantity, we are once more in the realm of the proprietary approach rather than the entity approach.

Thus, if we assume a realistic world in which relative prices change and there is technical progress, it seems unlikely that we can justify the maintenance of an entity in physical terms, whether output or assets. This issue has already been addressed in the discussion of replacement cost in Chapter 4. Once we concede the case for defining capital maintenance in monetary terms, without reference to a specific collection of assets, we have conceded the case for a proprietary approach to capital maintenance. This regards the capital of the firm as a fund of general purchasing power which can be switched to its most profitable use, rather than being tied to the preservation of a particular physical activity.[9] It also allows appreciation of asset values to be treated as profit. Thus, a 'real terms' proprietary approach treats real holding gains as profits, and real holding losses as losses.[10]

Proponents of the entity approach (such as Merrett and Sykes, 1980)[11] sometimes object that asset cost prices can rise without product sale prices rising, so that the holding gain on the asset recognised by the proprietary approach is illusory. In order to examine this argument, we shall consider the three possible alternative relationships between asset costs and product sale prices:

1. *Prices immediately compensate for cost increases.* In this case, replacement cost of assets employed can be passed on immediately in price rises without loss of sales volume, and the holding gain resulting from the rise in replacement cost of assets already held will be realised when the output is sold, so that it is indisputably accurate to describe this as a realisable gain.

2. *Prices compensate for cost increases after a time lag, to reflect the costs of actual replacement.* In this case, the firm may pass on increased replacement costs through price increases when the output being sold has involved the use of assets purchased at the new replacement cost. This will cover the actual replacement costs incurred but not the holding gains on assets held at the time of the cost increase. In the meantime, it will price on the basis of historical cost, so that the holding gain on assets held at the time of the cost increase will not be realised.

In this case, the entity approach will charge the enhanced replacement cost of assets consumed against revenue, irrespective of whether the assets used to earn the revenue were purchased at that cost, and will not recognise a realisable holding gain.[12] The proprietary approach will also charge current replacement cost against revenue, but it will also recognise the realisable holding gain which occurs when (at the time of the cost increase) replacement cost rises above the historical acquisition cost of the assets already held. Thus, the proprietary approach recognises a realisable holding gain when the replacement cost increases; the subsequent realisation occurs when the asset is used and charged (at replacement cost rather than historical cost) against revenue. The entity approach charges the realisation against profit but does not credit the holding gain, i.e. it treats appreciation and depreciation asymmetrically.[13] In a period of rising prices, this results in an ultra-conservative profit figure, profit being charged with depreciation of holding gains which have not been recognised as profit when they occurred.

3. *Prices never compensate for cost increases.* This case might seem to be one which favours the entity approach. However, the argument of the preceding paragraph can still be invoked in support of a proprietary approach. Although profits, after charging replacement cost, will be reduced permanently by the cost increase, during the transitional period the firm will still benefit, to the extent of the holding gain, by having capital goods in stock which were bought at the lower historical cost, rather than the higher current replacement cost. The proprietary approach will recognise this, and the entity approach will not. To take a simple example, suppose that a firm purchases stock at the beginning of each period and sells and replaces at the end. It has been trading, up to time $t$, with stock costing £100 and selling at a mark-up of 50 per cent. The profit calculation for periods ending not later than $t$ will be:

|  | £ |
|---|---|
| Sales | 150 |
| *Less* Replacement Cost of Sales | 100 |
| Profit | £50 |

This will be the same on both the proprietary and the entity basis, if we assume that all prices have remained constant. Now, assume that replacement cost at time $t + 1$ rises by 20 per cent but selling prices remain constant. The proprietary approach would report profit for the period ending $t + 1$ as follows:

|  | £ |
|---|---|
| Sales | 150 |
| *Less* Replacement Cost of Sales | 120 |
| Operating Profit | 30 |
| *Add* Holding Gain | 20 |
| Total Profit | £50 |

The entity approach, on the other hand, would report profit as follows:

|  | £ |
|---|---|
| Sales | 150 |
| *Less* Replacement Cost of Sales | 120 |
| Profit | £30 |

In this case, the holding gain of £20 would be credited to a capital reserve. Thus, the proprietary approach would maintain a capital of £100 and the entity approach a capital of £120. Both systems recognise the enhanced asset value in the balance sheet, so the question of the possibly lower economic value of the assets due to the decline in profit margin is irrelevant to the choice between systems. Equally, the operating profit figure in the proprietary system conveys the same information as that in the entity system. The essential difference between the systems is that the proprietary approach regards the gain as profit, whereas the entity approach regards it as being a necessary part of maintaining existing capital. Again, the entity approach is asymmetrical in its treatment of gains and losses, excluding the holding gain from profit but charging the enhanced stock value (including the gain) against profit, as cost of sales.

In this context, the argument about lower profit margins can be turned against the entity approach, because it is questionable whether the maintenance of existing stocks is justified when margins have declined. If replacement did not take place, but the company instead liquidated its investment, the proprietary approach undoubtedly gives a more informative profit figure: the total profit of £50 does represent the surplus of the cash which the proprietors would have on liquidation, over the amount of their capital interest at the beginning of the period, if the stock were not replaced.

Thus, the entity approach has questionable foundations, although it may be relevant in producing a sub-division of income which is useful. The concept of operating profit, for example, may be found useful, and the separation of this from holding gains can be regarded as reconciling the entity approach (profit after charging replacement cost but excluding holding gains) with the proprietary approach (holding gains added).[14] The Sandilands Committee's proposals for current cost accounting could be interpreted as an example of this approach, their operating profit before deducting interest being an entity measure of income,[15] and total gains being a proprietary measure. It should, however, be noted that, for implementation in a world characterised by general inflation, the gains would have to be abated by a general price-level adjustment (strongly opposed by Sandilands) in order to produce a 'real terms' proprietary measure. The Sandilands Committee emphasised that its measure of operating profit is not based on physical capital maintenance (Sandilands Report, 1975, para. 129): the capital which it preserves is based upon the 'value to the business' rather than the replacement cost of the assets of the firm. However, 'value to the business' is assessed according to the characteristics of the specific assets of the firm, and it may typically be expected to equal replacement cost (Gee and Peasnell, 1976), so that it does not seem unreasonable to classify the Sandilands operating profit as an entity measure: certainly, its exclusion of all holding gains precludes it from being regarded as a proprietary approach.

To conclude the discussion of the entity approach, we shall briefly consider two details of its application about which its proponents differ in their preferred method. These are, respectively, backlog depreciation and the treatment of monetary working capital.

## 6.4 BACKLOG DEPRECIATION

Backlog depreciation arises when the accumulated depreciation provision is inadequate to cover the cost of replacement, the gap being backlog depreciation. A simple example is as follows:

Assume that an asset cost £100 and is to be written off over 5 years on the straight-line basis. After 2½ years, the replacement cost of the asset rises to £150, and remains at this level until the end of the fifth year. Replacement cost depreciation would be provided as follows:

| | Within-year basis | | | End-year basis | |
|---|---|---|---|---|---|
| Time | Annual Provision | Accumulated Provision | Time | Annual Provision | Accumulated Provision |
| 1 | 20 | 20 | 1 | 20 | 20 |
| 2 | 20 | 40 | 2 | 20 | 40 |
| 3 | 25 | 65 | 3 | 30 | 70 |
| 4 | 30 | 95 | 4 | 30 | 100 |
| 5 | 30 | 125 | 5 | 30 | 130 |

The backlog depreciation is £25 (= £150 − £125) in the case of the 'within-year' basis and £20 (= £150 − £130) in the case of the 'end-year' basis. This is because the provision made for the period before the cost rise was based on a cost lower than that at which replacement ultimately takes place. Strictly, there are two distinct backlog problems, the between-year problem and the within-year problem. The former is the problem of under-provision for past years (years 1 and 2 in the example), whereas the latter is the problem of under-provision for the current year, which arises if we charge depreciation on the basis of cost at the time of use (the within-year basis). The end-year basis bypasses the latter problem by charging on the basis of end-year costs, although this is difficult to justify if we regard depreciation as reflecting cost at the time of use.

The backlog problem arises from regarding depreciation as a fund for the replacement of specific assets. If we regard depreciation as merely an allocation of costs, no problem arises. In that case, we are no longer concerned with the total accumulated provision but merely with the charge for the relevant period: if that charge was adequate to represent cost at the time of use, no problem arises. However, even if we are concerned with the total accumulated provision, this raises no problems for the proprietary theorist, because any increase in depreciation will be offset by a holding gain. Suppose, for example, we wished to provide backlog depreciation in period 3, and we were using the mid-year method, which best reflects cost at the time of use. We would revalue the asset at replacement cost, crediting a holding gain:

|  | Debit | Credit |
|---|---|---|
| Cost of Asset | £50 | |
| Holding Gain | | £50 |

We would provide backlog depreciation, debiting this to the holding gain

|  | Debit | Credit |
|---|---|---|
| Holding Gain | £25 | |
| Accumulated depreciation | | £25 |

The net effect would be to record the revaluation of the unde-preciated portion of the asset as a net holding gain. An entity theorist would not, however, treat the holding gain on the asset as part of income but would charge normal depreciation to income. This creates a choice either of charging the backlog depreciation against income, without any offsetting holding gain, or of treating backlog depreciation differently from current depreciation, debiting it to capital rather than income. The latter procedure is the most commonly adopted (e.g. by Gynther, 1966, and by the Sandilands Committee, 1975, para. 606). It can be justified by assuming that accounts are concerned with periodic income, rather than with the life cycle of asset ownership. It is therefore sufficient that the depreciation for the period should measure the replacement cost of assets used up during the period. It may further be argued that depreciation should only meet the cost of replacement at the precise time when the asset was used up: this would justify the 'mid-year' rather than the 'end-year' method.

Income measurement is concerned with charging the cost of the asset at the time of its use, not with providing funds, so that the concept of depreciation as a fund for replacement is not relevant to income measurement. Even if it were, nevertheless, considered important[16] that current depreciation charges should reflect the current burden of replacement on the funds of the firm, it should be noted that charging replacement cost depreciation would not necessarily achieve this, because the replacement requirements of a period will typically differ from the replacement cost of assets used up during that period. Domar (1953) demonstrates that, with a growing stock of fixed assets and rising replacement prices, historical cost depreciation can be adequate to cover the replacement requirements of a period, because it is the oldest (and, with a growing stock, the least numerous) assets which require replacement.

## 6.5 MONETARY ITEMS AND THE MONETARY WORKING CAPITAL ADJUSTMENT

The treatment of monetary items also lends itself to a variety of alternative interpretations under the entity capital maintenance convention. Monetary items are those assets and liabilities whose realisable value is fixed in nominal money amounts, such as trade debtors and creditors, loans, deposits and cash itself. Under the proprietary approach, their treatment is simple: we either maintain money values, in which case the nominal value of $M_t$ and $-L_t$ are maintained, or we maintain real values, in which case we apply general index adjustment, $M_t(1 + p)$ and $-L_t(1 + p)$, giving rise to a loss on holding money and a gain on borrowing, when $p$ is positive, as discussed earlier in Chapter 5 (particularly in relation to equation (5.5)).

Under the entity approach, we have already seen (Chapter 4, particularly equation (4.7)) that it is possible to maintain the current value of non-monetary assets by applying specific indices to them, but to maintain net monetary assets (assets, less liabilities) at their nominal amount, making no allowances for changes in the general price level in the capital maintained. However, committed entity theorists, such as Gynther (1966), advocate a specific index approach to monetary working capital (the credit received and given, and cash held, in order to conduct business) in which a specific maintenance factor $s$ is substituted for $p$ in the preceding definitions. They also question relevance of the 'gain on borrowing' when this applies to long-term finance loans. From the entity's perspective it is argued that both equity interests and long-term borrowing are sources of finance and that there should be no differentiation in their treatment, no 'gain on borrowing' being recognised on either element of long-term capital.

The specific index approach to monetary assets and liabilities that are part of working capital is consistent with the spirit of entity capital maintenance. It attempts to extend the concept of the entity beyond its physical assets (including financial assets whose value is not fixed in money terms) to its monetary assets and liabilities. Physical working capital, in the form of stocks and work-in-progress, is already included as part of the non-monetary capital to be maintained, and it is a natural step for an entity theorist to argue that it is just as necessary for the smooth running of the business to hold cash and give trade credit to customers as it is for it to hold stocks. Thus, if we can define a specific index, s, which reflects appropriately the change in the firm's need for monetary working capital arising from price changes during the period, in order to maintain its level of output, we can define the monetary working capital to be maintained as $M_t(1 + s) - L_t(1 + s)$. This is described as a *monetary working capital adjustment* (MWCA).

This definition of the MWCA is strictly appropriate only if $L$ consists entirely of borrowing that necessarily arises from current operations, i.e. working capital. If some of the borrowing finances the non-monetary assets of the business (sometimes characterised loosely as 'long-term borrowing', although rolling short-term borrowing programmes can be used to finance longer term investment), an entity perspective may suggest that it is not be appropriate to index it on the same basis as the MWCA (because it does not arise from the requirement for working capital), and probably not at all (because loan financing is regarded as a claim on the net assets of the business similar to that of equity). The latter view implies that the possible gain to equity shareholders resulting from loan financing (tradition-ally known as *gearing* in the UK and *leverage* in the US) will be ignored in the accounts, because it does not represent a gain (or loss) to the entity but rather a transfer between the owners of the long-term finance of the entity: debt and equity. In order to remedy this possible deficiency of the entity approach as information specifically for share-holders (equity), the *gearing adjustment* has been proposed. This is discussed in the following section of this chapter. In implementing the MWCA, many problems arise when we try to define $s$ precisely for a particular item or class of items, and consequently there are many practical variations on this basic theme. For example, we might have different indices for trade debtors (whose needs presumably reflect product selling price) and trade creditors (which presumably reflect the purchase price of inputs), although some writers, such as Gibbs (1976), prefer to regard trade credit net, rather than gross, regarding an increase in creditors as a natural offset to an increase in debtors as the money value of output rises. There are also difficult concep-tual and practical problems involved in separating monetary working capital from other forms of monetary capital attached to the firm. This is most obvious in the case of cash and deposits, which may be necessary to meet the normal flow of payments (the transactions motive), or may be held in reserve to meet unforeseen fluctuations in payments (the precautionary motive) or may be held as an investment (the speculative motive). Equally, bank overdrafts and short-term lia-bilities may be held for a variety of motives and are, to some extent, substitutes for long-term liabilities, which are not usually regarded as part of monetary working capital. Even trade credit is not exempt from ambiguity: the concept of the level of trade credit necessary for the maintenance of output cannot be defined in absolute terms, inde-pendently of financial conditions. Giving and receiving trade credit entails costs and brings benefits to the firm, and the amount which it is appropriate to give and receive will depend not only on the level of output, but also on the level of interest rates, the financial state of the firm, its suppliers and customers and the competitiveness of the markets in which the firm operates.

Thus, the maintenance of a specific level of monetary working capital is consistent with the entity approach and brings with it the ambiguities inherent in that approach. Once we move away from concepts of money or general purchasing power, it is extremely difficult to define clearly and measure precisely what is meant by the entity and therefore what is required in order to maintain it intact.

## 6.6 THE GEARING ADJUSTMENT

We now turn to a capital maintenance concept which has both proprietary and entity elements, that which uses the gearing adjustment. This has been of practical importance because it was a feature of the UK's standard on current cost accounting (SSAP16, Accounting Standards Committee, 1980). The gearing adjustment is an eclectic capital maintenance concept. In its purest form, it involves the entity approach to maintaining equity capital but a proprietary approach (using money, rather than general purchasing power) to long-term borrowing. The argument for this usually starts from an entity view of the profit of the firm but then points out that there is an additional profit accruing to equity shareholders[17] in a period of inflation due to the fact that the ownership of the firm shifts from those providers of long-term capital with a fixed money claim ('gearing') to the residual claimants, the equity shareholders. Thus the gearing adjustment is an adjustment indicating how the equity shareholders have gained at the expense of long-term lenders (important proprietary information): it indicates changes in the allocation of profit and claims to capital amongst these groups, but does not tell us anything about the firm's profitability in trading and dealing with outsiders (the focus of entity information).

The gearing adjustment was originally a German creation, the basic idea being the creation of Schmidt; his 1930 and 1931 papers are an accessible account of his ideas for English readers.[18] His work was the main source of inspiration for the 1975 recommendation by the German Institute of Chartered Accountants, which was the first professional pronouncement to advocate a form of gearing adjustment.

The German recommendations, and their relationship to the work of Schmidt, are described in Coenenberg and Macharzina (1976).

However, the gearing adjustment was reinvented, apparently independently, by a group of British writers, Godley and Cripps, Kennedy and Gibbs in a series of articles published in *The Times* between 1974 and 1976. This literature has been surveyed by Kennedy (1978a). It was clearly influential in the thinking behind the Hyde Guidelines (Accounting Standards Committee, 1977), and SSAP16 (Accounting Standards Committee, 1980).

The origins of the gearing adjustment in the UK lay in the corporate liquidity crisis of 1974. Merrett and Sykes (1974) observed a situation in which wage inflation combined with price controls had depressed operating margins but taxable and distributable profits were swelled by stock appreciation, and interest rates were high so that external finance could not be substituted for internal funds. This led them to advocate a measure of profit which was based on the entity capital maintenance principle: the specific assets of the firm must be maintained before any distribution could be made to shareholders or to the tax authorities. Their article was influential in the introduction of stock appreciation relief, which removed stock appreciation from the tax base, in the autumn of 1974, reducing the tax burden, and therefore easing the liquidity problem. The entity principle of eliminating holding gains in the calculation of operating profit was followed by the Sandilands Report (1975).[19]

Godley and Wood (1974) objected to Merrett and Sykes' entity approach in the case of a loan-financed business, showing by means of numerical examples that the shareholders of such a business did make a distributable profit from stock appreciation and should therefore be taxed on this gain.

The gearing adjustment, proposed by Godley and Cripps (1975)[20] reconciled these two views. Holding gains on assets should be treated as profit to the extent that they were loan financed. Therefore, a proportion of holding gains should be credited to profits, the proportion being the gearing ratio of the firm. As Kennedy (1978a) points out, this implies that, insofar as assets are loan financed, the holding gain recognised is the same as that under 'real terms' accounting (as, for example, proposed by the CCAB, 1975), although the latter would divide the gain, in a period of general inflation, into a gain on borrowing and a real holding gain. Insofar as assets are equity financed, however, the gearing adjustment leaves holding gains 'below the line' and they are not recognised as part of profit, because equity capital is up-dated by the index appropriate to the specific assets of the entity. Thus, insofar as there are real holding gains in an equity-financed firm, they will not be included in profit under the gearing adjustment system, and this profit will therefore be less than 'real terms' profit.[21]

In algebraic terms, the Godley/Cripps/Gibbs/Kennedy gearing adjustment is as follows.

To opening money capital, we add the following:

$$N_t''.s \left[ 1 - \frac{L_t - M_t}{L_t - M_t + P_t''} \right]$$

where $N_t''.s$ is the 'entity' adjustment necessary to provide fully for the replacement of non-monetary assets (as explained earlier in Chapter 4, equation (4.7)). If a monetary working capital adjustment is made, its components should be classified as part of $N_t''$, rather than $M_t$ or $L_t$. The proportion of opening non-monetary assets[22] which is financed by gearing is:

$$\left[ \frac{L_t - M_t}{L_t - M_t + P_t''} \right] \quad \text{(since } L_t - M_t + P_t'' = N_t'' \text{)}$$

Thus, geared income is current cost profit, as defined earlier in (4.7), modified by abating the current cost capital maintenance adjustment to reflect gearing:

$$
\begin{aligned}
Y_G = P_{t+1}'' &- \left[ P_t + N_t''.s \left( 1 - \frac{L_t - M_t}{L_t - M_t + P_t''} \right) \right] \\
&= (M_{t+1} - M_t) + (N_{t+1}'' - N_t'') \\
&- N_t''.s \left( 1 - \frac{L_t - M_t}{L_t - M_t + P_t''} \right) - (L_t - L_t)
\end{aligned}
\tag{6.4}
$$

This is the simplest and most self-consistent form of gearing adjustment. Apart from the dating problem already noted, SSAP16 and its predecessors had the peculiarity of arbitrarily restricting the holding gains which are recognised, by applying the gearing adjustment only to realised holding gains, i.e. the gearing adjustment is applied as an abatement of depreciation, the cost of sales adjustment (stock appreciation removal) and the monetary working capital adjustment, but is not applied to the appreciation of fixed assets which are still held at the end of the period. This ultra-conservative approach was condemned by proponents of the gearing adjustment, such as Kennedy (1978a) and Gibbs and Seward (1979), and will not be discussed further. When the gearing adjustment is applied to a system with an adjustment for monetary working capital (as in SSAP16), the definition of gearing has to exclude the monetary working capital elements of $M_t$ and $L_t$.

It is possible to question the usefulness of profit calculations based upon the gearing adjustment, and their superiority to 'real terms' accounting based on the proprietary approach. The 'entity' valuation of equity capital, which excludes real holding gains from profit assumes that the firm remains intact in its present form, and that no profit results even when the current value of that form rises in real terms.

The difficulties of justifying and implementing the entity approach were discussed earlier in this chapter. Kennedy (1978a) describes operating profit, less interest and after the gearing adjustment, as 'proprietary profit'. This *is* a proprietary concept insofar as these two adjustments have been made in order to reflect profit attributable to equity, but the method of *measuring* equity for capital maintenance purposes is *entity* based, reflecting the values of the specific assets of the firm which are assumed to be maintained,[23] rather than proprietary, reflecting the general purchasing power of shareholders (reflecting a 'financial' rather than a 'physical' view of capital). It is therefore possible to contest Kennedy's view that his 'proprietary profit' is 'the most suitable figure for use as a *base* for dividend distribution policy', because it does not reflect the perspective of an equity shareholder.[24]

A second deficiency of the gearing adjustment system is the failure to separate the gain on borrowing from holding gains on assets. To anyone who accepts the proprietary approach with constant purchasing power as the ideal measurement standard (such as Sweeney, 1936; Edwards and Bell, 1961; Baxter, 1975), this involves a serious loss of information, pooling gains on financing (the borrowing gain) with gains on investment (asset gains). Kennedy proposes a system which should combine this information with the gearing adjustment.[25]

Finally, the relationship of the gearing adjustment to particular uses is ill-specified. Merrett and Sykes (1974) were clearly concerned with a liquidity crisis rather than a profits crisis (unrealised holding gains do not give rise to a cash flow even when they can be regarded as an economic gain which is of the nature of a profit). A concern with liquidity remained throughout the debate, particularly in the writings of Gibbs (1975, 1976, 1979), and it is not entirely clear whether the central concern was with profit or with cash flow. Taxation appeared to be a central concern of Godley and Wood (1974) and Godley and Cripps (1975), although Kennedy (1978a) avoided any commitment on this issue.

## 6.7 ECLECTIC INCOME STATEMENTS

Kennedy (1978a) proposed a 'simplified income statement' which would record 'real terms' proprietary profit in addition to various income measures suggested by proponents of the gearing adjustment and of the entity approach. It is difficult to quarrel with this eclectic approach to the income statement, which seems to be one way to achieve the reporting of 'different incomes for different purposes'. This would have the benefit of reducing the emphasis on a single income number, and would be an application of the 'useful information' approach (or what the Sandilands Report, para. 540, described as a 'building block' approach) exemplified by the work of Edwards and

Bell (1961). It is possible to incorporate a variety of capital maintenance concepts in the same set of accounts because capital maintenance affects only income measurement, and can therefore be dealt
with in the profit and loss account. It will be recalled that reporting a variety of asset valuation bases was more difficult because
this would entail re-stating individual assets in the balance sheet,
as well as various components (such as depreciation) of the profit and
loss account. Thus, the valuation problem entails multiple-column
accounting, whereas the capital maintenance problem involves only
multiple rows in the income statement, since it merely requires alternative statements of a single item, the income number.

For illustrative purposes, Kennedy's (1978a) proposal will be
discussed, although many alternatives exist in the literature, and the
gearing adjustment in particular may be an unnecessary complication.
Kennedy's 'simplified income statement' is as follows:

|  |  | £ |
|---|---|---|
|  | *Current cost operating profit* | <u>X</u> |
| Plus | Interest received from net monetary assets | X |
| Minus | Adjustment for maintenance of real value of | |
|  | net monetary assets | <u>(X)</u> |
| Equals | *Entity profit* | <u>X</u> |
| Minus | Interest paid on monetary liabilities | (X) |
| Plus | Geared holding gains | <u>X</u> |
| Equals | *Proprietary profit* | <u>X</u> |
| Plus | Ungeared holding gains | <u>X</u> |
| Equals | *Total proprietary gain* | <u>X</u> |
| Minus | Inflationary element of ungeared holding | |
|  | gains | <u>(X)</u> |
| Equals | *Inflation-corrected proprietary gain* | <u>X</u> |

Each of the italicised rows represents a different profit concept.
We start with current cost operating profit, which uses an entity capital maintenance concept based upon the replacement of the value to

the owner of physical assets: $P_t'' + N_t''.s$. After the addition of financial income (which could include dividends as well as interest), there is an entity adjustment to allow for the maintenance of net monetary assets in real terms, i.e. a monetary working capital adjustment. This adjusts opening capital to be maintained by $(M_{c,t} - L_{c,t}).s$, to give a total of $P_t'' + N_t''.s + (M_{c,t} - L_{c,t}).s$, where the subscript $c$ indicates $M$ and $L$ items which are part of working capital. It should be noted that $s$ is a specific index which may vary with asset type. The result of this adjustment is a complete entity profit figure, based on maintaining the business intact. It suffers from the conceptual problems discussed earlier; the precise nature of what is being maintained, especially with respect to monetary working capital, is not as clear as might be wished.

The next step involves a move to 'proprietary profit', using a gearing adjustment. Interest paid is deducted, since this is an apportionment of entity profit to the non-proprietary element of net worth (the geared element). Geared holding gains are then added back: as explained earlier, this represents an abatement of the capital maintenance concept to allow for the fact that the gearing element is fixed in monetary terms, so that there is a net gain to proprietors (equity). If we define long-term borrowing (for fixed capital) as $L_f$ and short-term borrowing (for working capital) as $L_c$, the entity capital maintenance concept was $P_t'' + N_t''.s + (M_{c,t} - L_{c,t}).s$ and Kennedy's proprietary capital maintenance concept becomes

$$P_t'' + \left(1 - \frac{L_{f,t}}{L_{f,t} + P_t''}\right)(N_t''.s + [M_{c,t} - L_{c,t}].s) \qquad (6.5)$$

where the term $L_{f,t}/(L_{f,t} + P_t'')$ is the gearing ratio.[26] The effect of this adjustment is that a money capital maintenance concept is applied to geared capital but equity capital $(P_t'')$ is still maintained on an *entity* basis, i.e. applying an index, $s$, which is specific to the firm. This becomes obvious in the ungeared case, when the term in the first bracket becomes unity. This is not, therefore, a proprietary concept in the sense in which this was defined earlier in this chapter, but is rather a product of the gearing adjustment which was discussed critically in the previous section. It should be noted that this form of gearing adjustment embraces all holding gains: the SSAP16 form used in the UK in the early 1980s excluded unrealised holding gains.

The next stage is to add back to profit the ungeared holding gains (the product of the two bracketed components in equation (6.5)), to apply the simple capital maintenance concept, $P_t''$. This is proprietary capital in money terms, as discussed earlier, and the proprietary profit measure which it yields is described by Kennedy as Total Proprietary Gain.

Finally, an adjustment is made to derive 'real terms' proprietary profit, which Kennedy describes as the Inflation-corrected Proprietary Gain. The correct method of doing this is to add to the capital maintenance concept (i.e. deduct from profit) the general price adjustment of equity, $P_t''.s$, to give a total capital to be maintained, $P_t''.(1 + p)$. Kennedy makes an arithmetic slip here in deducting from profit the 'Inflationary element of all holding gains',[27] $p.(P_t'' + L_{f,t})$, rather than merely the inflationary element of *ungeared* holding gains, $p.P_t''$. From the proprietors' standpoint it is unnecessary to index geared capital, because it requires maintenance (or repayment) only in money terms, the excess of the re-stated real terms amount over the money amount being the gain on borrowing.

It is therefore possible to disagree with Kennedy's detailed proposals for an eclectic income statement. The gearing adjustment may be unnecessary and it might be preferable to make the distinction between realised and unrealised holding gains (following Sweeney, 1936, or Edwards and Bell, 1961). It would also be desirable to show the gain on borrowing separately. The monetary working capital adjustment also is contentious. However, it is difficult to disagree with the broad principle of reporting a variety of alternative income measures which can be used to meet the specific informational needs of different users for different purposes. Kennedy also deals effectively with a common criticism of this type of proposal:

> The suggestion that more than one measure of profit in the main statement of the accounts will confuse the users of the accounts has been greatly exaggerated. A user of accounts can simply pick on the line in the statement most appropriate for his purpose. In any case, even if he is confused, it is definitely preferable that he should remain so than that he should be misled by a single profit figure that he has not properly understood. *(Kennedy, 1978a, pp. 63–64)*

Since the time of Kennedy's proposal, financial reporting standards and practice have moved in the direction of eclectic income statements. In particular, there has been increasing acceptance of a 'comprehensive' income measure, encompassing all gains and losses, with sub-divisions such as operating profit which could potentially incorporate different capital maintenance concepts (as in the proposals of Kennedy and the Sandilands Report), although the debate continues as to the precise nature of those sub-divisions and the extent to which they should be prescribed by standards (Barker, 2010).[28]

## 6.8 CONCLUSION

The capital maintenance concept is a crucial component of income measurement. The measure of income, whether for pricing, taxation, dividend distributions, wage bargaining or share valuation, was a central concern of participants in the inflation accounting debate and has continued to underlie the subsequent debate about improving the income statement to meet the needs of users. A variety of alternative concepts has been proposed. Fortunately, it is possible to devise an income statement which shows several alternative income numbers, based on different capital maintenance concepts. The three concepts which are most widely canvassed in the literature are the entity concept, the money proprietary concept and the real proprietary concept. The former raises the problem of defining the nature of the entity to be maintained, but if this issue can be resolved it seems likely that it will be useful to have a profit measure which excludes that portion of revenue which is pre-empted by the need to maintain the entity intact when the relative price of its assets is rising. The money proprietary concept has strong traditional and intuitive roots, and reflects the perspective of the shareholder, but it needs to be modified for some purposes, particularly in a period of inflation, by general price-level adjustment, to yield income after providing for real proprietary capital maintenance.

Each of these three basic concepts can be incorporated in a single income statement, so they need not be regarded as being mutually exclusive. The steps in the reconciliation are open to debate. Kennedy (1978a) proposed that these should include a gearing adjustment, but discussion of this adjustment failed to establish that it is anything other than an awkward compromise between the entity and the proprietary approaches. An alternative route would apply the general purchasing power adjustment across all sources of capital, as in a real terms system, separating real holding gains (and losses) from fictitious gains due to inflation (or losses due to deflation, if that were to come about), and identifying the gain on borrowing and loss on holding monetary assets in a period of inflation. It might also be useful to separate realised holding gains from unrealised gains.

The exposition of this chapter has been mainly verbal and algebraic. In order to aid comprehension, Appendix A provides a set of simple numerical illustrations of alternative capital maintenance concepts. The argument has been conducted mainly in terms of a priori reasoning, but there is considerable scope for empirical work in order to establish the realism of the empirical assumptions of competing arguments, the materiality of the differences between capital maintenance concepts, and the utility of the resulting measures. Appendix B reviews the results of the empirical work which has been published to date. Chapter 7 attempts to provide an overview of the discussion in this and previous chapters.

## APPENDIX A: A NUMERICAL ILLUSTRATION OF ALTERNATIVE CAPITAL MAINTENANCE CONCEPTS

### A.1 INTRODUCTION

This appendix provides a numerical illustration of two important capital maintenance concepts not illustrated in the earlier chapters. These are the gearing adjustment (in its 'pure' Godley/Cripps/ Kennedy/Gibbs form) and the general index 'real terms' adjustment, applied to a current valuation base. Finally, the Kennedy Income Statement is used to reconcile the profit figures resulting from using different concepts of capital maintenance.

The facts assumed are those of the 'Old Fred' example used in earlier chapters, the particular starting point for this illustration being Appendix B to Chapter 4, which gave current cost accounts, using replacement cost as the valuation base, and reporting both a money proprietary and an entity view of capital maintenance, in the spirit, if not the letter, of the Sandilands Report. Obviously, there is a bewildering variety of variations on the current value base (which were indicated in Chapter 4) and on the capital maintenance concept (which were indicated in Chapter 6). A valuable survey of capital maintenance concepts which have been proposed for practical application is provided by Tweedie (1979), and a thorough discussion of the relative merits of different capital maintenance concepts, focusing on 'physical' versus 'financial' concepts, is provided by Sterling and Lemke (1982).

The object of the following examples is to illustrate the basic workings of some of the more popular techniques, rather than to deal exhaustively with all possible techniques and circumstances. The latter type of guidance will be found in the guidance notes and manuals published in association with accounting standards. For example, UK practice, which incorporated a form of gearing adjustment (restricted to realised holding gains) and a monetary working capital adjustment, was defined in SSAP16 (Accounting Standards Committee, 1980) and the *Guidance Notes* appended to it.

Mallinson (1980) provides a thorough technical discussion of its implementation.

## A.2 THE GEARING ADJUSTMENT

*Period 1*: It will be recalled from Chapter 4, Appendix B, that Old Fred's opening balance sheet, on a current cost basis, was:

Balance Sheet at *t*

| | £ | | £ |
|---|---|---|---|
| *Proprietor's Capital* | 150 | *Fixed Asset* | |
| *Loan* | 50 | Cart (at cost) | 100 |
| | | *Current Asset* | |
| | | Cash | 100 |
| | £200 | | £200 |

It will be observed that the gearing ratio is 1/4 (= 50/200), i.e. one quarter of the long-term capital is provided by loans. Applying this ratio to the current cost accounts for the period, as given in Chapter 4, Appendix B, a simple form of gearing adjustment will give us the following income statement:

Income Statement for period 1, *t* to *t* + 1

| | £ |
|---|---|
| Sales | 120 |
| *Less* Current Cost of goods sold | 104 |
| | 16 |
| *Less* Depreciation | 10 |
| Current Cost Operating Profit | 6 |
| *Add* Gearing Adjustment | 7.50 |
| Distributable Profit | £13.50 |

It will be observed that this profit and loss account is the same as that for the current cost accounts (Chapter 5, Appendix B) up to the calculation of current cost operating profit. Current Cost Operating Profit is based upon an entity concept of capital maintenance, holding gains being excluded from profit and treated as increases in the value of capital to be maintained. The gearing adjustment adds back that proportion of the holding gains which is financed by debt. In this particular case, the calculation is 1/4 (the gearing ratio) times £30 (the holding gain on stocks). The resulting profit figure (£13.50) is described here as 'distributable profit' because it is that profit which proponents of the gearing adjustment would regard as being distributable to the proprietor (or, in the case of a company, the shareholders) without impairing the substance of the entity (i.e. the specific assets of the business, financed by a constant gearing ratio), on the assumption that further borrowing is possible in order to maintain the initial gearing ratio.

It should be noted that a number of variants of the gearing adjustment is possible. These include:

1. UK practice under SSAP16 (1980) was to apply the gearing ratio only to realised holding gains, but this practice was rejected by the original authors of the adjustment (Godley, Cripps, Gibbs and Kennedy), so we shall ignore it here.
2. Gearing can be measured (as in SSAP16 in the UK) as the average for the year, rather than by reference to the beginning of year balance sheet.
3. In the case of a company, preference shares may be regarded either as gearing (as in the earlier Hyde Guidelines for the UK) or as part of the proprietors' interest (as in the case of the later SSAP16).
4. Long-term fixed-interest loan stocks, or fixed dividend preference stocks, could be shown at market value, rather than nominal value, for the purpose of measuring gearing. Market value would be consistent with the *current* basis of current cost accounting, but nominal value is preferred in practice as being simpler to calculate and not subject to fluctuations as market interest rates change.
5. The range of monetary liabilities and assets to be taken into account in determining gearing can be defined in various ways. Gearing is

usually considered to be relevant to long-term financing, and short-term liabilities are often considered as an offset to current assets in determining net monetary working capital, for the purposes of a monetary working capital adjustment. In the simple example of period 1, shown earlier, we assume no short-term liabilities, so that the latter problem does not arise. We also assume that the cash holding in the opening balance sheet was immediately converted into stocks, so that there was no monetary working capital during the period.

The closing balance sheet is the same as that for the current cost accounts (Chapter 4, Appendix B), except that the apportionment of the proprietor's capital is different, the ungeared holding gain (£22.50) being regarded as an undistributable capital maintenance reserve.

Balance Sheet at $t + 1$

| | £ | | £ | £ |
|---|---|---|---|---|
| *Proprietor's Capital* | | *Fixed Asset* | | |
| Opening balance | | Cart (at cost) | 100 | |
| (at *t*) | 150 | *Less* | | |
| *Add* Capital reserve | 22.50 | Accumulated | | |
| Distributable profit | 13.50 | depreciation | 10 | |
| | 186 | | | 90 |
| *Less* Drawings | 30 | *Current Assets* | | |
| Closing balance (at | | Stock (at | | |
| *t* + 1) | 156 | current cost) | 26 | |
| *Loan* | 50 | Cash | 90 | |
| | | | | 116 |
| | £206 | | | £206 |

*Period 2:* The gearing ratio in the opening balance sheet, calculated on the same basis as for Period 1, is 50/206. Applying this to the £50 holding gains shown in the current cost accounts

(Chapter 4, Appendix B) gives the following final section of the income statement.

**Gearing adjustment to the Period 2, Current Cost Income Statement**

| | £ |
|---|---|
| Current Cost Operating Loss | (37) |
| *Add* Gearing adjustment $\left(50 \times \dfrac{50}{206}\right)$ | 12.14 |
| Distributable Loss | £(24.86) |

The proprietor's capital in the balance sheet again must equal that in the current cost accounts (by definition, since it must equal $N_{t+1} + M_{t+1} - L_{t+1}$) but the division between distributable profits and undistributable reserves occurs under the gearing adjustment system:

| | £ |
|---|---|
| *Proprietor's Capital* | |
| Opening balance (at $t + 1$) | 156.00 |
| *Add* Appropriation to capital maintenance | |
| reserve (ungeared holding gains) | 37.86 |
| Distributable (loss) | (24.86) |
| | 169.00 |
| *Less* Drawings | 106.00 |
| Closing balance (at $t + 2$) | £63.00 |

In this example, we have implicitly assumed that a monetary working capital adjustment is inappropriate. However, the firm did have net monetary working capital of £14 during period 2, if we make the assumption (as for Chapter 4, Appendix B) that purchase transactions and settlement of initial debts took place at the beginning of the period, whereas sales took place at the end. This consists of £52 credit received from the supplier, less £38 held as a cash balance. The cash balance is assumed to be necessary for the running of the business, and therefore part of monetary working capital, i.e. in terms of the notation of Chapter 6, we define $M_{c,t+1}$ as £38 and $L_{c,t+1}$ as £52. We assume that the appropriate index by which to adjust the monetary working capital is the rise in the price of stocks during the period, $1.38 (= 1.80/1.30)$.

The monetary working capital adjustment is analogous to the cost of sales adjustment (i.e. the additional charge for the excess of replacement cost over historical cost) for stocks. When a net amount is invested in monetary working capital, the increase required to maintain this amount in real terms (according to the specific index chosen) is charged to the profit and loss account in arriving at current cost operating profit. This charge is then abated by the gearing adjustment, because a proportion of the net monetary working capital is financed by long-term debt and, on the assumption of a constant gearing ratio, would not require maintenance by the proprietors of the entity. When, as in the present case, net monetary working capital is negative, i.e. borrowings exceed lendings and cash holdings, it is an addition (credit) to Profit and Loss, rather than a charge (debit), and so offsets the additional charge for replacement cost of stocks.

These adjustments would be implemented as follows.

The effect of introducing the monetary working capital adjustment in this example is that the current cost operating loss is reduced by the full amount of the adjustment (£2.80) and the distributable loss is reduced by the ungeared proportion (£2.12). This results in a transfer of £2.12 from the capital maintenance reserve, to reduce the distributable loss, but the closing balance of proprietor's interest in the balance sheet is unchanged. This demonstrates that the monetary working capital adjustment is a capital maintenance concept, assisting the separation of capital from profit, but not affecting the evaluation of the proprietor's aggregate interest in the firm, which depends upon the valuation basis adopted for assets and liabilities (since $P_{t+2} \equiv N_{t+2} + M_{t+2} - L_{t+2}$).

Income Statement for Period 2, $t + 1$ to $t + 2$, with Monetary Working Capital and Gearing Adjustments

|  | £ | £ |
|---|---|---|
| Sales |  | 135.00 |
| *Less* Current Cost of Goods Sold | 162.00 |  |
| Monetary Working Capital |  |  |
| Adjustment (£14 [180/150 – 1]) | (2.80) |  |
|  |  | 159.20 |
| Trading (Loss) |  | (24.20) |
| *Less* Current Cost Depreciation |  | 10.00 |
| Current Cost Operating (Loss) |  | (34.20) |
| *Add* Gearing |  |  |
| Adjustment $\left(\dfrac{50}{206}[\$50 - \$2.80]\right)$ |  | 11.46 |
| Distributable (Loss) |  | £(22.74) |

Balance Sheet at $t + 2$, Proprietor's Capital section

|  | £ |
|---|---|
| Opening balance (at $t +1$) | 156.00 |
| *Add* Appropriation to Capital Maintenance |  |
| Reserve (£37.86 – £2.12) | 35.74 |
| Distributable (Loss) | (22.74) |
|  | 169.00 |
| *Less* Drawings | 106.00 |
| Closing Balance (at $t + 2$) | £63.00 |

If net monetary working capital had been positive (assets exceeding liabilities), the effect of the monetary working capital adjustment would, of course, have been arithmetically opposite, increasing the capital maintenance reserve and reducing distributable profit.

It should be noted that the monetary working capital adjustment is subject to a wide variety of possible definitions. Of particular importance are the specification of the constituent assets and liabilities (e.g. whether cash should be included), the appropriate index or indices to be used (e.g. buying prices, selling prices or general purchasing power index), and the calculation technique (e.g. whether the adjustment should be based on the precise dating of transactions, as in the preceding example, or on some averaging method).

*Period 3:* The net borrowing during this period (as calculated in Chapter 5, Appendix B) was £215. Of this, £50 was a long-term loan. If we define the remaining components (creditors £180, less cash £15) as monetary working capital, the net borrowing during the period for the purposes of the adjustment is £165. Purchase prices rose during the period from £1.80 to £1.90, giving a specific index of approximately 1.06, which we assume to be appropriate

The Monetary Working Capital Adjustment is therefore

$$\$165 \times \left( \frac{1.9}{1.8} - 1 \right) = \$9.17$$

The Gearing Ratio, based upon the opening balance sheet is

$$\frac{50}{50 + 63} = 0.4425$$

The holding gains for the period (as in Chapter 4, Appendix B) are £51. The monetary working capital adjustment will, in this example (of net borrowing) be deducted from the holding gains in calculating the gearing adjustment:

Gearing Adjustment: (£51 – £9.17) 0.4425 = £18.51

This is added to distributable profit, the remainder, £23.32 (= £51 – £9.17 – £18.51) being added to the capital maintenance reserve.

These adjustments appear in the accounts as follows:

Income Statement for Period 3

|  | £ | £ |
|---|---|---|
| Sales |  | 180.00 |
| *Less* Current Cost of Goods Sold | 171.00 |  |
| Monetary Working Capital Adjustment | (9.17) |  |
| Current Cost Depreciation | 15.00 |  |
|  |  | 176.83 |
| Current Cost Operating Profit |  | 3.17 |
| *Add* Gearing Adjustment |  | 18.51 |
| Distributable Profit |  | £21.68 |

The Proprietor's Capital section of the closing balance sheet, at $t + 3$, appears as follows:

| *Proprietor's Capital* | £ |
|---|---|
| Opening balance (at $t + 2$) | 63.00 |
| *Add* Appropriation to capital maintenance reserve | 23.32 |
| Distributable Profit | 21.68 |
| | 108.00 |
| *Less* Drawings | 10.00 |
| Closing balance (at $t + 3$) | £98.00 |

*Period 4:* The gearing and monetary working capital adjustments are not really appropriate to this period, as they are based upon the assumption of continuity of the business, whereas the business is being liquidated during the period. The only holding gain is a realised gain (on the cart) for which no replacement is intended. It is not therefore necessary to amend the accounts given in Chapter 5, Appendix B, showing a trading profit of £6 and total gains of £21. In the context of the impending liquidation, all of the gains are distributable.

### A.3 REAL TERMS ACCOUNTING

Here, we adjust the current cost accounts, given in Chapter 4, Appendix B, to show a 'real terms proprietary' concept of capital maintenance, i.e. the money value of the proprietor's capital, as calculated by deducting liabilities from the current value of assets (as defined for current cost accounting purposes), is increased by reference to a general price-level index, for capital maintenance purposes. A similar exercise was carried out using historical cost accounts in Chapter 5, Appendix B. In this example, we assume that all sales took place either at the end of the period, or after all price changes of the period (both specific and general) had taken place, so that all figures in the accounts are expressed in end-of-period £s. Otherwise, if we wished to obtain a full set of 'real terms' accounts, measured in constant value £s, we should have to translate some of the profit and loss figures into year-end £s, as described in Chapter 5. It should also be noted that, for purposes of inter-period comparison, a full 'real terms' system would require that the accounts of previous periods be translated into current £s (or £s of any other common date, in which case the present period's accounts should be stated in the same unit), as described in Chapter 5. This is a purely mechanical piece of arithmetic which will not be demonstrated here.

Obviously, there are a great number of variations possible on the method of implementing real terms accounting. Very valuable sources of reference both for discussion and for numerical examples are the classic works of Edwards and Bell (1961) and of Sweeney (1936), particularly Chapter 3 of the latter.

*Period 1*: This starts with the same opening balance sheet (at $t$) as for the examples of current cost accounting (Chapter 4, Appendix B) and the gearing adjustment (A.2). The 'real terms' capital maintenance concept is, however, to maintain the proprietor's capital $P_t$ in real terms by multiplying by a general index $p$. The relevant values for period 1 are $P_t = £150$ and $p = 1.1$, so that closing capital to be maintained is £165, the increase of £15 being credited to a capital maintenance reserve. The Income Statement is as follows:

Real Terms Income Statement for period 1, $t$ to $t + 1$

|  | £ |
|---|---|
| Sales | 120 |
| *Less* Current cost of Goods Sold | 104 |
|  | 16 |
| *Less* Depreciation | 10 |
| Current Cost Operating Profit | 6 |
| *Add* Real Holding Gains | 15 |
| Total Real Gains | £21 |

The real holding gains constitute the holding gains on stocks of £30 (from Chapter 4, Appendix B), less the transfer to capital maintenance reserve (£15) which is necessary to maintain opening capital in real terms. Alternatively, by looking at opening capital from the other side of the balance sheet, in terms of the components of net worth (i.e. as $N_t + M_t - L_t$ rather than $P_t$), we can attribute the real holding gains to particular classes of asset and liability held during the period, as follows:

£

*Real Holding Gains*

| | |
|---|---:|
| Gain on Stocks (£30 − [£100 × 0.1]) | 20 |
| Gain on Borrowing (£50 × 0.1) | 5 |
| Loss on Cart (£100 × 0.1) | (10) |
| | £15 |

The real gains and losses are calculated by deducting each item's indexed ('real') opening value from its actual closing value, i.e. in the case of an asset whose money value has not changed, by multiplying opening value by − 0.1 (= 1 − 1.1). The monetary gain on stocks (£30) was calculated in Chapter 4, Appendix B. The loss on the cart arises because its replacement price did not keep pace with inflation. The loss was partly realised (in the form of the depreciation charge) and partly unrealised (in the form of the net value of the cart, appearing in the closing balance sheet).

The closing balance sheet reflects the 'real terms' approach in the proprietor's capital section, the assets and liabilities being the same as in the current cost case.

Real terms Balance Sheet as at $t + 1$

| | £ | | £ | £ |
|---|---:|---|---:|---:|
| *Proprietor's Capital* | | *Fixed Asset* | | |
| Opening balance (at $t$) | 150 | Cart (at cost) | 100 | |
| *Add* capital | | *Less* depreciation | 10 | |
| maintenance reserve | 15 | | | 90 |
| | 165 | *Current Assets* | | |
| *Add* Real Gains | 21 | Stock (at current | | |
| | 186 | cost) | 26 | |
| *Less* Drawings | 30 | Cash | 90 | |
| Closing balance (a $t + 1$) | 156 | | | 116 |
| *Loan* | 50 | | | |
| | £206 | | | £206 |

*Period 2*: The opening balance sheet (at $t + 1$) shows capital to be maintained of £156. Adjusting this by the rate of general

price-level change for the period, $p = 0.2$, gives an allocation to capital maintenance reserve of £31.20.

The income statement will start with a calculation of current cost operating profit, as for current cost accounting (Chapter 4, Appendix B), but the final section will be:

|  | £ |
| --- | --- |
| Current Cost Operating (Loss) | (37.00) |
| *Add* Real Holding Gains[†] | 18.80 |
| Total Real (Loss) | £(18.20) |

[†] £50 nominal holding gains (Chapter 4, Appendix B),
     *Less* £31.20 capital maintenance reserve.

The real holding gains can be decomposed as follows:

|  | £ |
| --- | --- |
| Gain on stocks (£50 − [£130 × 0.2]) | 24 |
| Gain on borrowing (£102 × 0.2) | 20.40 |
| Loss on holding money (£38 × 0.2) | (7.60) |
| Loss on cart (£90 × 0.2) | (18.00) |
| Net real holding gains | £18.80 |

As for the previous period, these gains and losses are calculated by deducting indexed opening value from actual closing value, in the case of assets and liabilities held during the period.

The closing balance sheet again (necessarily) shows the same proprietor's net worth as in the current cost case (£63), since the valuation basis is the same. The division between capital and profit is as follows:

|  | £ |
| --- | --- |
| *Proprietor's Capital* |  |
| Opening balance (at $t + 1$) | 156.00 |
| *Add* Allocation to capital maintenance reserve | 31.20 |
|  | 187.20 |
| *Add* Real (Loss) | (18.20) |
|  | 169.00 |
| *Less* Drawings | 106.00 |
| Closing balance (at $t + 2$) | £63.00 |

*Period 3:* The proprietor's capital at the start of the period (at $t + 2$) was £63. Indexing this by the inflation rate during the period (10 per cent, see Chapter 4, Appendix B) gives a transfer to capital maintenance reserve of £6.30. The adjustment to the income statement is as follows:

|  | £ |
|---|---|
| Current Cost Operating (Loss) | (6) |
| *Add* Real Holding Gains[†] | 44.70 |
| Total Real Gains | £38.70 |

[†] £51 (as in Chapter 4, Appendix B), *less* £6.30 capital maintenance.

The decomposition of the holding gains is as follows:

|  | £ |
|---|---|
| Gain on Fixed Asset (£40 – [£80 × 0.1]) | 32 |
| Gain on borrowing ([£180 + £50] × 0.1) | 23 |
| Loss on holding money (£15 × 0.1) | (1.50) |
| Loss on holding stocks (£11 – [£198 × 0.1]) | (8.80) |
|  | £44.70 |

It is notable that there was a real loss on holding stocks during this period, because the replacement cost of stocks failed to keep pace with the change in the general price level $(p)$.

The proprietor's capital in the balance sheet appears as follows:

|  | £ |
|---|---|
| *Proprietor's Capital* |  |
| Opening balance (at $t + 2$) | 63.00 |
| *Add* Allocation to capital maintenance reserve | 6.30 |
|  | 69.30 |
| *Add* Real Gains | 38.70 |
|  | 108.00 |
| *Less* Drawings | 10.00 |
| Closing Balance (at $t + 3$) | £98.00 |

*Period 4:* The opening balance of proprietor's capital (at $t + 3$) is £98 and the general price-level change ($p$) is 5 per cent, so the amount required for the capital maintenance reserve is £4.90 (= £98 × 0.05).

Income Statement for period 4, $t + 3$ to $t + 4$

| | £ |
|---|---|
| Sales | 44.00 |
| *Less* Current cost of goods sold | 38.00 |
| Current Cost profit | 6.00 |
| *Add* Real holding gains | 10.10 |
| Total Real Gains | £16.10 |

The real holding gains are calculated as the realised gain of £15 (Chapter 4, Appendix B), less the real capital maintenance requirement (£4.90). Alternatively, the gains and losses can be attributed to specific assets and liabilities as follows:

| | £ |
|---|---|
| Gain on cart(£15 – [£105 × 0.05]) | 9.75 |
| Gain on borrowing (£50 × 0.05) | 2.50 |
| Loss on holding cash (£5 × 0.05) | (0.25) |
| Loss on holding stocks (£38 × 0.05) | (1.90) |
| | £10.10 |

The real loss on holding stocks arises because it is assumed that their replacement cost did not rise during the period before sale, so that their current cost value failed to keep pace with inflation.

Balance Sheet at $t + 4$

| | £ | | £ |
|---|---|---|---|
| *Proprietor's Capital* | | | |
| Opening balance (at $t + 3$) | 98.00 | Cash | 169.00 |
| *Add* Allocation to capital | | | |
| maintenance reserve | 4.90 | | |
| | 102.90 | | |
| *Add* Real Gains | 16.10 | | |
| Closing Balance (at $t + 4$) | 119.00 | | |
| *Loan* | 50.00 | | |
| | £169.00 | | £169.00 |

A.4 THE KENNEDY INCOME STATEMENT

In this section, we illustrate Kennedy's 'simplified income statement', which was described in Section 6.7. This has the advantage of displaying a variety of information, including the 'geared' and 'real terms' profit figures illustrated earlier, and it provides a clear reconciliation of these figures. Alternative income statements of this broad type are illustrated and discussed in Edwards and Bell (1961).

*Period 1*

|  | £ |
|---|---|
| *Current Cost Operating Profit* | 6.00 |
| *Add* Geared Holding Gains | 7.50 |
| *Proprietary Profit* | 13.50 |
| *Add* Ungeared Holding gains | 22.50 |
| *Total Proprietary Gain* | 36.00 |
| *Less* Inflationary element of ungeared holding gains | 15.00 |
| *Inflation-corrected Proprietary Gain* | £21.00 |

The format of this statement is identical with that illustrated in the text, except that lines which do not apply to this illustration (such as interest received) have been omitted. The numbers may be compared with those in the 'geared' and 'real terms' statements which were illustrated earlier in this appendix. 'Proprietary Profit' here is what was called 'distributable profit' in the gearing example, and 'Inflation-corrected Proprietary Gain' is the same as 'real profit' in the real terms example. 'Total Proprietary Gain' is the same as 'total gains' in Chapter 4, Appendix B (illustrating current value accounting) and the holding gains calculated there are the sum of the geared and ungeared holding gains reported here.

*Period 2*

|  |  | £ |
|---|---|---:|
| | *Current cost operating profit (loss)* | (37.00) |
| *Add* | Adjustment for maintenance of real value | |
| | of monetary assets | 2.80 |
| | *Entity Profit* | (34.20) |
| *Add* | Geared holding gains | 11.46 |
| | *Proprietary Profit (loss)* | (22.74) |
| *Add* | Ungeared holding gains | 35.74 |
| | *Total Proprietary Gain* | 13.00 |
| *Less* | Inflationary element of ungeared holding | |
| | gains | 31.20 |
| | *Inflation-corrected Proprietary Gain (Loss)* | £(18.20) |

The only innovation in this period is the introduction of the monetary working capital adjustment (line 2), which was not relevant in the previous period. Because net monetary working capital was negative (net borrowing), this item is an addition to, rather than a deduction from, current cost operating profit.

*Period 3*

|  |  | £ |
|---|---|---:|
| | *Current cost operating profit (loss)* | (6.00) |
| *Add* | Adjustment for maintenance of real value | |
| | of monetary assets | 9.17 |
| | *Entity Profit* | 3.17 |
| *Add* | Geared holding gains | 18.51 |
| | *Proprietary Profit* | 21.68 |
| *Add* | Ungeared holding gains | 23.32 |
| | *Total Proprietary Gain* | 45.00 |
| *Less* | Inflationary element of ungeared holding | |
| | gains | 6.30 |
| | *Inflation-corrected Proprietary Gain* | £38.70 |

*Period 4*

Here, the gearing and monetary working capital adjustments were not considered relevant, so the statement will be simpler, the first three lines being taken from the current cost accounts (Chapter 4, Appendix B). The inflationary element of holding gains (£4.90) is the general price-level adjustment calculated earlier for real terms accounting.

|  |  | £ |
|---|---|---|
|  | *Current cost operating profit* | 6.00 |
| *Add* | Holding gains | 15.00 |
|  | *Total Proprietary Gain* | 21.00 |
| *Less* | Inflationary element of holding gains | 4.90 |
|  | *Inflation-corrected Proprietary Gain* | £16.10 |

## APPENDIX B: EMPIRICAL EVIDENCE RELATING TO ALTERNATIVE CAPITAL MAINTENANCE CONCEPTS

The capital maintenance concept is an essential ingredient in a profit calculation, so that the case studies described in Chapter 4, Appendix A and Section 5.9, which compare the results of computing alternative profit measures, necessarily involve a choice of capital maintenance concepts and often involve a comparison of the use of alternative capital maintenance concepts. Thus, for example, the study by Hope (1974) involves a comparison of money proprietary, real proprietary and entity capital maintenance concepts, and the studies by Gibbs (listed in Gibbs, 1979), include estimates for individual companies of the effects of implementing gearing adjustments, and alternative capital maintenance concepts. Inevitably, shortage of data has meant that less of these studies have been concerned with entity concepts, which require current value data, the comparison of money proprietary (which is commonly the basis of published accounts) with real proprietary measures (which require only additional knowledge of movements in a general price index) being much more common.

Empirical research on capital maintenance concepts in isolation from income measurement is relatively rare, but some interesting lines of research were started during the worldwide inflation of the 1970s and some might be fruitful areas for further research, although lack of empirical data has been a problem since the end of the short-lived experiments with current cost accounting in the 1980s. One such line of research is the question of whether geared companies do, in fact, gain on borrowing in a period of inflation, as suggested by 'real terms' capital maintenance concepts. Briscoe and Hawke (1976) found that UK companies with high gearing did not appear to have particularly high gains in shareholder wealth, in the inflationary period 1965–74. They attributed this result to price competition, which caused gains on borrowing to be passed on in lower prices. Peasnell and Skerratt (1976b) have criticised this study on methodological grounds (in particular, the Briscoe and Hawke study did not allow for the effects of factors other than gearing, which might wrongly be attributed to gearing) and, more fundamentally, have argued that the basic hypothesis is not relevant to the case for general price-level adjustment of capital. Even if heavily geared companies performed badly in times of inflation, this does not mean that they did not gain from borrowing, but merely implies that other aspects of their performance were bad. The latter criticism is particularly telling: the basic hypothesis certainly requires clearer specification before implications for accounting can be drawn. For example, the gain on borrowing is an offset to the interest rate, and companies will gain net from borrowing only if the interest rate fails to anticipate inflation fully. Furthermore, the issue of whether there has been a gain on debt should be separated, for financial reporting purposes, from the issue of whether this gain has benefitted shareholders (through higher profits) or customers (through lower prices). It is clear that fuller specification of the theory and the empirical methodology is required before the tests of the debtor/creditor hypothesis can give insights into the choice of accounting method.[29]

Another relevant area of empirical research is the question of the adequacy of depreciation funds to finance new investment. This is relevant to the entity capital maintenance concept and its implication that a backlog depreciation problem might arise, although it was made clear in the earlier discussion (Section 6.4) that this is a problem of liquidity rather than income measurement. Several of the papers by economists referred to in Chapter 4, Appendix A (such as Meeks, 1974; Merrett and Sykes, 1974, 1980) have been concerned, *inter alia*, with this problem. A study by Nguyen and Whittaker (1976), based on data for thirty-one industrial groups in the UK, suggested that a rate of inflation in excess of sixteen per cent would lead to a serious shortfall of amortisation funds, calculated on the conventional historical cost basis, in relation to replacement requirements. There is clearly scope for much more work of this type, using better data, particularly at the level of the individual firm, and exploring the implications of such a shortfall, e.g. in terms of dividend policy or the appropriate rates of capital allowance for tax purposes.

Finally, the controversial question of the relevance to individual shareholders of general index adjustments, as used in 'real terms' capital maintenance, has been explored by Peasnell and Skerratt (1978). They test the 'heterogeneity hypothesis', that changes in different individuals' purchasing power are not captured by changes in a general index, and find a 'remarkable degree of commonality' between groups, which leads them to reject the hypothesis and favour general index adjustment. Their study is based upon comparing the purchasing power of different income groups of individuals with changes in the general index, and this is an important limitation of the study. There is scope for further work, studying individuals, preferably selected from amongst the shareholders of a particular firm.

We have already noted (Chapter 4, Appendix A) that the current cost accounting experiments in the US (FAS33, FASB, 1979b) and the UK (SSAP16, Accounting Standards Committee, 1980) gave rise to research programmes to evaluate the consequences.

In the UK, the Carsberg Report (Carsberg and Page, 1984) explicitly included capital maintenance within its scope. The conclusion, as summarised by the leading author (Carsberg, 1984, pp. 40–42) was that the current cost operating income, based on operating capability, was used by analysts, government regulators and investors (as reflected in its impact on stock prices). However, the gearing adjustment (a component of the SSAP 16 system) was less popular, partly because it was based only on abating realised gains and therefore not a full gearing adjustment. There was also limited evidence that 'real terms' adjustments produced information that affected share prices. Hence, the provisional conclusion was that operating capital maintenance was a useful concept within a wider framework of income measurement which included proprietary measures, as in the Kennedy framework illustrated previously.

The research in the US was focused on the impact of different earnings measures on the stock market, rather than with the particular effect of different capital maintenance concepts. However, measuring earnings requires a capital maintenance concept, and replacement cost earnings implies an entity (operating capability) capital maintenance concept. Hence, the Beaver and Landsman (1983) study which rejected the usefulness (measured as impact on share prices) of replacement cost earnings might be interpreted also as a rejection of the entity measure of capital maintenance. However, general price-level adjustment, which implies proprietary capital maintenance, also failed Beaver and Landsman's test, although, as we have already noted, some later studies challenged the early Beaver and Landsman conclusions. Hence, the bulk of the studies done in the US at this time did not illuminate the question of choice of capital maintenance concept. An exception was the study by Haw and Lustgarten (1988), who examined the relationship between security returns and holding gains, as disclosed under the SEC's replacement cost requirements (ASR190, 1976) and the subsequent requirements of the FASB (FAS33, 1979). They found a statistically significant positive relationship between security returns and holding gains, consistent with the view that holding gains contain useful information for investors. Holding gains are part of comprehensive income, based on proprietary capital maintenance, but are excluded from an entity concept. Hence, this result suggests that the wider concept of capital maintenance is relevant, although it may still be useful to separate holding gains from other income, as is the result of applying proprietary capital maintenance, because holding gains may have a differential impact from that of other elements of comprehensive income.

In conclusion, relatively little empirical work has been done which relates specifically to the choice of capital maintenance concepts. This can be explained by the short-lived nature of the 'current cost revolution' of the late 1970s and early 1980s, which failed to generate sufficient data (partly because of its short life and partly because of its poor adoption rate) or to maintain sufficient interest from policy makers to justify the serious attention of researchers. However, such evidence as is available is broadly consistent with the view that both entity and proprietary measures of capital can yield useful information and that the eclectic approach of combining the two in a single comprehensive income statement, as advocated by Kennedy and others, has merit.

NOTES

1 Sterling and Lemke (1982) prefer to use the term 'physical', contrasting it with 'financial', rather than proprietary. This distinction is common in the literature, but it leads to some arid debates about the inappropriateness of physical replication rather than economic replacement.

2 Discounted net present value of future receipts is the measure of capital implicit in Hicks' No. 1 definition, so that this situation is one in which the Hicks No. 1 and No. 2 definitions of income lead to an identical measure, i.e. maintaining net present value in money terms maintains consumption in money terms. Alternatively if the No. 1 definition is taken to imply maintenance of net present value in real terms, it will be consistent with the No. 3 definition, real consumption maintenance, in this situation. The accountant's traditional approach to capital

maintenance is not, of course, based upon maintenance of net present value.

3 It is therefore necessary to adjust figures for previous years into current pounds, for comparative purposes. It is also desirable to adjust the flows in the profit and loss account from average pounds for the year to closing pounds, to achieve consistency with the closing balance sheet (Edwards and Bell, 1961, p. 253; Gynther, 1966, Chapter 12).

4 This is illustrated in Chapters 5 and 6 of Edwards and Bell's (1961) book.

5 A general review of Baxter's work, with further comment on this point, is Whittington (1975).

6 He deducts the full replacement cost (rather than merely CPP-adjusted historical cost) of goods sold and depreciation, in calculating 'current operating profit' (as in a CCA system) but then adds back 'real depreciation' (the excess of the replacement costs over CPP-adjusted historical cost) to obtain a 'Profit before Tax' which equals CPP-adjusted historical cost profit.

7 The converse is not true: certain advocates of replacement cost (notably Edwards and Bell) do not adopt an entity approach to capital maintenance. Samuelson (1980) argues that the entity view of capital is the only one which is consistent with replacement cost valuation. 'Current cost' and 'value to the owner' can be regarded as modified replacement cost, for present purposes.

8 Schmidt (1930) also includes a gearing adjustment. This is discussed in Section 6.6.

9 An alternative and more detailed discussion of the case against the entity approach is in Baxter (1975, Chapter 8).

10 Gynther (1966, Chapter 15) points out that the Philips system treats real holding gains as capital (an entity approach) but real holding losses as losses (a proprietary approach).

11 A critical commentary on their argument is Whittington (1980b).

12 For simplicity, we are assuming no inflation in this argument. If inflation occurs, the proprietary approach must be interpreted in real terms (i.e. with a general index adjustment) and the holding gain should be defined as a real holding gain.

13 Samuelson (1980), in an interesting paper advocating the entity approach, appears not to realise that, by rejecting the 'cost-saving' argument for holding gains as being based upon a hypothetical opportunity, he is also

rejecting the argument for preferring replacement cost depreciation rather than historical cost depreciation.

14 We should, however, remember that, as noted in Chapter 5, the validity and utility of this distinction have been questioned (Drake and Dopuch, 1965; Prakash and Sunder, 1979). In many business operations, holding assets is an integral activity and it is essentially arbitrary to distinguish between 'holding' and 'operating' gains.

15 Their 'current cost profit' is not strictly an entity concept, because, as Kennedy (1978a) points out, it is calculated after deducting interest, which is the financial return to the geared portion of the entity capital. Concentration on returns to proprietors, as represented by equity interests, is characteristic of the 'proprietary' approach, whereas a pure entity approach would focus on the returns to the total long-term capital of the entity, irrespective of the method of finance.

16 This is often the case when tax allowances are based upon depreciation charges: the consequent reduction in the tax burden may provide a significant proportion of the funds for replacement investment (Domar, 1953).

17 Preference shares have a fixed claim and conceptually are part of the gearing, although SSAP16 does not treat them as such.

18 The essential idea of the gearing adjustment appears on pp. 237–38 of the 1930 paper.

19 Although the Report did not specifically come down in favour of operating profit rather than total gains as the tax base.

20 The two other notable contemporary advocates of the gearing adjustment were Gibbs (1975, 1976) and Kennedy, who has provided an excellent summary of the debate (Kennedy, 1978a).

21 This is demonstrated rigorously in Forker (1980).

22 ED24 and SSAP16 use *average* gearing, rather than opening gearing, but the reason for this is not explained.

23 The entity orientation of the 'specific index' approach to equity capital maintenance can be seen clearly in Schmidt (1930).

24 Kennedy (1978a, p. 63). The whole question of using profit measures to determine dividend distribution is explored thoroughly by Egginton (1980), who concludes that income measures should be supplemented by liquidity measures for this purpose.

25 Although his system suffers from a minor error of double counting, which is demonstrated by Forker (1980) and discussed later.

26 This assumes that all monetary assets are classified as working capital, $M_{c,t}$, or are maintained only in nominal terms, and are not deducted from $L_f$ in calculating gearing.

27 This slip has been corrected in the illustration given earlier.

28 In the UK an important development was FRS3 (ASC, 1992), which proposed a Statement of Total Recognised Gains and Losses. The US introduced a Comprehensive Income Statement in FAS130 (FASB, 1997). Progress was slower in international standards (Camfferman and Zeff, 2007, pp. 292–93) but the revision of IAS1 (1997) made a tentative move towards comprehensive income, through a statement of changes in equity, and further progress has been made in subsequent revisions by the IASB.

29 Some American studies of the debtor/creditor hypothesis are surveyed in Freeman (1978).

# 7 Review

## 7.1 INTRODUCTION

The object of this chapter is to review the previous discussion (Section 7.2), and then to focus on three themes arising from it: firstly to identify the major issues that have to be resolved in order to select an appropriate measurement system for financial accounting (Section 7.3), secondly to identify the contribution of research (Section 7.4), and thirdly to review the evolution of practice (Section 7.5).

It should be clear from the earlier discussion that it is not appropriate to offer uniquely 'correct' solutions. The approach here is rather to discuss rational alternatives, each of which has its merits and its disadvantages, which might be more or less appropriate in different circumstances.

## 7.2 REVIEW OF THE EARLIER DISCUSSION

The discussion has focused on the problems raised by changing prices for financial accounting, i.e. the periodic reporting of the economic performance of a whole business entity to shareholders and other users of financial information who are external to the entity, in the sense that they are not involved in day-to-day management. This restriction still leaves us with a wide variety of users and uses which financial accounting information has to satisfy. These were discussed in Chapters 1 and 2. In a realistic world of uncertainty and imperfect and incomplete markets, it is unlikely that it will be possible to identify unique measures of value, capital and income which will satisfy all of these needs. Even when prices do not *change*, there will be a choice of *different* prices and values (such as historical cost, replacement cost, selling price and value in use) for any particular item in the accounts. Thus, financial accounting faces serious problems, in defining the appropriate range of information which should be disclosed, even in the absence of price changes. The discussion of price changes is often complicated by the fact that it proceeds from an inadequately specified view of the role and content of accounts in their absence: thus, the problems of changing prices become intertwined with the fundamental problems of financial accounting.

The accountant's traditional basis for financial reporting is a profit and loss account (which we have described by the more inclusive term 'income statement') and balance sheet based upon *historical cost*. This was discussed critically in Chapter 3. Historical cost has the advantage of providing a record of actual transactions, which gives it an important use for control purposes. The transactions base also imparts a degree of objectivity to financial reports based upon historical cost, although the assessment of accruals (accumulated costs and benefits, recorded in the closing balance sheet) is an important exception to this, involving either a degree of subjectivity or the application of completely arbitrary allocation rules. Outside the unrealistic conditions of the 'stationary state' (in which all prices remain constant), historical cost valuation is seriously deficient in failing to record in the balance sheet the changes in value of assets[1] which take place between the date of acquisition (historical cost) and the date of the balance sheet (current values, the changes being unrealised holding gains and losses). The historical cost profit and loss account also fails to record separately the difference between historical cost and value at the time of use (current cost, the difference being realised holding gains and losses). Thus, historical cost accounts fail, in the presence of relative price changes but the absence of general inflation, to provide measures of value and income which are likely to be adequate for assessing the economic performance of the accounting entity. These problems are exacerbated by the presence of general inflation (or deflation) which tends to widen the gap between current values and historical cost, due to the decline (or increase) in the value of the monetary unit, in addition to any distortion caused by relative price changes.

*Inflation* is commonly taken to imply an increase in the general price level, i.e. a declining value of money relative to goods. This can, in theory, occur when the prices of goods relative to one another remain constant. A method of eliminating the effects on accounts of general inflation is the Constant (or Current) Purchasing Power method (CPP) discussed in Chapter 5. This method is theoretically satisfactory, provided that inflation is of the pure 'no relative price change' variety. In practice, this is not usually the case, and we are faced with difficulties both in asset (and liability) valuation and in defining the capital to be maintained for income measurement purposes. The valuation problem can be dealt with by adopting current values of the specific assets and liabilities concerned, although, as we saw in Chapter 4, the precise choice of current value method is problematic in practice.

A current asset valuation base combined with CPP adjustment of items other than asset values yields 'real terms' accounting. The capital maintenance problem is dealt with in this system by applying a general purchasing power index, a 'proprietary' measure of capital, but some theorists have argued that an index specific to the assets of the firm should be adopted, implementing an 'entity' approach which aims to preserve the productive power of the entity intact. The divergence between the two capital maintenance concepts depends upon there being changes in the prices of the firm's assets relative to the general price index. It can also be argued that the CPP adjustment method is ill-founded because the general index used does not reflect changes in the cost of living of individual shareholders: this argument also depends on there being relative price changes, although the relevant comparison is now between the cost of goods consumed by the individual shareholder (rather than the business) and the general index.

It must, however, be stressed that given the limitations of accounting measurement, such as the failure to recognise many intangible assets that are internally generated, neither the isolation of the effects of general inflation nor the introduction of current values into accounts is likely to produce unambiguously 'true' figures for income or capital. The most that can be hoped for is that the accounts will yield a set of information relating to the economic progress of the entity, which will be relevant to a wide range of external users of financial information. In Chapter 4, various alternative valuation bases were examined from this standpoint. The two main competing bases are replacement cost and net realisable value. Both of these bases are based upon market prices and may therefore be regarded as being objective when such prices are available, although it is easy to conceive of situations in which they are unlikely to be available, e.g. in calculating the value of a partly used plant which has a highly specialised function. Each basis is clearly relevant to particular uses and circumstances. Replacement cost has obvious relevance for assessing the economic performance of a continuing business in which realisation is indirect (involving use in association with other factors of production) and replacement will take place, but net realisable value is relevant to situations and purposes in which direct realisation is contemplated, e.g. in assessing the security for a loan. It is also clear that each basis requires a precise definition of the assumed uses and circumstances before it can be implemented in practice, e.g. replacement cost requires a definition as to whether it is to be based upon physical replacement ('reproduction cost'), replacement of the service ('maintenance of operating capacity') or some alternative criterion, and the choice of definition will be determined by the use to which the information is to be put, as well as the specific circumstances of the business, e.g. replacement cost requires an assumption that future profit margins will justify replacement. It is difficult to avoid the conclusion that both replacement cost and net realisable value would be of potential interest to a wide range of users of accounts and should therefore both be reported, either in a multiple-column format or in the notes to the accounts, if that could be achieved reliably and without undue complexity and cost. However, most writers on the subject have espoused a single valuation basis to the exclusion of all others.

A recent example of the apparent pursuit of a single valuation base has been the support for fair value which was apparent in some of the early pronouncements of the IASB (Whittington, 2008b). However, more recently, the IASB (2015), in its Exposure Draft on the revision of the conceptual framework, has supported the use of a variety of valuation methods, the method used for a particular item being selected on the basis of how that item will be used by the business.

A third valuation basis, which is potentially important for decision making, is present value, i.e. the discounted present value of the expected future cash flows generated by assets in their current use. This suffers from the obvious problem of subjectivity, depending entirely upon estimates of future cash flows and discount rates. This makes it unsuitable for reporting purposes, apart from special circumstances such as impairment measurement, although one possible practical approach is to select other market values as surrogates for present value. This, however, amounts to using closeness to present value as a means of selecting between the two more objective, market-validated bases (replacement cost and net realisable value), rather than being a direct application of the present value basis. Furthermore, there are conceptual difficulties in relation to the level of aggregation appropriate for present value calculations, because the joint nature of income generation means that it is difficult to separate out the individual contributions of specific assets to future cash flows (an example of the allocation problem in accounting, which was explored by Thomas, 1969, 1974). Moreover, the aggregate value of the firm will include intangible assets, notably goodwill (Johnson and Petrone, 1998) which are commonly regarded as too uncertain in their existence or outcome to justify recognition in financial accounts except when their value is confirmed by a market transaction such as a take-over.

If the object of the information is to provide a present value of the whole firm (as might be the case if shareholders wished to value their investment) the whole firm should be valued, rather than summing estimates for individual assets. This is a formidable task (especially as different shareholders might wish to apply different discount rates) and it might be more realistically accomplished by providing information which might be the basis of estimates by individual users of accounts, rather than by attempting a direct estimate in the accounts. Moreover, even if present values were reported, they should, for many purposes, be compared with valuations based on alternative assumptions about the disposition of assets (such as net realisable values), so that their use should not preclude the multiple measures approach.

An alternative to reporting either a single 'pure' valuation basis (such as replacement cost) or multiple reporting of several measurement bases is to adopt an eclectic valuation basis which selects the valuation most appropriate to the circumstances of the particular asset being valued. An example of this is 'value to the owner' (deprival value) which selects one of replacement cost, net realisable value or present value in use, according to their relative values (alternatively expressed as replacement cost or 'recoverable amount', whichever is the lower). Although this seems to be a sensible pragmatic principle if it is essential to report only one value, the calculation of value to the owner would require knowledge of its three components (net realisable value, replacement cost and value in use). Thus, multiple-column reporting would be possible at no additional cost to the preparers of accounts and would provide more information to users, although it might raise the problem of 'information overload'. Another possible criticism of deprival value from an aggregation perspective is that different items in the same accounts may be reported on different valuation bases (depending upon which of the three components becomes deprival value) so that summing them amounts to 'adding apples and pears' (aggregating heterogeneous measurements), but this criticism is valid only if it is intended that the individual items in the accounts should sum to ideal measures such as the value of shareholders' equity interests.

Profit measurement is usually assumed to be an important purpose of accounts, and this requires a *capital maintenance* concept

as well as a valuation basis. The main competing capital maintenance concepts were discussed in Chapter 6. The two central concepts
of capital maintenance are the proprietary approach and the entity
approach. The proprietary approach views the capital of the firm as a
fund of wealth attributable to the proprietors (or equity shareholders).
When the general price level is stable, the money amount of opening
capital must be maintained before a profit is recognised. When the
general price-level changes, giving rise to inflation or deflation, it is
the real purchasing power of opening capital which is to be maintained, real purchasing power being derived by the application of a
general price index, to yield a capital measure which aims to maintain
command over goods and services in general. The entity approach, on
the other hand, aims to preserve the productive power of the business intact. When all prices are constant, this again leads to money
capital maintenance, but when there are relative price changes, the
entity approach requires the adjustment of opening money capital by
changes in specific indices, so that the cost of maintaining the specific
assets necessary to maintain productive capacity is deducted from revenue before a profit is recognised. Both of these approaches have their
problems (e.g. of defining the appropriate indices to be applied when
prices change) and both have their uses, but fortunately, as we saw in
Chapter 6, both can be reported in a single income statement, without resorting to multiple-column reporting, so that they need not be
regarded as mutually exclusive alternatives.

One eclectic capital maintenance concept was discussed
because it has received considerable attention in the theoretical literature and as a basis for practical reform of financial accounting,
although it has not become a permanent feature of accepted practice. This treats the geared (loan financed) portion of the firm's net
assets on the money capital maintenance basis (i.e. the proprietary
basis with no inflation adjustment). The ungeared portion (equity-
financed) is treated on an entity basis, i.e. specific assets must be
maintained before a profit is recognised. The gearing adjustment can
be used as a step in the process of moving from an entity basis to a

proprietary basis within a single appropriation statement, so that it need not be regarded as competing with the other bases. However, it is possible to question the value of the gearing adjustment relative to alternative intermediate steps which might, for example, divide holding gains on assets into real and fictitious (due to changes in the purchasing power of money) elements and recognise the gain on borrowing fixed money sums and the loss on holding fixed money sums during periods of inflation. However, the precise definition and measurement of holding gains is itself not without difficulty, especially in businesses in which holding assets is an integral part of operating activities.

## 7.3 THE MAJOR ISSUES IN MEASUREMENT

It is clear from this review of the earlier discussion that the primary problem in measurement for financial accounting is to establish what accounting system is appropriate in the presence of relative price changes but in the absence of general inflation. Only when this prior problem is solved is it possible to define clearly what additional problems are introduced by general inflation and to suggest possible solutions. It is also clear that, although a wide range of possible models is available, it is unlikely, given the uncertainties and imperfections of the markets to which accounting information relates, that any single model will be appropriate to all users and uses. Indeed, it seems unlikely that a single model will be sufficient to meet the needs of any particular use or user in all circumstances. Thus, another important issue is the question of how much variety of information can be reported without imposing excessive costs on the reporting entity or creating confusion in the minds of potential users.

The following are important issues in deciding the appropriate form of reporting, even in the absence of general inflation:

1. *The scope of the reports.* Balance sheets and income statements are the fundamental *ex post* financial statements. The degree of detail offered is an important issue, but more fundamental is the question

of providing additional statements, such as statements of changes in equity (to provide a complete reconciliation between comprehensive income statements and the equity interest reported in the associated balance sheets), segmental reports or cash flow statements. Perhaps of even greater importance is the question of providing *ex ante* data, which are of clear relevance to decision making but are highly subjective.

2. *The valuation basis.* If it is not possible to produce a wide variety of valuations of each asset or obligation, we must decide which are the most important valuation bases to be used in accounts. We must devise methods for choosing between them if they cannot all be reported in the same statements.

3. *The capital maintenance concept.* It seems likely that income measurement in some form will remain an important objective of financial reporting for some time to come, even if the emphasis might be on components of comprehensive income (such as trading profit) rather than a single aggregate measure. It is therefore essential to specify which capital maintenance concepts should be used, e.g. a cost-based measure may be appropriate for measuring operating profit but a financial measure may be more appropriate for measuring holding gains. Fortunately, it is possible to report a variety of capital maintenance measures, based upon alternative concepts, without undue complication, so that the choice of capital maintenance concept does not raise such acute problems as the choice of valuation base. Reporting a variety of measures may have a useful educational effect on those users who are 'functionally fixated' on a single profit measure, wrongly believing it to be a 'true' measure which is valid in all uses and circumstances.

Having established the appropriate form of financial reporting, we need to establish the problems raised by inflation, i.e. general price-level changes. These problems may be subsumed under a single heading: *the choice of the unit of measurement.* The essential choice is between choosing a monetary unit whose value will depend upon the date of the transaction or the valuation date and one whose value is constant in real terms. The difference between the two measuring units will be most apparent in the case of historical cost systems, in which a high proportion of asset values will be recorded in past purchasing power units of different dates. Current value systems largely eliminate this problem for asset and liability values, since current values are, by definition, recorded consistently in current currency units, but the capital to be maintained when measuring income and gains will still need to be translated into current units if a 'real terms' proprietary measure is used. If an entity measure is used, the application of replacement costs or specific indices will ensure that the capital to be maintained is automatically expressed in current currency units. The remaining real terms adjustment to be made to conventional current value accounts will be to translate the transactions recorded in the profit and loss account into current (year-end) purchasing power units, where they are recorded in average-for-the-year prices. The time lag involved is relatively short, so this adjustment should not be very large, unless the rate of inflation during the year has been high. Finally, for comparative purposes, when current purchasing power is the standard unit (as opposed to constant purchasing power with a base in the past) data for past years should be translated into current purchasing power, and forecasts for future years should also be expressed in current units.

There are two important issues relating to the choice between a variable money unit ('actual £s') and a constant unit ('current £s'). First, there is the question of whether the concept of constant purchasing power has any operational meaning, and, secondly, it is important to recognise that, in many uses of accounting data, monetary measures are preferable to constant purchasing power measures. It has been argued, notably by the Sandilands Committee, that there is no such thing as a general price level, merely movements of individual prices, and it is not possible, therefore, to construct a unit of constant purchasing power using general indices. This view was discussed at some length in Chapter 5. In its more extreme form it might be taken to imply that inflation does not exist and there can be no problem of inflation accounting. On a more pragmatic level it leads to an argument about the construction of price indices and their utility to users of accounts. The second issue is less contentious: it is clear that not all accounting measures should be measured in 'real' units for all purposes for which they are used. For example, if we wish to evaluate an accounting income measure in terms of an interest rate observed in the market (e.g. by discounting the income measure to give an estimate of present value) no inflation adjustment of the income measure is appropriate, since the market interest rate is applicable to money returns (in 'actual £s') not real returns ('current £s'). Equally, various forms of ratio analysis eliminate or reduce the scale effects of the changing value of the monetary unit, and this was suggested by the Sandilands Report as a method of avoiding the need for comparative historical data expressed in real terms. Thus, there is a case for expressing accounts in both 'money' and 'real' terms, and most reform proposals have adopted this approach, by making various inflation adjustments in supplementary statements rather than the main accounts.

This summarises the main theoretical issues which have to be considered in deciding upon the appropriate method or methods of measurement to be used in financial reporting. There are, however, at least two types of practical constraint which have to be considered. First, there are the constraints on the volume of information which can be included in the accounts. On the supply side we have to consider the cost to the firm of providing a broad range of information, and on the demand side we have to consider the limitations of the user's capacity to absorb and interpret information. Secondly, there are the constraints imposed by the institutional environment in which accounting standards are framed. The practical reform of accounting practice is constrained by the current state of practice and the past experience and beliefs of accountants, managers, users of accounts and governments. This theme will be developed in the final sections of this chapter.

## 7.4 THE CONTRIBUTION OF RESEARCH

Most of the ideas and systems discussed in earlier chapters have been the result of what might be described as research. In the earlier days, this was done by practitioners who may or may not have been attached to academic institutions. In the early twentieth century, practitioner-academics were particularly prominent contributors, examples being Limperg in the Netherlands, Schmidt and Schmalenbach in Germany, and Sweeney in the US. They were able to draw upon both the ideas of academics, particularly economists, and practical experience of the problems of implementation. The style of this research was theoretical, in the sense that it attempted to devise and advocate measurement systems on the basis of theoretical assumptions, supported by deductive reasoning. Watts and Zimmerman (1978) describe this approach pejoratively as 'normative', i.e. saying how accounting *ought* to be done. Some empirical work was also done at this time, but it was mainly limited to the case study approach, demonstrating the practicality or materiality of alternative measurement methods.

By the mid-twentieth century, accounting had become more firmly established in universities, and research on measurement debate became mainly the province of academics, although they were often involved with practitioners through professional and regulatory bodies. Examples were Chambers (1966), Edwards and Bell (1961), Gynther (1966), Revsine (1970) and Sterling (1970). They introduced greater theoretical sophistication, often drawing upon economics (e.g. Edwards and Bell's residual income approach to valuation) and created in the 1960s what Carl Nelson (1973) memorably described as 'a golden Age in the history of a priori research in accounting'.

This 'Golden Age' was focused on the development of ambitious models of measurement which attempted to prescribe (hence the description 'normative') a single measurement technique that should be applied to all elements in the accounts. These models provided fuel for the vigorous debate on accounting for price changes, which was particularly active during the late 1960s and 1970s, but it became clear that they could not provide a definitive solution. Theoretical models depend upon assumptions, and different assumptions will lead to different conclusions. Hence, Watts and Zimmerman (1979), in their influential paper, characterised 'normative' theory as supplying 'the market for excuses'. This harmonised well with the mood of the time, because current cost accounting was very controversial and soon to be abandoned by standard-setters, despite its theoretical appeal. Watts and Zimmerman advocated 'positive accounting theory', by which they meant theory supported by empirical testing. This too harmonised with contemporary developments, because, following pioneering papers by Ball and Brown (1968), Beaver (1968) and other young researchers, aided by developments in computing, empirical research in accounting (on such issues as stock market reaction to the publication of accounting results) had reached a new level of sophistication (econometric testing of models rather than surveying and describing) and was about to dominate academic research for several decades. It was therefore particularly apt that the ultimate rejection of CCA in the US and the UK was supported by empirical research evidence (the Beaver and Landsman report in the US and the Carsberg Report in the UK, as discussed earlier in Chapter 4, Appendix A). However, we have seen that this evidence was not decisive, so its use could be interpreted as an indication that empirical evidence too can be used to supply the 'market for excuses'.

An important theoretical paper published in 1979 was by Beaver and Demski. This analysed the informational role of financial accounts, starting from the assumption that they are only needed when markets are imperfect and incomplete (perfect markets are fully informed, so that the accounts add no information). In such markets, such measures as profit or value are ill-defined ('fuzzy'), depending on the needs and preferences of the individual user. Hence, the role of accounting is to provide information that will help users to make their own subjective judgements rather than providing precise global answers to their needs. In other words, accounting provides useful *information* as input to users' models rather than precise *measures* of variables such as income or value. This approach provides a rationale for rejecting some of the grand models of the Golden Age and for adopting a more specific and limited approach to research in accounting measurement, such as has been adopted by most researchers (both empirical and theoretical) since that time.

The research that has been carried out since 1980 has been reviewed briefly in appendices to earlier chapters. A review that relates research on measurement during this period to developments in practice is Whittington (2015). Empirical research, which was the predominant paradigm of the period, is constrained by the availability of data which, in turn, depends upon the methods used in practice. Hence, after the brief experiments with CCA in English-speaking countries in the early 1980s, there was little further opportunity to study the practical consequences of CCA systems. There were limited opportunities to study the effects of CPP in hyper-inflationary economies, but the greatest opportunity for empirical research lay in the piecemeal use of current values (usually described loosely as 'fair values') for certain types of asset or liability, within what was otherwise a historical cost system. The most obvious of these was financial instruments, which, depending upon circumstances, could be measured either at amortised cost or at fair value. The empirical evidence relating to fair value measurements is surveyed by Landsman (2007). The picture that emerges is, as might be expected, not decisive. The banking crisis which started in 2007 stimulated theoretical and empirical research to examine the allegation that the crisis was facilitated by fair value accounting, which provided a transmission mechanism when markets became illiquid (Plantin et al., 2008). This research focused on the banks' holdings of financial instruments, rather than econometric modelling. The broad conclusion to emerge was that fair value was not a significant contributor to the crisis in the actual circumstances that prevailed (Amel-Zadeh and Meeks, 2013).

Theoretical research was not constrained by data availability but it became unfashionable after Watts and Zimmerman's 'market for excuses' critique, although this unpopularity may have owed less to Watts and Zimmerman than to the general disillusion with the indecisive conclusion to the Golden Age debates on measurement and the subsequent collapse of CCA in the accounting standards arena. It was also probably encouraged by the changing technology of research (large databases, greater computing power and easily accessed econometric software packages) and the changing skills of researchers (better training in finance and econometrics and less training in accounting techniques). Despite this constraint, theoretical work continued, and some of it has been described in earlier chapters. It was mainly confined to specific circumstances and objectives, rather than developing global 'best' measures, as in the Golden Age, but this was perhaps a more fruitful approach.

The analysis of Value to the Business (VTB) continued. A notable contribution was Edwards et al. (1987), which demonstrated the relevance of VTB to the detection of monopoly profits. This was particularly relevant to the public-sector regulatory use of VTB which persists to the present time. Other notable contributions include Stark (1997), which introduces real options into the VTB calculus, and Horton et al. (2011), which considers the application of VTB to contract liabilities (and hence to revenue recognition).

Fair Value was much discussed, and sometimes adopted, by standard-setters during this period. It was not as prominent in the theoretical academic literature as in the empirical literature, perhaps reflecting the contemporary emphasis on empirical research. However, there was some theoretical discussion of fair value. For example, it was supported by Barth (2007) and Hague (2007) on the grounds of its consistency with the conceptual frameworks of the FASB and the IASB, and a contrary view was expressed by Whittington (2008a), who argued against the 'fair value view' implicit in the IASB Framework on the ground that it made unrealistic assumptions about the perfection and completeness of markets. The latter argument became particularly pertinent during the Financial Crisis of 2007 onwards, when the collapse of liquidity rendered selling prices hypothetical for many financial instruments. Fair Value was also critiqued by, amongst others, Penman (2007) and Nissim and Penman (2008), who suggested that cost measures were a better basis than fair value for valuing the ongoing operations of a business, whereas fair value was more appropriate for measuring assets held for sale.

Apart from research specifically directed towards measurement methods, there has been a considerable volume of empirical and theoretical research on the broader context of financial reporting which both informs and constrains the choice of measurement method. An accessible survey of this research insofar as it relates to the role of financial reporting in informing capital providers is Cascino et al. (2013): its twenty-four-page list of references demonstrates that its volume and variety are too great to be given a proper discussion here. However, some of the implications for measurement require acknowledgement.

An important strand in this contextual research is *stewardship*, i.e. the accountability of management to capital providers and also to others to whom it has a responsibility. This has been an important issue in the discussion of the IASB/FASB Conceptual Framework revision, which, in its early stages, gave prominence to decision-usefulness, relegating stewardship to a subsidiary role. A stewardship perspective draws attention to the informational asymmetry between the steward (management) who prepares the accounts and the external recipient of the accounts who fulfils a monitoring role. This has been analysed theoretically by applying agency theory (Wagenhofer, 2015), the steward being the agent. The agent often has incentives to misrepresent the situation (e.g. because remuneration may be based on accounting performance), so the principal requires information that can be relied upon to minimise potential misrepresentation. This leads to conventions such as conservatism, the asymmetric recognition of gains and losses (Watts, 2003a, 2003b). Conservatism may express itself in the choice of measurement method, as in the traditional valuation rule for current assets 'historical cost or market value, whichever is the lower'. Stewardship and conservatism are current subjects both of research and of policy, particularly in relation to the IASB Conceptual Framework.

Another important strand is *valuation* of the business entity as a whole, or its equity capital. This is an important aspect of decision-usefulness, which is generally accepted as one (if not the principal) use of financial reports. There have been many empirical studies of how investment analysts and others use accounts for this purpose (e.g. Barker, 1999). Professional analysts appear to use valuation methods based on discounting expected earnings. These usually incorporate a finite time horizon, beyond which earnings cannot be predicted reliably, and this requires an estimate of terminal value (capital value at the horizon) to complete the valuation. Important theoretical insights into this type of model, supported subsequently by extensive empirical studies, have been provided by the work of Ohlson (Ohlson, 1995; Feltham and Ohlson, 1995, and subsequent extensions).[2]

The Ohlson model was originally designed as a theoretical analysis of the fundamental relationship between accounting and valuation. By assuming that accounting income is calculated on a *clean surplus* basis (as in our definition, in earlier chapters, of comprehensive income), Ohlson demonstrates that the dividend valuation model can be re-expressed in terms of accounting profits rather than dividends. His derivation of value divides it into two components, the book (accounting) value of the business, upon which a normal rate of return (cost of capital) is required, and the present value of abnormal profits, which are profits in excess of the normal cost of capital times book value. This is a residual income model, which has origins in earlier theoretical work (Preinreich, 1936; Edwards and Bell, 1961; Peasnell, 1982). Ohlson adds to this model a structure which determines the expected future pattern of abnormal profits. Essentially, this structure, which is described as 'linear information dynamics', assumes that abnormal profits will gradually disappear over time, so that their present value is finite. Adding this value to book value gives the present value of the proprietorship interest in the business.

The Ohlson model has focused attention on the fundamental valuation role of financial accounts, consistent with the 'decision-usefulness' objective. Whereas the earlier empirical research, exemplified by Ball and Brown (1968), had focused on the incremental effect of accounting information (typically earnings) on changes in share prices, the Ohlson model explored the relationship of aggregate accounting information to total share price. As a practical valuation model, empirical tests suggest that the Ohlson model performs better than the traditional dividend valuation models (Walker, 1997), which project dividends up to a finite time horizon and add a terminal value for returns beyond the horizon, often based on questionable assumptions such as constant future growth.

An important limitation of the Ohlson approach is that it does not address directly the question of which measurement method is most appropriate in the financial statements. It does have a concept of 'unbiased accounting', which requires book value to equal the net present value of expected future cash flows at the time when abnormal profits converge to zero, but the measurement technique that will achieve this is not discussed. Some commentators (such as Walker, 1997) have suggested that current cost might be an appropriate measurement basis for book value, because the decay of abnormal profits is attributable to market competition which would tend to drive down profits to a normal rate of return on entry cost (current cost). In practice, empirical studies use actual accounting data, and their results suggest that book values are under-stated, so that abnormal profits converge to a positive amount rather than zero. This amount is usually referred to as a measure of accounting conservatism (Watts, 2003a, 2003b), attributable both to the choice of measurement method (including historical cost) and conservative recognition criteria (such as the non-recognition of many internally generated intangible assets).

The Ohlson approach has produced important insights into the role of financial accounts in the valuation of proprietary interests in businesses, but it has not produced definitive guidance on what accounting measurement techniques will best suit this purpose. In particular, the role of 'dirty surplus' (non-articulating) profit and loss items needs further exploration. These were advocated, for example, in Black's (1980, 1993) discussion of accounting earnings measures that would serve as inputs into valuation (essentially an informational rather than a measurement approach). Equally, there is the possibility that further disaggregation of the income statement will produce more refined information for valuation purposes. For example, Nissim and Penman's (2008) study uses a valuation model derived from Ohlson but separates operating assets (recorded at historical cost) from assets held for sale value (recorded at fair value).

To summarise, the research of recent years has clarified many aspects of financial accounting, and particularly measurement. This has led to useful insights rather than the grand global solutions that were proposed during the Golden Age. This more modest approach is consistent with contemporary developments in practice, which are reviewed briefly in the following section. In particular, the use of multiple measurement methods, based on the facts and circumstance surrounding a particular asset or liability, is consistent with an informational perspective, and the emphasis on providing comprehensive income measures (together with others) is consistent with the 'clean surplus' assumption that was a core element of the Ohlson model.

## 7.5 MEASUREMENT IN ACCOUNTING PRACTICE

The earlier discussion has concentrated on explaining the alternative theoretical models which are available, with occasional references to the often scanty empirical evidence. The variety of alternative models available, combined with the indecisiveness and piecemeal nature of the empirical results, would be quite sufficient to explain the lack of consensus in both academic and professional circles on the best system of measurement in accounting. However, it would be misleading to suggest that this difficulty can be resolved merely by more research, refining and clarifying alternative theories and testing their assumptions and practicality. The reason for this is that the debate on measurement in accounting is a historical and political process.

The receptiveness of various groups and individuals to ideas relating to measurement is coloured by their education and past experience and by the current state of accounting practice,[3] all of which are historical facts. Equally, different groups have different interests in relation to accounting data, and accounting standard-setting is therefore inevitably a political process, compromising between the interests of different groups. For example, it is not surprising that professional bodies have tended initially to favour historical-cost-based CPP systems as a method of inflation accounting (Tweedie and Whittington, 1984): the index adjustments made in CPP rely on indices which are publicly available and accepted as being objective, so that their application involves professional practitioners in much less risk of controversy than if they become involved in the more subjective valuations required by current value accounting. Equally, business managers, faced by rising production costs in a period of inflation, are likely to favour replacement cost or current cost accounting (probably excluding all holding gains from income) because it gives them an apparent justification for meeting the threat of rising costs by increasing prices, and possibly also by holding down wages (since the form of accounting which shows the lowest profit will presumably favour management's case in wage negotiations), and by paying less taxes and dividends.

This interpretation of the accounting measurement debate is not new. Sweeney, the great American pioneer of inflation accounting, explained developments during the inter-war period as follows:

'A period of inflation causes business management to arise in unanimous protest. For then expenses become understated, profits and income taxes overstated, and union-and-stockholder desires insatiable. Business management is well informed, well financed, and well organized. It likes to bask in the spurious glory of overstated profits – but it likes to blast the accompanying excessive wages, income taxes and dividends'. (Sweeney, 1964, p. xxv)

A number of later writers have made similar observations. McRae and Dobbins (1974) surveyed the inflation accounting debate in Britain and concluded that technical arguments had been used 'to obscure the true issues which concern the personal interests of the various groups affected by inflation adjustment'. Aranya (1974) provides a historical survey of the evolution of British financial reporting, interpreted in terms of the conflicting interests of suppliers and users of reports. Beja and Aharoni (1977) demonstrate that many of the problems of inflation accounting are caused by the operation of legal and institutional constraints, such as tax laws, dividend rules and debt levels. Mumford (1979) compares the pattern of the inflation accounting debate in the UK during the 1948–54 inflation with that in the 1973–78 period, finding certain parallels between the two periods. Watts and Zimmerman (1978) propose a 'positive theory of accounting', based upon the assumption that managers' attitudes to accounting standards are formed by the implications of the standards for their self-interest in such matters as taxes, public regulation and management compensation (salaries): from this they predict that large firms will favour changes which reduce reported earnings, and this is confirmed by an empirical analysis of corporate submissions in response to the FASB's Discussion Memorandum on General Price Level Adjustment. Watts and Zimmerman's later 1979 paper concludes that 'the predominant function of accounting theories is now to supply excuses which satisfy the demand created by the political process; consequently accounting theories have become increasingly normative' (Watts and Zimmerman, 1979, p. 300).

Watts and Zimmerman's position is extreme and they admit that their evidence 'is somewhat "casual", and not as rigorous as we would like' (Watts and Zimmerman, 1979, p. 289). However, it is clear that the debate on price-change accounting during the inflationary period of the 1960s and 1970s, on which they based their analysis, was not resolved by theoretical discussion alone, and the outcome was determined by a process of negotiation between interested parties which can be described broadly as political, although both theory and empirical evidence did play a part. Since that time, the debate on measurement has continued to be contested by interested parties. For example in the discussion of whether fair value contributed to the Financial Crisis, it was a convenient excuse for bankers to assert that the root of the problem lay with the accountants (through the instability resulting from marking financial securities to market) rather than with their own behaviour (by investing heavily in risky financial securities). In recent years, many researchers have followed Watts and Zimmerman by studying the effects of lobbying behaviour on accounting standards and the factors determining the accounting choices made by individual firms. There have also been historical studies of the accounting standard-setting process (such as Camfferman and Zeff's, 2007, 2015, studies of the IASC and the IASB) which have recorded the complex interactions involved.

Measurement has continued to be a central issue in the accounting standard-setting process. We have seen in earlier chapters that the inflation accounting debate resulted in an experiment (notably in the US and the UK) with supplementary disclosure of current cost information, which was abandoned in the early 1980s. The withdrawal of current cost accounting can be explained substantially by economic events, notably the greater stability of prices (Tweedie and Whittington, 1997). However, subsequent events indicated a continuing need to consider alternatives to historical cost. In the 1990s, the growth and increasing sophistication of financial markets and treasury activities by companies meant that there was a need for some method of attributing a current value to financial instruments in some circumstances. The solution to this, as adopted in FASB standards and in the IASC standard (IAS 39, 1998) which substantially followed them, was fair value, based on selling price rather than cost as the current value, although the definition of fair value was not clarified until much later. Fair value was then adopted by the IASC in its final standards, on investment property (IAS 40, 2000) and on agriculture (IAS 41). When the IASB took over the work of the IASC (2001), it appeared to favour fair value in a number of new applications (Whittington,

2008a), but this changed during the Financial Crisis of 2007 onwards, when economic events again intervened to change the direction of accounting standards policy. The crisis drew attention to the fact that market selling prices are not always available or susceptible to reliable estimation. They might therefore be therefore particularly unsuitable for stewardship purposes, and many critics of the IASB objected to its proposal to eliminate stewardship as a primary objective (equal with decision-usefulness) in its conceptual framework revision (International Accounting Standards Board, 2010). Subsequently, the IASB withdrew from this provision and proposed to reinstate the stewardship objective (International Accounting Standards Board, 2015). Also, it adopted a more eclectic view of measurement, accepting that different measurement methods might be appropriate for different items in the accounts. The current position of the IASB, as indicated in the measurement section of the latest Exposure Draft from its conceptual framework revision project (International Accounting Standards Board, 2015), is that alternative valuation methods should be allowed in financial reporting standards, the method should be chosen according to the nature of the asset and the purpose for which it is held, and guidance on the measurement method appropriate to particular types of transaction will be provided at the standards level rather than in the conceptual framework. However, this is still (as of 2016) under discussion.

Meanwhile, standard -setting continues at the IASB, including decisions about measurement. Historical cost remains the predominant measurement method, particularly on initial recognition of an item in the accounts. Impairment testing is widely applied, to reduce asset values to a lower recoverable amount when the previous carrying amount is not recoverable. Recoverable amount is a current value, but not fair value, and impairment testing is asymmetrical (assets are not written up to a higher recoverable amount), so that it is an application of prudence, which is particularly relevant to the stewardship role of financial reporting. Where assets (and liabilities) are held with the intention of realising gains and losses on their capital value (as with investment properties and some financial instruments) they may be recorded at current value, which is usually an exit price such as fair value or fair value, less cost to sell. However, the calculation of fair value (as in FRS 13, 2011, which is based on the FASB standard) acknowledges that market prices may not be available, and allows proxies (particularly model-based estimates) which are far removed from the pure exit price concept. Current cost measures, including deprival value, do not feature explicitly in the IASB's current standards, although entry prices are allowed as proxies when exit prices are not available and, if impairment testing (lower recoverable amount) is added to that, the resulting measure is, in practical terms, deprival value.

Hence, the state of current practice is one of eclectic measurement methods, choosing between a variety of methods on the basis of which is considered to be appropriate in the circumstances. This is remarkably consistent with the *information* perspective (as opposed to the *measurement* perspective) which was described in our earlier discussion of theory. This recognises that ideal, objective measures provided by complete and perfect markets are not attainable, so that the accounts can give only partial information to meet the needs of particular users. Hence, different measures may be appropriate in different circumstances. In the absence of an ideal measurement method with universal application, the challenge to the accounting standard-setter is to define which measures are appropriate in particular circumstances, and to do this in a way that provides consistency, transparency and coherence to the accounts, so that the user understands the information and can make appropriate use of it. The conceptual framework is intended to help in this process by providing a consistent context for the standard-setter's judgements, but it is still incomplete.

## 7.6 CONCLUSION

This book has attempted to survey the various models which have been proposed to deal with the problems of accounting in conditions of changing prices, including relative price changes and changes in the general price level (inflation). The general drift of the argument should by now be clear: there is no universally 'correct' measurement method which will serve all uses and users well in all circumstances. Financial reports should therefore provide a range of information, the precise contents being determined by a trade-off between utility to the user and cost to the preparer. This trade-off involves difficult judgements which should be assisted by the use of a conceptual framework (such as that being developed by the IASB) which should aid consistency. For some purposes, such as taxation, it may be necessary to prepare an entirely different set of accounts, but even this decision is not independent of the decision about the contents of the main financial reports: if, for example, expensive information about current values is necessary for taxation purposes, the additional cost of providing this information in the financial reports will be much reduced.

Although it is not possible to discern a single correct method it is clear what types of information are most useful and that there are trade-offs between them. Utility for decision making implies relevance to current or future decisions, and this in turn implies an emphasis (but not exclusive reliability) on current rather than historical values and information which assists the understanding of future prospects. However, the stewardship or agency role of financial reports means that the accounting information should also provide a reliable record of past events and be as free as possible from bias induced by the interests of management. The latter role has traditionally been catered for by a historical cost measurement basis, supplemented by prudence (as in 'cost or market value, whichever is the lower') but the former (current and future information for decision-usefulness) has tended to be neglected. It is therefore encouraging to see that current values are increasingly used in practice and by standard-setting bodies, often as additional disclosures which enable the traditional stewardship information to be retained.

The reporting of current values as additional information runs the risk of informational overload for users of financial reports. Hence, the provision of such information should be disciplined and parsimonious. Several methods have been identified in earlier chapters which might ease this problem. One of these is the presentation of the income statement: the Kennedy format (and possible variations on it) enables income to be reported on a variety of capital maintenance bases within the same statement in a manner which combines subtlety with clarity. Another income statement methodology is the concept of comprehensive income, which reconciles the income statement to value changes in the balance sheet and, appropriately sub-divided, has the potential to add clarity to the contribution of different types of activity (such as trading and asset holding) to the entity's income. With regard to measurement techniques, deprival value (or Value to the Business) provides an economically meaningful algorithm for choosing between alternative current values where that is necessary. Deprival Value has fallen out of favour following the retreat from current cost accounting, but it may be revived now that eclectic valuation methods seem to be finding favour, although the IASB has not shown any enthusiasm for it.

Theoretical and empirical research have an important role to play in determining the evolution of accounting practice in relation to price changes. The fact that accounting reports have economic consequences, which affect different groups differently, and so bring accounting into the political sphere, should increase rather than diminish the importance of identifying the assumptions and implications of alternative models. However, it may be that the theoretical work summarised in this book has explored, if not exhausted, the most promising lines of theoretical research into comprehensive models, of the 'grand design' general purpose type. Recent research has more limited aims, concentrating on the specific information needs of particular users, and with much more emphasis on empirical research to establish both the materiality and the utility of particular types of information.

Nevertheless, the theoretical work of the past has given important insights into the problem of measurement in financial accounting, and the practical debate on accounting standards has not always reflected a satisfactory level of understanding of these insights: even such basic distinctions as those between valuation and the capital maintenance concept or between relative price changes and changes in the general price level, which were well known to writers such as Sweeney almost a century ago, are still ignored or misunderstood by some contributors to the debate on accounting practice. One reason for this is that accounting is a relatively new profession and that its practitioners are, in the main, unconvinced that the theory of the subject is worthy of serious study. One objective of this book has been to help to remedy this situation by demonstrating that the theory of accounting is not only important, offering insights into the solution of practical problems, but also has accumulated an interesting literature and has enough unsolved problems to offer a serious challenge to intelligent people.

NOTES

1 Liabilities should be included in this definition as, conceptually, 'negative assets'.

2 Penman (2015) provides a comprehensive and accessible review of alternative valuation models.

3 E.g. if some form of current value accounting had been the traditional method, and therefore the basis of generally accepted accounting principles, there would probably be strong resistance within the accounting profession (by individuals who would, no doubt, be described as 'backwoodsmen') to the idea of introducing a historical cost basis.

# Bibliography

Abdel-Khalik, A. R. and McKeown, J. C. (1978), 'Disclosure of estimates of holding gains and the assessment of systematic risk', *Journal of Accounting Research*, Vol. 16(Suppl.), pp. 46–77.

Aboody, D., Barth, M. E. and Kasznik, R. (1999), 'Revaluations of fixed assets and future firm performance: evidence from the UK', *Journal of Accounting and Economics*, Vol. 26, No. 1, pp. 149–78.

— (2004), 'SFAS No. 123 stock-based compensation expense and equity market values', *The Accounting Review*, Vol. 79, No. 2, pp. 251–75.

Accounting Principles Board (1969), *Statement No. 3, Financial Statements Restated for General Price-Level Changes (APB3)*, AICPA, Washington, DC, June.

Accounting Standards Board (1992), *FRS 3, Reporting Financial Performance*, ASB, London, October.

— (1999), *Statement of Principles for Financial Reporting*, ASB, London, December.

Accounting Standards Committee (1975), *Statement of Standard Accounting Practice No. 10, Statements of Source and Application of Funds*, ASC, London, July.

— (1976), *ED18, Current Cost Accounting*, ASC, London, 30 November.

— (1977), *Inflation Accounting – an Interim Recommendation by the Accounting Standards Committee ('The Hyde Guidelines')*, ASC, London, 4 November.

— (1979), *ED 24, Current Cost Accounting*, ASC, London, 30 April.

— (1980), *Statement of Standard Accounting Practice No. 16, Current Cost Accounting ('SSAP16')*, ASC, London, March.

— (1985), *ED 35, Accounting for the Effects of Changing Prices*, ASC, London, July 1984.

Accounting Standards Steering Committee (1971), *Inflation and Accounts, Discussion Paper and Fact Sheet*, Accountancy Publications, London.

— (1973), *ED8: Accounting for Changes in the Purchasing Power of Money*, ASSC, London, 17 January.

— (1974), *Provisional Statement of Standard Accounting Practice No. 7, Accounting for Changes in the Purchasing Power of Money ('PSSAP7')*, ASSC, London, May.

— (1975), *The Corporate Report*, ASSC, London, July.

Adkerson, R. C. (1978), 'Discussion of DAAM: the demand for alternative accounting measurements', *Journal of Accounting Research*, Vol. 16(Suppl.), pp. 31–36.

Afriat, S. N. (1977), *The Price Index*, Cambridge University Press, Cambridge.

Alexander, S. S. (1948), 'Income measurement in a dynamic economy'. Originally pp. 1–97 of Study Group on Business Income (1948). Revised by David Solomons and reprinted in Baxter and Davidson (1977), pp. 35–85.

Allen, R. G. D. (1975), *Index Numbers in Theory and Practice*, Macmillan, London.

Allen, William A. (1999), 'Inflation targeting: the British experience'. Lectures, Bank of England, London.

Amel-Zadeh, A. and Meeks, G. (2013), 'Bank failure, mark-to-market and the Financial Crisis', *Abacus*, Vol. 49, No. 3, pp. 308–39.

American Accounting Association, Committee on Concepts and Standards for External Financial Reports (1977), *Statement on Accounting Theory and Theory Acceptance*, American Accounting Association, Sarasota, Florida.

American Institute of Certified Public Accountants, Accounting Research Division (1963), *Reporting the Financial Effects of Price-Level Changes*, Accounting Research Study No. 6 ('ARS6'), American Institute of Certified Public Accountants, New York.

Anderson, J. A. (1976), *A Comparative Analysis of Selected Income Measurement Theories in Financial Accounting*, Studies in Accounting, 12, American Accounting Association, Sarasota, Florida.

Anthony, R. N. (1976), 'The case for historical costs', *Harvard Business Review*, Vol. 54, No. 6, November/December.

Appleyard, A. and Strong, N. (1984), ' The impact of SSAP 16 current cost accounting disclosures on security prices', pp. 235–44 of Carsberg and Page (1984).

Aranya, N. (1974), 'The influence of pressure groups on financial statements in Britain', *Abacus*, Vol. 10, No. 1, pp. 3–12.

Archer, S. and Steele, A. (1984), 'The implementation of SSAP 16, current cost accounting, by UK listed companies', vol. 4 of Carsberg and Page (1984).

Armitage, S. (2005), *The Cost of Capital: Intermediate Theory*, Cambridge University Press, Cambridge.

Arnold, J. and El-Azma, M. (1978), *A Study of the Relative Usefulness of Six Accounting Measures of Income*, The Institute of Chartered Accountants in England and Wales, London.

Association of Certified and Corporate Accountants, Taxation & Research Committee (1952), *Accounting for Inflation, a Study of Techniques under Conditions of Changing Price Levels*, Gee.

Australian Accounting Research Foundation (AARF) (1998), *Measurement in Accounting*, Accounting Theory Monograph 10, AARF, Melbourne.

Ball, R. and Brown, P. (1968), 'An empirical evaluation of accounting income numbers', *Journal of Accounting Research*, Vol. 6, No. 2, pp. 159–78.

Barker, R. (1999), 'The role of dividends in valuation models used by analysts and fund managers', *European Accounting Review*, Vol. 8, No. 2, pp. 195–218.

— (2004), 'Reporting financial performance', *Accounting Horizons*, Vol. 18, No. 2, pp. 157–72.

— (2010), 'On the definitions of income, expenses and profit in IFRS', *Accounting in Europe*, Vol. 7, No. 2, pp. 147–58.

Barniv, R. (1999), 'The value relevance of inflation-adjusted and historical-cost earnings during hyperinflation', *Journal of International Accounting, Auditing and Taxation*, Vol. 8, No. 2, pp. 269–87.

Barth, M. E. (2007), 'Standard-setting measurement issues and the relevance of research', *Accounting and Business Research*, Vol. 37(Suppl.), pp. 7–15.

Barth, M. E., Beaver, W. H. and Landsman, W. R. (1996), 'Value-relevance of banks' fair value disclosures under SFAS No. 107 (Digest Summary)', *Accounting Review*, Vol. 71, No. 4, pp. 513–37.

Barth, M. E. and Clinch, G. (1998), 'Revalued financial, tangible, and intangible assets: associations with share prices and non-market-based value estimates', *Journal of Accounting Research*, Vol. 36, pp. 199–233.

Barth, M. E. and Landsman, W. R. (1995), 'Fundamental issues related to using fair value accounting for financial reporting', *Accounting Horizons*, Vol. 9, No. 4, p. 97.

Barth, M. E., Landsman, W. R. and Wahlen, J. M. (1995), 'Fair value accounting: effects on banks' earnings volatility, regulatory capital, and value of contractual cash flows', *Journal of Banking and Finance*, Vol. 19, No. 3, pp. 577–605.

Barton, A. D. (1974), 'Expectations and achievements in income theory', *The Accounting Review*, Vol. 49, No. 4, pp. 664–81.

— (1975), *An Analysis of Business Income Concepts*, ICRA Occasional Paper No. 7, International Centre for Research in Accounting, University of Lancaster, Lancaster, UK.

— (1976), 'Surrogates in income theory: a reply', *The Accounting Review*, Vol. 51, No. 1, pp. 160–62.

Basu, S. (1977), *Inflation Accounting, Capital Market Efficiency and Security Prices*, The Society of Management Accountants of Canada, Hamilton, Ontario.

Baxter, W. T. (1959), 'Inflation and the accounts of steel companies', *Accountancy*, May, pp. 250–57 and June, pp. 308–14.

— (1967), 'Accounting values: sale price versus replacement cost', *Journal of Accounting Research*, Vol. 5, No. 2, pp. 208–14.

— (1971), *Depreciation*, Sweet and Maxwell, London.

— (1975), *Accounting Values and Inflation*, McGraw-Hill, New York.

— (1976), 'Monetary correction: adjustments to inflation in three South American countries', *Bank of London and South America Review*, Vol. 10, No. 4/76, pp. 184–94.

— (1982), 'Lessors' depreciation and profit – an approach via deprival value', *Journal of Business Finance and Accounting*, Vol. 9, No. 1, pp. 1–18.

— (2003), *The Case for Deprival Value*, Institute of Chartered Accountants of Scotland, Edinburgh.

Baxter, W. T. and Davidson, S. (eds) (1977), *Studies in Accounting*, 3rd ed., Institute of Chartered Accountants in England and Wales, London.

Beaver, W. H. (1968), 'The information content of annual earnings announcements', *Journal of Accounting Research*, Vol. 6(Suppl.), pp. 67–92.

— (1973), 'What should be the FASB's objectives?', *Journal of Accountancy*, Vol. 136, No. 2, pp. 49–56.

— (1981), 'Market efficiency', *The Accounting Review*, Vol. 56, No. 1, pp. 23–37.

— (1989), *Financial Accounting: An Accounting Revolution*, Prentice Hall, Englewood Cliffs, NJ.

Beaver, W. and Demski, J. (1979), 'The nature of income measurement', *The Accounting Review*, Vol. 54, pp. 38–46.

Beaver, W. H. and Landsman, W. R. (1983), *Incremental information content of Statement 33 disclosures*, Research Report, Financial Accounting Standards Board, Stamford, CT.

Beja, A. and Aharoni, Y. (1977), 'Some aspects of conventional accounting profits in an inflationary environment', *Journal of Accounting Research*, Vol. 15, No. 2, pp. 169–78.

Bell, P. W. (1971), 'On current replacement costs and business income', Chapter 2, pp. 19–32 of Sterling (1971).

Bell, P. W. and Peasnell, K. (1997), 'Another look at the deprival value approach to depreciation', pp. 122–146 of Cooke and Nobes (eds) (1997).

Benston, G. J. and Krasney, M. A. (1978), 'DAAM: The demand for alternative accounting measurements', *Journal of Accounting Research*, Vol. 16(Suppl.), pp. 1–30.

Berliner, R. W. (1983), 'Do analysts use inflation-adjusted information? Results of a survey', *Financial Analysts Journal*, Vol. 39, No. 2, pp. 65–72.

Bierman, H. and Smidt, S. (2007), *The Capital Budgeting Decision: Economic Analysis of Investment Projects*, 9th ed., Routledge, New York.

Bildersee, J. S. and Ronen, J. (1987), 'Stock returns and real activity in an inflationary environment: the informational impact of FAS No. 33', *Contemporary Accounting Research*, Vol. 4, No. 1, pp. 89–110.

Bilgic, F. A. and Ibis, C. (2013), 'Effects of new financial reporting standards on value relevance – a study about Turkish stock markets', *International Journal of Economics and Finance*, Vol. 5, No. 10, pp. 126–40.

Black, E. L., Sellers, K. F. and Manly, T. S. (1998), 'Earnings management using asset sales: an international study of countries allowing noncurrent asset revaluation', *Journal of Business Finance and Accounting*, 25(9–10), pp. 1287–1317.

Black, F. (1980), 'The magic in earnings: economic earnings versus accounting earnings', *Financial Analysts journal*, Vol. 36, No. 6, pp. 19–24.

— (1993), 'Choosing accounting rules', *Accounting Horizons*, Vol. 7, No. 4, pp. 1–17.

Boer, G. (1966), ' Replacement cost: a historical look', *The Accounting Review*, Vol. 41, No. 1, pp. 92–97.

Bonbright, J. C. (1937), *Valuation of Property* (2 vols), McGraw-Hill, New York.

Bourn, M., Stoney, P. J. M. and Wynn, R. F. (1976), 'Price indices for current cost accounting', *Journal of Business Finance and Accounting*, Vol. 3, No. 3, pp. 149–72.

— (1977), 'Price indices for current cost accounting: a rejoinder', *Journal of Business Finance and Accounting*, Vol. 4, No. 1, pp. 145–47.

BP (2015), *Annual Report and Form 20-F, 2015*, BP plc, London.

Brink, H. and Langendijk, H. (1995), 'Actuele waarde in de jaarrekening', in H. L. Brink and L. G. van der Tas (eds), *Jar in Jar uit 9*, Kluwer, Deventer.

Briscoe, G. and Hawke, G. (1976), 'Long-term debt and realisable gains in shareholder wealth: an empirical study', *Journal of Business Finance and Accounting*, Vol. 3, No. 1, pp. 125–35.

Bromwich, M. (1975a), 'Asset valuation with imperfect markets', *Accounting and Business Research*, Vol. 5, No. 20, pp. 242–53.

— (1975b), 'Individual purchasing power indices and accounting reports', *Accounting and Business Research*, Vol. 5, No. 18, pp. 118–22.

— (1976), *The Economics of Capital Budgeting*, Penguin, New York.

— (1977a), 'The use of present value valuation models in published accounting reports', *The Accounting Review*, Vol. 52, No. 3, pp. 587–96.

— (1977b), 'The general validity of certain "current" value asset valuation bases', *Accounting and Business Research*, Vol. 7, No. 28, pp. 242–49.

Bublitz, B., Frecka, T. J. and McKeown, J. C. (1985), 'Market association tests and FASB Statement No. 33 disclosures: A reexamination', *Journal of Accounting Research*, Vol. 23, No. 3, pp. 1–23.

Buckmaster, D. A., Copeland, R. M. and Dascher, P. E. (1977), 'The relative predictive ability of three accounting income models', *Accounting and Business Research*, Vol. 7, No. 27, pp. 177–86.

Burgert, R. (1972), 'Reservations about 'replacement value' accounting in the Netherlands', *Abacus*, Vol. 8, No. 2, pp. 111–26.

Bush, T. (2005), *'Divided by a Common Language': Where Economics Meets the Law: US versus Non-US Financial Reporting Models: Dialogue in Corporate Governance*, ICAEW, London.

Business Statistics Office (1986), *Business Monitor, MA3, Company Finance*, 17th issue, HMSO, London.

— (1988), *Business Monitor MA3, Company Finance*, 19th issue, HMSO, London.

Buzby, S. L. and Falk, H. (1978), 'Discussion of DAAM: the demand for alternative accounting measurements', *Journal of Accounting Research*, Vol. 16(Suppl.), pp. 37–45.

Byatt, I. C. (1986), *Accounting for Economic Costs and Prices: A Report to HM Treasury by an Advisory Group* [the Byatt Report] (2 vols), HMSO, London.

Camfferman, K. (1998), ' Deprival value in the Netherlands: history and current status', *Abacus*, Vol. 34, No. 1, pp. 18–27.

Camfferman, K. and Zeff, S. A. (2007), *Financial Reporting and Global Capital Markets: A History of the International Accounting Standards Committee*, Oxford University Press, Oxford.

— (2015), *Aiming for Global Accounting Standards: The International Accounting Standards Board, 2001–2011*, Oxford University Press, Oxford.

Canning, J. B. (1929), *The Economics of Accountancy: A Critical Analysis of Accounting Theory*, Ronald Press, New York.

Carsberg, B. (1984), 'The usefulness of current cost accounting: a report on a research programme', Vol. 1 of Carsberg and Page (1984), pp. 1–70.

Carsberg, B. and Hope, A. (1976), *Business Investment Decisions under Inflation*, The Institute of Chartered Accountants in England and Wales, London.

Carsberg, B., Morgan, E. V. and Parkin, M. (eds) (1974), *Indexation and Inflation*, Financial Times Publications, London.

Carsberg, B. and Page, M. (1984), *Current Cost Accounting: The Benefits and the Costs* [the Carsberg Report] (2 vols), Prentice Hall, Englewood Cliffs, NJ.

Cascino, S., Clatworthy, M., Osma, B. G., Gassen, J., Imam, S. and Jeanjean, T. (2013), *The Use of Information by Capital Providers: Academic Literature Review*, The Institute of Chartered Accountants of Scotland and the European Financial Reporting Advisory Group, Edinburgh.

CCAB (1975), *Initial Reactions to the Report of the Inflation Accounting Committee*, Accounting Standards Committee, London, October.

Chambers, R. J. (1966), *Accounting, Evaluation and Economic Behaviour*, Prentice Hall, Englewood Cliffs, NJ.

— (1970), 'Second thoughts on continuously contemporaneous accounting', *Abacus*, Vol. 6, No. 1, pp. 39–55.

— (1971a), 'Evidence for a market-selling price-accounting system', Chapter 4, pp. 74–96 of Sterling (1971).

— (1971b), 'Value to the owner', *Abacus*, Vol. 7, No. 1, pp. 62–72.

— (1972), 'Multiple column accounting – "cui bono?" and "quo vado?"', *Chartered Accountant in Australia*, Vols 42 and 43, pp. 4–8 and 13–15.

— (1976), *Current Cost Accounting – A Critique of the Sandilands Report*, ICRA Occasional Paper No. 11, University of Lancaster, Lancaster, UK.

— (1977), *An Autobibliography*, ICRA Occasional Paper No. 15, International Centre for Research in Accounting, University of Lancaster, Lancaster, UK.

— (1978), 'The use and abuse of a notation: a history of an idea', *Abacus*, Vol. 14, No. 2, pp. 122–44.

— (1979), 'Canning's *The Economics of Accountancy* – after 50 years', *The Accounting Review*, Vol. 54, No. 4, pp. 764–75.

Chatfield, M. (1974), *A History of Accounting Thought*, The Dryden Press, Hinsdale, IL.

Clarke, F. L. (1998), ' Deprival value and optimized deprival value in Australasian public sector accounting: unwarranted drift and contestable serviceability', *Abacus*, Vol. 34, No. 1, pp. 8–17.

Coenenberg, A. and Macharzina, K. (1976), 'Accounting for price changes: an analysis of current developments in Germany', *Journal of Business Finance and Accounting*, Vol. 3, No. 1, pp. 53–68.

Cohen, K. J. and Cyert, R. M. (1975), *Theory of the Firm: Resource Allocation in a Market Economy*, 2nd ed., Prentice Hall, Englewood Cliffs, NJ.

Committee of Inquiry into Inflation and Taxation (1975), *Report: Inflation and Taxation* [the Mathews Report], Australian Government Publishing Service, Canberra.

Companies Act (2006), HMSO, London, December.

Company Law Review Steering Group (2001), *Modern Company Law for a Competitive Economy, Final Report* (2 vols), Department of Trade and Industry, London, June.

Cook, J. S. and Holzmann, O. J. (1976), 'Current cost and present value in income theory', *The Accounting Review*, Vol. 51, No. 4, pp. 778–87.

Cooke, T. and Nobes, C.(eds) (1997), *The Development of Accounting in an International Context: A Festschrift in Honour of RH Parker*, Routledge, New York.

Craswell, A. (1976), *A Manual on Continuously Contemporaneous Accounting*, Inflation Accounting Research Project, Department of Management Studies, University of Waikato, Hamilton, New Zealand.

Cutler, R. S. and Westwick, C. A. (1973), 'The impact of inflation accounting on the stock exchange', *Accountancy*, Vol. 84, No. 955, pp. 15–24.

Daines, H. C. (1929), 'The changing objectives of accounting', *The Accounting Review*, Vol. 4, pp. 94–110. Reprinted in Zeff (1976).

Davidson, S., Stickney, C. P. and Weil, R. L. (1976), *Inflation Accounting: A Guide for the Accountant and the Financial Analyst*, McGraw-Hill, New York.

Davidson, S. and Weil, R. L. (1975), 'Inflation accounting: what will general price level adjusted income statements show?', *Financial Analysts Journal*, January–February, pp. 27–31 and 71–84.

Davis-Friday, P. Y. and Rivera, J. M. (2000), 'Inflation accounting and 20-F Disclosures: evidence from Mexico', *Accounting Horizons*, Vol. 14, No. 2, pp. 113–35.

Day, A. C. L. (1974), article in *The Observer*, 3 November.

Dean, J. (1951), 'Measurement of profits for executive decisions', *Accounting Review*, Vol. 26, No. 2, pp. 185–96.

— (1954), 'Measurement of real economic earnings of a machinery manufacturer', *The Accounting Review*, Vol. 29, No. 2, pp. 255–66.

Deane, P. M. (1979), 'Inflation in history', pp. 1–36 of David Heathfield (ed.), *Perspectives on Inflation, Models and Policies*, Longman, New York.

Deaton, A. S. (1980), 'Measurement of welfare: theory and practical guidelines', LSMS Working Paper No. 7, The World Bank Development Research Center, Washington, DC, October.

Deaton, A. S. and Muellbauer, J. (1980), *Economics and Consumer Behavior*, Cambridge University Press, Cambridge.

Devon, P. C. and Kolodny, R. (1978), 'Price-level reporting and its value to investors', *Accounting and Business Research*, Vol. 9, No. 33, pp. 19–24.

Domar, E. D. (1953), 'Depreciation, replacement and growth', *The Economic Journal*, Vol. 63, pp. 1–32.

Dopuch, N. and Revsine, L. (eds) (1973), *Accounting Research 1960–1970: A Critical Evaluation*, Center for International Education and Research in Accounting, University of Illinois, Urbana-Champaign.

Drake, D. F. and Dopuch, N. (1965), 'On the case for dichotomizing income', *Journal of Accounting Research*, Vol. 3, pp. 192–205.

Dyckman, T. R. (1969), *Investment Analysis and General Price-Level Adjustments*, Studies in Accounting Research, No. 1, American Accounting Association, Evanston, Illinois.

— (1975), 'The Effects of restating financial statements for price-level changes: a comment', *The Accounting Review*, Vol. 50, No. 4, pp. 796–808.

Dyckman, T. and Morse, D. (1986), *Efficient Capital Markets: A Critical Analysis*, Prentice Hall, Englewood Cliffs, NJ.

Edey, H. C. (1974), 'Deprival value and financial accounting', pp. 75–83 of H. C. Edey and B. S. Yamey (eds), *Debits, Credits, Finance, and Profits*, Sweet and Maxwell, London.

— (1979), 'Sandilands and the logic of current cost', *Accounting and Business Research*, Vol. 9, No. 35, pp. 191–200.

Edwards, E. O. (1975), 'The state of current value accounting', *The Accounting Review*, Vol. 50, No. 2, pp. 235–45.

Edwards, E. O. and Bell, P. W. (1961), *The Theory and Measurement of Business Income*, University of California Press, Berkeley, California.

Edwards, J. S. S., Kay, J. A. and Mayer, C. P. (1987), *The Economic Analysis of Accounting Profitability*, Clarendon Press, Oxford.

Edwards, R. S. (1938), 'The nature and measurement of income', *The Accountant*, July–October. Revised and reprinted in Baxter and Davidson (1977), pp. 96–140.

Egginton, D. A. (1980), 'Distributable profit and the pursuit of prudence', *Accounting and Business Research*, No. 41, Winter, pp. 1–14.

Emanuel, D. (1976), *A Manual on Current Purchasing Power Accounting*, Inflation Accounting Research Project, Department of Management Studies, University of Waikato, Hamilton, New Zealand.

Fama, E. (1970), 'Efficient capital markets: a review of theory and empirical work', *Journal of Finance*, Vol. 25, No. 2, pp. 383–417.

Fane, G. (1975), 'The case for indexation', pp. 1–13 in Liesner and King (1975).

Financial Accounting Standards Board (1974), *Exposure Draft: Financial Reporting in Units of General Purchasing Power*, FASB, Stamford, CT, 31 December.

— (1977), *Field Tests of Financial Reporting in Units of General Purchasing Power*, FASB, Stamford, CT, May.

— (1978), *Proposed Statement of Financial Accounting Standards: Financial Reporting and Changing Prices*, FASB, Stamford, CT, 28 December.

— (1979a), *Exposure Draft: Constant Dollar Accounting*, FASB, Stamford, CT, 2 March.

— (1979b), *Statement of Financial Accounting Standards No. 33 (FAS33): Financial Reporting and Changing Prices*, FASB, Stamford, CT, September.

— (1981), *Invitation to Comment on the Need for Research in Financial Reporting and Changing Prices*, FASB, Stamford, CT, 15 June.

— (1984), *FAS82: Financial Reporting and Changing Prices: Elimination of Certain Disclosures – an Amendment of FASB Statement No. 33*, FASB, Stamford, CT, November.

— (1986), *SFAS 89: Financial Reporting and Changing Prices*, FASB, Stamford, CT, December.

— (1997), *SFAS 130: Reporting Comprehensive Income*, FASB, Norwalk, CT, June.

— (2006), *Statement of Financial Accounting Standards No. 157 (SFAS 157): Fair Value Measurements*, FASB, Norwalk, CT, September.

Fells, J. M. (1919), 'Some principles governing the ascertainment of cost', *Incorporated Accountants' Journal*, November, p. 34.

Feltham, G. A. and Ohlson, J. A. (1995), 'Valuation and clean surplus accounting for operating and financial activities', *Contemporary Accounting Research*, Vol. 11, No. 2, pp. 689–731.

Fisher, F. M. and McGowan, J. J. (1983), 'On the misuse of accounting rates of return to infer monopoly profits', *American Economic Review*, Vol. 73, March, pp. 82–97.

Fisher, I. (1911), *The Purchasing Power of Money*, Macmillan, New York.

— (1920), *Stabilizing the Dollar: A Plan to Stabilize the General Price Level without Fixed Individual Prices*, Macmillan, New York.

— (1930), 'The economics of accountancy', *American Economic Review*, Vol. 20, No. 4, pp. 603–18.

Flemming, J. S. (1976), *Inflation*, Oxford University Press, Oxford.

Flemming, J. S., Price, L. D. D. and Ingram, D. H. A. (1976), 'Trends in company profitability', *Bank of England Quarterly Bulletin*, Vol. 16, No. 1, pp. 36–52.

Forker, J. J. (1980), 'Capital maintenance concepts, gains from borrowing and the measurement of income', *Accounting and Business Research*, Vol. 10, No. 40, pp. 393–402.

Frank, W. (1969), 'A study of the predictive significance of two income measures', *Journal of Accounting Research*, Vol. 7, No. 1, pp. 123–36.

FRC (2011), *Cutting Clutter: Combating Clutter in Annual Reports*, FRC, London, April.

Freeman, R. N. (1978), 'On the association between net monetary position and equity security prices', *Journal of Accounting Research*, Vol. 16(Suppl.), pp. 111–45.

Friedman, M. (1974), *Monetary Correction*, IEA Occasional Paper 41, Institute of Economic Affairs, London.

Frisch, R. (1936), 'The problem of index numbers', *Econometrica*, Vol. 4, pp. 1–38.

Gee, K. P. (1977), *Management Planning and Control in Inflation*, Macmillan, New York.

Gee, K. and Peasnell, K. V. (1976), 'A pragmatic defence of replacement cost', *Accounting and Business Research*, Vol. 6, No. 24, pp. 242–49.

Gellein, O. S. (1971), 'Response' (to Staubus, 1971), pp. 70–73 of Sterling (1971).

Gibbs, M. (1975), 'Why Sandilands is not the full answer', *The Times*, 18 September.

— (1976), 'A better answer to the problem of inflation accounting', *The Times*, 23 February.

— (1979), 'Inflation accounting and company taxation', *Fiscal Studies*, Vol. 1, No. 1, pp. 11–19.

Gibbs, M. and Seward, W. (1979), *ED24 – Morpeth's New Proposals*, Phillips and Drew, 30 April.

Godley, W. and Cripps, F. (1975), 'Profits, stock appreciation and the Sandilands Report', *The Times*, 1 October.

Godley, W. and Wood, A. (1974), 'Stock appreciation and the crisis of British industry', Department of Applied Economics, Cambridge, mimeo, October. Later published in *The Economic Policy Review*, 1975.

Goudeket, A. (1960), 'An application of replacement value theory', *Journal of Accountancy*, July, pp. 37–47. Revised and reprinted, with a postscript by E. B. MacDonald, in Baxter and Davidson (1977), pp. 234–49.

Gray, S. J. (1975), 'Price changes and company profits in the securities market', *Abacus*, Vol. 11, No. 1, pp. 71–85.

— (1976), 'Accounting for price changes: a case study of a multinational company', *Journal of Business Finance and Accounting*, Vol. 3, No. 1, pp. 1–14.

Gress, E. J. (1972), 'Application of replacement cost accounting: a case study', *Abacus*, Vol. 8, No. 1, pp. 3–13.

Grossman, S. J. and Stiglitz, J. E. (1980), ' On the impossibility of informationally efficient markets', *The American Economic Review*, Vol. 70, No. 3, pp. 393–408.

Gynther, R. S. (1966), *Accounting for Price-Level Changes: Theory and Procedures*, Pergamon, New York.

— (1974), 'Why use General Purchasing Power?', *Accounting and Business Research*, Vol. 4, No. 2, pp. 141–57.

Hague, I. P. (2007), 'The case for fair value', Chapter 4, pp. 32–45, of Walton (2007).

Harcourt, G. C. (1958), 'The quantitative effect of basing company taxation on replacement costs', *Accounting Research*, Vol. 9, No. 1, pp. 1–16.

— (1965), 'The accountant in a Golden Age', *Oxford Economic Papers*, Vol. 17, pp. 66–80. Reprinted in Parker and Harcourt (1969).

Haw, I. M. and Lustgarten, S. (1988), 'Evidence on income measurement properties of ASR No. 190 and SFAS No. 33 data', *Journal of Accounting Research*, October, pp. 331–52.

Heath, L. C. (1972), 'Distinguishing between monetary and nonmonetary assets and liabilities in general price-level accounting', *The Accounting Review*, Vol. 47, No. 3, pp. 458–68.

Heintz, J. A. (1975), 'The effects of restating financial statements for price-level changes: a reply', *The Accounting Review*, Vol. 50, No. 4, pp. 809–14.

Hicks, J. R. (1946), *Value and Capital*, Clarendon Press, Oxford. pp. 171–181 of the second edition (1946) are reprinted in Parker and Harcourt (1969), pp. 74–82.

Hillison, W. A. (1979), 'Empirical investigation of general purchasing power adjustments on earnings per share and the movement of security prices', *Journal of Accounting Research*, Vol. 17, No. 1, pp. 60–73.

Hirshleifer, J. (1958), 'On the theory of the optimal investment decision', *The Journal of Political Economy*, Vol. 66, No. 4, pp. 329–52.

Hope, A. (1974), *Accounting for Price Changes – a Practical Survey of 6 Methods*, Research Committee Occasional Paper No. 4, Institute of Chartered Accountants in England and Wales, London.

Hopper, T., Northcutt, D. and Scapens, R. (eds) (2007), *Issues in Management Accounting*, 3rd ed., Pearson Education, Mahwah, NJ.

Horngren, C. T., Sundem, G. L., Stratton, W. L., Burgstahler, D. and Schatzberg, J. O. (2013), *Introduction to Management Accounting*, 16th ed., Pearson Education, Mahwah, NJ.

Horton, J. and Macve, R. (1995), *Accounting Principles for Life Insurance: A True and Fair View?* Institute of Chartered Accountants in England and Wales Research Board, London.

Horton, J., Macve, R. and Serafeim, G. (2011), 'Deprival value vs. fair value measurement for contract liabilities: how to resolve the revenue recognition conundrum?', *Accounting and Business Research*, Vol. 41, No. 5, pp. 491–514.

Hume, A. (1976), *A Manual on Current Cost Accounting*, Inflation Accounting Research Project, Department of Management Studies, University of Waikato, Hamilton, New Zealand.

Ijiri, Y. (1971), 'A defence for historical cost accounting', Chapter 1, pp. 1–14 of Sterling (1971).

— (1976), 'The price-level restatement and its dual interpretation', *The Accounting Review*, Vol. 51, No. 2, pp. 227–43.

— (1979), 'A simple system of cash flow accounting', Chapter 3, pp. 57–71 of Sterling and Thomas (1979).

Inflation Accounting Steering Group (1976), *Background Papers to the Exposure Draft on Current Cost Accounting*, Tolley Publishing Co. and the Institute of Chartered Accountants in England and Wales, London.

Institute of Chartered Accountants in Australia and Australian Society of Accountants (1975), *A Method of 'Current Value Accounting'*, Preliminary Exposure Draft, Institute of Chartered Accountants in Australia, Melbourne, June.

Institute of Chartered Accountants in England and Wales (1952), 'Accounting in relation to changes in the purchasing power of money', *Recommendations on Accounting Principles*, N15, Institute of Chartered Accountants in England and Wales, London, 30 May.

Institute of Chartered Accountants in England and Wales, General Educational Trust (1973), *Accounting for Inflation, a Working Guide to the Accounting Procedures, Part 1: Text* and *Part 2: Tables*, Institute of Chartered Accountants in England and Wales, London.

Institute of Chartered Accountants in England and Wales, Research Committee (1968), *Accounting for Stewardship in a Period of Inflation*, Research Foundation of the Institute of Chartered Accountants in England and Wales, London.

Institute of Cost and Works Accountants, Research and Technical Committee (1952), *The Accountancy of Changing Price Levels*, The Institute of Cost and Works Accountants, London.

International Accounting Standards Board (2003), *IAS 21 (Amended), The Effects of Changes in Foreign Exchange Rates*, International Accounting Standards Board, London.

— (2004), *IFRS 3, Business Combinations*, International Accounting Standards Board, London.

— (2005a), *Discussion Paper: Measurement Bases for Financial Accounting – Measurement Initial Recognition*, International Accounting Standards Board, London.

— (2005b), *IFRS 7, Financial Instruments: Disclosures*, International Accounting Standards Board, London.

— (2006), *Discussion Paper: Preliminary Views on an Improved Conceptual Framework for Financial Reporting: The Objective of Financial Reporting and Qualitative Characteristics of Decision-Useful Financial Reporting Information*, International Accounting Standards Board, London, July.

— (2009a), *IFRS 9, Financial Instruments*, International Accounting Standards Board, London. Revised 2014.

— (2009b), *Exposure Draft: Fair Value Measurement*, International Accounting Standards Board, London.

— (2010), *Conceptual Framework Revision*, Chapters 1 and 2, International Accounting Standards Board, London.

— (2011), *IFRS 13, Fair Value Measurement*, International Accounting Standards Board, London, May.

— (2015), *Exposure Draft: Conceptual Framework for Financial Reporting*, International Accounting Standards Board, London, May.

International Accounting Standards Committee (1977), *IAS6, Accounting Responses to Changing Prices*, International Accounting Standards Committee, London, March.

— (1981), *IAS15, Information Reflecting the Effects of Changing Prices*, International Accounting Standards Committee, London, June.

— (1989), *IAS29, Financial Reporting in Highly Inflationary Economies*, International Accounting Standards Committee, London, April.

— (1992), *IAS 7, Statement of Cash Flows* (revision), International Accounting Standards Committee, London.

— (1997), *IAS 1, Presentation of Accounting Statements* (revision), International Accounting Standards Committee, London.

— (1998), *IAS 39, Financial Instruments: Recognition and Measurement*, International Accounting Standards Committee, London, December.

— (2000a), *IAS 40, Investment Property*, International Accounting Standards Committee, London, March.

— (2000b), *IAS 41: Agriculture*, International Accounting Standards Committee, London, December.

IPSASB (2010), *Conceptual Framework Exposure Draft 1: Conceptual Framework for General Purpose Reporting by Public Sector Entities*, IFAC, Toronto.

Jackman, R. and Klappholz, K. (1975), *Taming the Tiger*, Hobart Paper 63, Institute of Economic Affairs, London.

Johnson, L. T. and Petrone, K. R. (1998), 'Commentary: is goodwill an asset?,' *Accounting Horizons*, Vol. 12, No. 3, pp. 1–14.

Jones, M. J. (2010), 'Accounting for the environment: towards a theoretical perspective for environmental accounting and reporting', *Accounting Forum*, Vol. 34, No. 2, pp. 123–38.

Jones, R. C. (1949), 'Effect of inflation on capital and profits: the record of nine steel companies', *The Journal of Accountancy*, January, pp. 9–27.

— (1955), *Price Level Changes and Financial Statements – Case Studies of Four Companies*, American Accounting Association, Sarasota, Florida.

— (1956), *Effects of Price Level Changes on Business Income, Capital, and Taxes*, American Accounting Association, Sarasota, Florida.

Jones, S. (ed.) (2015), *The Routledge Companion to Financial Accounting Theory*, Routledge, London and New York.

Kaldor, N. (1955), 'The concept of income in economic theory', in *An Expenditure Tax*, Allen and Unwin, London, pp. 54–78. Reprinted in Parker and Harcourt (1969).

Kay, J. A. (1976), 'Accountants, too, could be happy in a Golden Age: The Accountant's Rate of Profit and the Internal Rate of Return', *Oxford Economic Papers*, Vol. 28, No. 3, pp. 447–60.

— (1977), 'Inflation accounting – a review article', *The Economic Journal*, Vol. 87, No. 346, pp. 300–311.

— (1978), 'Accounting rate of profit and internal rate of return: a reply', *Oxford Economic Papers*, Vol. 30, No. 3, pp. 469–70.

Kay, J. A. and King, M. A. (1980), *The British System of Taxation*, 2nd ed., Oxford University Press, Oxford.

Kennedy, C. (1976), 'Inflation accounting, profits, profitability and share valuation', *Journal of Business Finance and Accounting*, Vol. 3, No. 1, pp. 137–46.

— (1978a), 'Inflation accounting: retrospect and prospect', *Cambridge Economic Policy Review*, No. 4, Chapter 7, pp. 58–64.

— (1978b), 'Fixed assets and the Hyde gearing adjustment', *Journal of Business Finance and Accounting*, Vol. 5, No. 4, pp. 393–406.

Ketz, J. E. (1978a), 'The validation of some general price level estimating models', *The Accounting Review*, Vol. 53, No. 4, pp. 952–60.

— (1978b), 'The effect of general price-level adjustments on the predictive ability of financial ratios', *Journal of Accounting Research*, Vol. 16(Suppl.), pp. 273–84.

King, M. A. (1975), 'The United Kingdom profits crisis: myth or reality?', *The Economic Journal*, Vol. 85, March, pp. 33–54.

Kirkulak, B. and Balsari, C. K. (2009), 'Value relevance of inflation-adjusted equity and income', *The International Journal of Accounting*, Vol. 44, No. 4, pp. 363–77.

Kratchman, S. H., Malcom, R. E. and Twark, R. D. (1974), 'An intra-industry comparison of alternative income concepts and relative performance evaluations', *The Accounting Review*, Vol. 49, No. 4, pp. 682–89.

— (1975), 'The comparison of alternative income concepts: a reply', *The Accounting Review*, Vol. 50, No. 4, pp. 865–68.

— (1976), 'Alternative income concepts and relative performance evaluations: a reply', *The Accounting Review*, Vol. 51, No. 2, pp. 421–26.

Kulkarni, D. (1980), 'The valuation of liabilities', *Accounting and Business Research*, Vol. 10, No. 39, pp. 291–97.

Landsman, W. R. (2007), ' Is fair value accounting information relevant and reliable? Evidence from capital market research', *Accounting and Business Research*, Vol. 37(Suppl.), pp. 19–30.

Landsman, W., Peasnell, K., Pope, P. and Yeh, S. (2006), 'Which approach to accounting for employee stock options best reflects market pricing?', *Review of Accounting Studies*, Vol. 11, No. 2–3, pp. 203–45.

Largay, J. A. and Livingstone, J. L. (1976), *Accounting for Changing Prices*, Wiley, Hoboken, NJ.

Laux, C. (2012), 'Financial instruments, financial reporting, and financial stability', *Accounting and Business Research*, Vol. 42, No. 3, pp. 239–60.

Laux, C. and Leuz, C. (2010), 'Did fair-value accounting contribute to the financial crisis?', *The Journal of Economic Perspectives*, Vol. 24, No. 1, pp. 93–118.

Lawson, G. H. (1971), 'Cash flow accounting', *The Accountant*, 28 October and 4 November, pp. 998–1002 and 1083–88.

Lee, T. A. (1972), 'A case for cash flow reporting', *Journal of Business Finance*, Vol. 4, No. 2, Summer 1972, pp. 27–36.

— (1979), 'The simplicity and complexity of accounting', Chapter 2, pp. 35–55 of Sterling and Thomas (1979).

— (1985), *Income and Value Measurement: Theory and Practice*, 3rd ed., Van Nostrand Reinhold, London.

Lennard, A. (2002), *Liabilities and How to Account for Them: An Exploratory Essay*, Accounting Standards Board, London.

— (2007), 'Stewardship and the objectives of financial statements: a comment on the preliminary views on an improved conceptual framework for financial reporting', *Accounting in Europe*, Vol. 4, No. 1, pp. 51–66.

Liao, S. S. (1975), 'The comparison of alternative income concepts: a comment', *The Accounting Review*, Vol. 50, No. 4, pp. 860–64.

Liesner, T. and King, M. A. (eds) (1975), *Indexing for Inflation*, IFS/Heinemann, London.

Lobo, G. J. and Song, I.-M. (1989), 'The incremental information in SFAS 33 income disclosures over historical cost income and its cash and accrual components', *The Accounting Review*, Vol. 64, No. 2, pp. 329–43.

London Society of Chartered Accountants (1977), *Submission on ED18*, May.

Ma, R. (1976), 'Value to the owner revisited', *Abacus*, Vol. 12, No. 2, pp. 159–65.

Macdonald, G. (1974a), 'Deprival value: its use and abuse', *Accounting and Business Research*, Vol. 4, No. 16, pp. 263–69.

— (1974b), *Profit Measurement: Alternatives to Historical Cost*, Haymarket, London.

MacFarlane, H. and Mortimer-Lee, P. (1994), 'Inflation over 300 years', *Bank of England Quarterly Bulletin*, Vol. 34, No. 2, pp. 156–62.

MacNeal, K. (1939), *Truth in Accounting*, University of Pennsylvania Press, Philadelphia.

MacNeill, J. H. (1971), 'Response' (to Ijiri, 1971), pp. 15–18 of Sterling (1971).

Macve, R. (2010), 'The case for deprival value', *Abacus*, Vol. 46, No. 1, pp. 111–19.

Mallinson, D. (1980), *Understanding Current Cost Accounting*, Butterworths, London.

Mason, P. (1956), *Price-Level Changes and Financial Statements: Basic Concepts and Methods*, American Accounting Association, Sarasota, Florida.

Mathews, R. L. (1965), 'Price-level changes and useless information', *Journal of Accounting Research*, Vol. 3, pp. 133–58.

— (1968), 'Income, price changes and the valuation controversy in accounting', *The Accounting Review*, Vol. 43, July, pp. 509–16.

Mathews, R. L. and Grant, J. M. (1958), *Inflation and Company Finance*, Law Book Co., Sydney.

McDonald, D. L. (1968), 'A test application of the feasibility of market based measures in accounting', *Journal of Accounting Research*, Vol. 6, No. 1, pp. 38–49.

McCafferty, I. (2013), 'Monetary policy in a changing economy'. Speech given at Bloomberg, London. Available at www.bankofengland.co.uk/publications/Pages/speeches/2013/267.aspx.

McIntyre, E. V. (1975), 'The effects of restating financial statements for price-level changes: a reply', *The Accounting Review*, Vol. 50, No. 4, pp. 815–17.

McKeown, J. C. (1971), 'An empirical test of a model proposed by Chambers', *The Accounting Review*, Vol. 46, No. 1, pp. 12–29.

McMonnies, P. N. (1988), *Making Corporate Reports Valuable*, Kogan Page, London.

McRae, W. T. and Dobbins, R. (1974), 'Behavioural aspects of the inflation accounting controversy', *Accounting and Business Research*, Vol. 4, No. 14, pp. 135–40.

Meade, J. E. (1978), *The Structure and Reform of Direct Taxation* [the Meade Committee Report], George Allen and Unwin, London.

Meeks, G. (1974), 'Profit illusion', *Bulletin of the Oxford Institute of Economics and Statistics*, Vol. 36, No. 4, pp. 267–85.

Merrett, A. J. and Sykes, A. (1974), article in *The Financial Times*, 30 September.

— (1980), 'Inflation accounting: how badly flawed is ED24?', *The Times*, 11 February.

Mey, A. (1966), 'Theodore Limperg and his theory of values and costs', *Abacus*, Vol. 2, No. 1, pp. 1–23.

Middleditch, L. (1918), 'Should accounts reflect the changing value of the dollar?', *The Journal of Accountancy*, Vol. 25, No. 2, pp. 114–20, reprinted in Zeff (1976).

Moonitz, M. (1973), *Changing Prices and Financial Reporting*, International Centre for Research in Accounting, University of Lancaster, Lancaster, UK.

Moore, B. (1980), 'Equity values and inflation: the importance of dividends', *Lloyds Bank Review*, No. 137, July, pp. 1–15.

Morris, R. C. (1975), 'Evidence of the impact of inflation accounting on share prices', *Accounting and Business Research*, Vol. 5, No. 18, pp. 82–90.

Moser, D. V. and Martin, P. R. (2012), 'A broader perspective on social responsibility research in accounting', *The Accounting Review*, Vol. 87, No. 3, pp. 797–806.

Most, K. S. (1977), *Accounting Theory*, Grid Inc., Columbus, OH.

Muller, K. and Riedl, E. (2002), 'External monitoring of property appraisal estimates and information asymmetry', *Journal of Accounting Research*, Vol. 40, No. 3, pp. 865–81.

Mumford, M. (1979), 'The end of a familiar inflation accounting cycle', *Accounting and Business Research*, Vol. 9, No. 34, pp. 98–104.

Murdoch, B. (1986), 'The information content of FAS 33 returns on equity', *The Accounting Review*, Vol. 61, No. 2, pp. 273–87.

Nelson, C. L. (1973), 'A priori research in accounting', in Dopuch and Revsine (1973).

Nguyen, D. T. and Whittaker, R. A. (1976), 'Inflation, replacement and amortisation funds: a case study of UK industries', *Journal of Business Finance and Accounting*, Vol. 3, No. 1, pp. 43–52.

Nissim, D. and Penman, S. H. (2008), *Principles for the Application of Fair Value Accounting*, CEASA, Columbia Business School, New York.

Nobes, C. W. (1977), 'Current cost accounting – valuation by intent?', *Accounting and Business Research*, Vol. 7, No. 26, pp. 95–99.

— (2011), 'On relief value (deprival value) versus fair value measurement for contract liabilities: a comment and a response', *Accounting and Business Research*, Vol. 41, No. 5, pp. 515–24.

Norby, W. C. (1983), 'Applications of inflation-adjusted accounting data', *Financial Analysts Journal*, Vol. 39, No. 2, pp. 33–39.

Norton, C. L. and Smith, R. E. (1979), 'A comparison of general price level and historical cost financial statements in the prediction of bankruptcy', *The Accounting Review*, Vol. 54, No. 1, pp. 72–87.

Office for National Statistics (2011), *Implications of the Differences between the Consumer Prices Index and Retail Prices Index*, Office for National Statistics, London.

Ohlson, J. A. (1995), 'Earnings, book values, and dividends in equity valuation', *Contemporary Accounting Research*, Vol. 11, No. 2, pp. 661–87.

Parker, J. E. (1977), 'Impact of price-level accounting', *The Accounting Review*, Vol. 52, pp. 69–96.

Parker, R. H. and Harcourt, G. C. (1969), *Readings in the Concept and Measurement of Income*, Cambridge University Press, Cambridge.

Parker, R. H., Harcourt, G. C. and Whittington, G. (1986), *Readings in the Concept and Measurement of Income*, 2nd ed., Philip Allan, Oxford.

Parker, Sir W. E. (1975), 'CPP accounting: what is the argument really about?', *The Accountant*, Vol. 172, No. 5231, pp. 426–28.

Patell, J. M. (1978), 'Discussion of the impact of price-level adjustment in the context of risk assessment and the effect of general price-level adjustments on the predictive ability of financial ratios', *Journal of Accounting Research*, Vol. 16(Suppl.), pp. 293–300.

Peasnell, K. V. (1977), 'A note on the discounted present value concept', *The Accounting Review*, Vol. 52, No. 1, pp. 186–99.

— (1978), 'Interaction effects in CCA valuation', *Accounting and Business Research*, Vol. 8, No. 30, pp. 82–91.

— (1982), 'Some formal connections between economic values and yields and accounting numbers', *Journal of Business Finance and Accounting*, Vol. 9, No. 3, pp. 361–81.

Peasnell, K. V. and Skerratt, L. C. L. (1976a), *Current Cost Accounting: The Index Number Problem*, International Centre for Research in Accounting, University of Lancaster, Lancaster, UK.

— (1976b), 'Long-term debt and shareholder wealth: a comment', *Journal of Business Finance and Accounting*, Vol. 3, No. 3, pp. 137–41.

— (1977a), 'How well does a single index represent the nineteen Sandilands plant and machinery indices?', *Journal of Accounting Research*, Vol. 15, No. 1, pp. 108–19.

— (1977b), 'Price indices for current cost accounting – a reply and some further evidence', *Journal of Business Finance and Accounting*, Vol. 4, No. 1, pp. 139–44.

— (1978), 'Income-group inflation rates and general purchasing power adjustments: an empirical test of the heterogeneity hypothesis', *Accounting and Business Research*, Vol. 9, No. 33, pp. 45–59.

Peasnell, K. and Whittington, G. (2010), 'The contribution of Philip W. Bell to accounting thought', *Accounting Horizons*, Vol. 24, No. 3, pp. 509–18.

Penman, S. H. (2007), 'Financial reporting quality: is fair value a plus or a minus?', *Accounting and Business Research*, Special Issue: International Accounting Policy Forum.

— (2015), 'Valuation models: an issue of accounting theory', Chapter 11, pp. 236–253, of Jones (ed.) (2015).

Petersen, R. J. (1973), 'Interindustry estimation of general price-level: impact on financial information', *The Accounting Review*, Vol. 48, No. 1, pp. 34–43.

— (1975), 'A portfolio analysis of general price level restatement', *The Accounting Review*, Vol. 50, No. 3, pp. 525–32.

— (1978), 'Interindustry estimation of a general price-level impact on financial information: more data and a reply', *The Accounting Review*, Vol. 53, No. 1, pp. 198–203.

Petri, E. and Gelfand, J. (1979), 'The production function: a new perspective in capital maintenance', *The Accounting Review*, Vol. 54, No. 2, pp. 330–45.

Picur, R. D. and McKeown, J. C. (1976), 'Alternative income concepts and relative performance evaluations: a comment and extension', *The Accounting Review*, Vol. 51, No. 2, pp. 415–20.

Plantin, G., Sapra, H. and Shin, H. (2008), 'Marking-to-market: panacea or Pandora's box?', *Journal of Accounting Research*, Vol. 46, No. 2, pp. 435–60.

Prakash, P. and Sunder, S. (1979), 'The case against separation of current operating profit and holding gains', *The Accounting Review*, Vol. 54, No. 1, pp. 1–22.

Preinreich, G. A. (1936), 'The fair value and yield of common stock', *The Accounting Review*, Vol. 11, No. 2, pp. 130–40.

Rayman, R. A. (1980). 'Is inflation accounting an academic confidence trick?', *The Financial Times*, 16 January, p. 13.

Revsine, L. (1970), 'On the correspondence between replacement cost income and economic income', *The Accounting Review*, Vol. 54, July, pp. 513–23.

— (1973), *Replacement Cost Accounting*, Prentice Hall, Englewood Cliffs, NJ.

— (1976), 'Surrogates in accounting theory: a comment', *The Accounting Review*, Vol. 51, No. 1, pp. 156–59.

Richardson Committee Report (1976), *The Report of the Committee of Inquiry into Inflation Accounting*, New Zealand Government Printer, Wellington.

Ross, H. (1969), *Financial Statements: A Crusade for Current Values*, Pitman, Canada.

Sale, T. and Scapens, R. (1978), 'Current cost accounting as a surrogate for dividend paying ability', *Accounting and Business Research*, Vol. 8, No. 31, pp. 208–16.

Samuelson, R. A. (1980), 'Should replacement-cost changes be included in income?', *The Accounting Review*, Vol. 55, No. 2, pp. 254–68.

Sandilands Committee (1975), *Inflation Accounting: Report of the Inflation Accounting Committee*, under the chairmanship of F. E. P. Sandilands, Cmnd 6225, HMSO, September.

Scapens, R. W. (1977), *Accounting in an Inflationary Environment*, Macmillan, New York.

Schmalenbach, E. (1959), *Dynamic Accounting*, trans. G. W. Murphy and K. S. Most, Gee.

Schmidt, F. (1921), *Die Organische Bilanz im Rahmen der Wirtschaft*, Gloeckner, Leipzig.

— (1930), 'The importance of replacement value', *The Accounting Review*, Vol. 5, pp. 235–42. Reprinted in Zeff (1976).

— (1931), 'Is appreciation profit', *The Accounting Review*, Vol. 6, pp. 289–93. Reprinted in Zeff (1976).

Schneider, D. (1998), 'German reflections on asset valuation', *Abacus*, Vol. 34, No. 1, pp. 31–35.

Scott, M. F. G. (1976), *Some Economic Principles of Accounting: A Constructive Critique of the Sandilands Report*, IFS Lecture Series, No. 7, Institute for Fiscal Studies, London.

Secretary of State for Trade (1977), *The Future of Company Reports: A Consultative Document*, Cmnd 6888, HMSO, July.

Securities and Exchange Commission (SEC) (1976), *Accounting Series Release No. 190 (ASR 190), Amendments to Regulation S-X Requiring Disclosure of Certain Replacement Cost Data in Notes to Financial Statements*, SEC, Washington, DC, 23 March.

Sen, A. K. (1979), 'The welfare basis of real income comparisons: a survey', *Journal of Economic Literature*, Vol. 17, March, pp. 1–45.

Short, D. G. (1978), 'The impact of price-level adjustment in the context of risk assessment', *Journal of Accounting Research*, Vol. 16(Suppl.), pp. 259–72.

Skerratt, L. C. L. and Thompson, A. P. (1984), 'Market reaction to SSAP16 current cost accounting disclosures', pp. 289–319 of Carsberg and Page (1984).

Solomon, E. (1966), 'Return on investment: the relation of book yields to true value', in *Research in Accounting Measurement*, ed. R. K. Jaedicke, Y. Ijiri and O. Nielsen, American Accounting Association,Sarasota, Florida.

Solomons, D. (1961), 'Economic and accounting concepts of income', *The Accounting Review*, Vol. 36, pp. 374–83. Reprinted in Parker and Harcourt (1969).

— (1966), 'Economic and accounting concepts of cost and value', Chapter 6, pp. 117–40, of M. Backer (ed.), *Modern Accounting Theory*, Prentice Hall, Englewood Cliffs, NJ.

— (1979), 'The politicization of accounting', pp. 25–39 of S. A. Zeff, J. Demski and N. Dopuch (eds), *Essays in Honor of William A. Paton*, University of Michigan, Ann Arbor.

— (1986), *Making Accounting Policy: The Quest for Credibility in Financial Reporting*, Oxford University Press, New York.

Stamp, E. (1971), 'Income and value determination and changing price levels: an essay towards a theory', *The Accountant's Magazine*, June, pp. 277–92.

— (1972), 'R. J. Chambers: quo vadis et cui bono', *Chartered Accountants in Australia*, August, pp. 10–12.

— (1979), 'Financial reports on an entity: ex uno plures', Chapter 8, pp. 163–80, of Sterling and Thomas (1979).

Stark, A. W. (1997), 'The impact of irreversibility, uncertainty and timing options on deprival valuations and the detection of monopoly profits', *Accounting and Business Research*, Vol. 28, No. 1, pp. 40–52.

Staubus, G. J. (1971), 'The relevance of evidence of cash flows', Chapter 3, pp. 42–69, of Sterling (1971).

Sterling, R. R. (1970), *Theory of the Measurement of Enterprise Income*, University Press of Kansas, Lawrence.

— (ed.) (1971), *Asset Valuation and Income Determination: A Consideration of the Alternatives*, Scholars, Houston, TX.

Sterling, R. R. and Lemke, K. W. (eds) (1982), *Maintenance of Capital: Financial versus Physical*, Scholars, Houston, TX.

Sterling, R. R. and Radosevitch, R. (1969), 'A valuation experiment', *Journal of Accounting Research*, Vol. 7, No. 1, pp. 90–95.

Sterling, R. R. and Thomas, A. L. (eds) (1979), *Accounting for a Simplified Firm Owning Depreciable Assets*, Scholars, Houston, TX.

Stone, J. R. N. and Stone, G. (1977), *National Income and Expenditure*, 10th ed., Bowes and Bowes.

Study Group on the Objectives of Financial Statements (1973), *Objectives of Financial Statements* [the Trueblood Report], American Institute of Certified Public Accountants, New York, October.

Sweeney, H. W. (1927), 'Effects of inflation on German accounting', *The Journal of Accountancy*, Vol. 43, No. 3, March. Reprinted in Zeff (1976).

— (1928), 'German inflation accounting', *The Journal of Accountancy*, Vol. 45, No. 2, February. Reprinted in Zeff (1976).

— (1933), 'Capital', *The Accounting Review*, Vol. 8, pp. 185–99. Reprinted in Zeff (1976).

— (1935), 'The technique of stabilized accounting', *The Accounting Review*, Vol. 10, pp. 185–205. Reprinted in Zeff (1976).

— (1936), *Stabilized Accounting*, Harper, New York. Reprinted 1964 by Holt, Rinehart and Winston, with a new foreword by W. A. Paton and an essay 'Forty years after: or stabilized accounting revisited' by H. W. Sweeney.

— (1964), 'Forty years after: or stabilized accounting revisited', pp. 17–39 of the 1964 reissue of *Stabilized Accounting*, Holt, Rinehart and Winston.

Thomas, A. L. (1969), *The Allocation Problem in Financial Accounting Theory*, Studies in Accounting Research, 3, American Accounting Association, Sarasota, Florida.

— (1974), *The Allocation Problem: Part Two*, Studies in Accounting Research, 9, American Accounting Association, Sarasota, Florida.

— (1979), 'Matching: up from our black hole', Chapter 1, pp. 11–33, of Sterling and Thomas (1979).

Tippett, M. (1979), 'ED24 – An inefficient means of information retrieval?', *The Accountant's Magazine*, Vol. 83, No. 881, pp. 465–68.

Trevithick, J. A. (1977), *Inflation: A Guide to the Crisis in Economics*, Penguin, New York.

Tweedie, D. P. (1977), 'Cash flows and realisable value: the intuitive accounting concepts? an empirical test', *Accounting and Business Research*, Vol. 8, No. 29, pp. 2–13.

— (1979), *Financial Reporting, Inflation and the Capital Maintenance Concept*, International Centre for Research in Accounting, University of Lancaster, Lancaster, UK.

Tweedie, D. P. and Whittington, G. (1984), *The Debate on Inflation Accounting*, Cambridge University Press, Cambridge.

— (1997), 'The end of the current cost revolution', pp. 149–76 of Cooke and Nobes (1997).

United Nations (1980), *World Economic Survey, 1979–80, Current Trends in the World Economy*, United Nations, New York.

United Nations (World Commission on Environment and Development) (1987), *Our Common Future* [the Brundtland Report], Oxford University Press, Oxford.

Van Zijl, T. and Whittington, G. (2006), ' Deprival value and fair value: a reinterpretation and a reconciliation', *Accounting and Business Research*, Vol. 36, No. 2, pp. 121–30.

Vatter, W. J. (1947), *The Fund Theory of Accounting*, University of Chicago Press, Chicago.

— (1966), 'Income models, book yield and rate of return', *The Accounting Review*, Vol. 41, No. 4, pp. 681–98.

Wagenhofer, A. (2015), 'Agency theory: usefulness and implications for financial reporting', Chapter 13, pp. 341–65, of Jones (ed.) (2015).

Walker, M. (1997), 'Clean surplus accounting models and market-based accounting research: a review', *Accounting and Business Research*, Vol. 27, No. 4, pp. 341–55.

Walton, P. (2007), *The Routledge Companion to Fair Value and Financial Reporting*, Routledge, New York.

Wanless, P. T. (1974), 'Reflections on asset valuation and value to the firm', *Abacus*, Vol. 10, No. 2, pp. 160–64.

— (1976), 'Current purchasing power accounting: a study of a cooperative venture', *Abacus*, Vol. 12, No. 1, pp. 61–72.

Wasserman, M. J. (1931), 'Accounting practice in France during the period of monetary inflation (1919–1927)', *The Accounting Review*, March. Reprinted in Zeff (1976).

Watts, R. L. (2003a), 'Conservatism in accounting part I: explanations and implications', *Accounting Horizons*, Vol. 17, No. 3, pp. 207–21.

— (2003b), 'Conservatism in accounting part II: evidence and research opportunities', *Accounting Horizons*, Vol. 17, No. 4, pp. 287–301.

Watts, R. L. and Zimmerman, J. L. (1978), 'Towards a positive theory of the determination of accounting standards', *The Accounting Review*, Vol. 53, No. 1, pp. 112–34.

— (1979), 'The demand for and supply of accounting theories: the market for excuses', *The Accounting Review*, Vol. 54, No. 2, pp. 273–305.

— (1980), 'On the irrelevance of replacement cost disclosures for security prices', *Journal of Accounting and Economics*, Vol. 2, No. 2, pp. 95–106.

Weetman, P. (2007), 'Comments on deprival value and standard setting in measurement: from a symposium to celebrate the work of Professor William T. Baxter', *Accounting and Business Research*, Vol. 37, No. 3, pp. 233–42.

Weston, F. T. (1971), 'Response' (to Chambers, 1971a), pp. 97–106 of Sterling (1971).

Westwick, C. A. (1980), 'The lessons to be learned from the development of inflation accounting in the UK', *Accounting and Business Research*, No. 40, Autumn, pp. 353–73.

Whittington, G. (1974), 'Asset valuation, income measurement and accounting income', *Accounting and Business Research*, Vol. 4, No. 14, pp. 96–101.

— (1975), 'Baxter on inflation accounting', *Accounting and Business Research*, Vol. 5, No. 20, pp. 314–17.

— (1976), 'Indexation: a review article', *Accounting and Business Research*, Vol. 6, No. 23, pp. 171–76.

— (1979), 'On the use of the accounting rate of return in empirical research', *Accounting and Business Research*, Vol. 9, No. 35, pp. 200–208.

— (1980a), 'Pioneers of income measurement and price-level accounting: a review article', *Accounting and Business Research*, Vol. 10, No. 38, pp. 232–40.

— (1980b), 'Inflation accounting – why the debate has gone off course', *The Times*, 10 March.

— (1981a), 'The British contribution to income theory', Chapter 1, pp. 1–29, of M. Bromwich and A. Hopwood (eds), *Essays in British Accounting Research*, Pitman, London.

— (1981b), *Inflation Accounting: All the Answers*, Deloitte, Haskins and Sells Lecture, University College of Cardiff Press, Cardiff.

— (1983), *Inflation Accounting, An introduction to the debate*, Cambridge University Press, Cambridge.

— (1985), 'The Carsberg Report: a review article', *The British Accounting Review*, Vol. 17, No. 1, pp. 59–70.

— (1994), 'Current cost accounting: its role in regulated industries', *Fiscal Studies*, Vol. 15, No. 4, pp. 102–18.

— (1997), 'The economic rate of return and the accountant', Vol. 2, Chapter 9, pp. 97–108, of P. Arestis, G. Palma and M. Sawyer, *Markets, Unemployment and Economic Policy, Essays in Honour of Geoff Harcourt*, Routledge, New York.

— (1998a), 'The role of current cost accounting for regulated industries', Chapter 3, pp. 41–61, of P. Vass (ed.), *The Financial Methodology of Incentive Regulation: Reconciling Accounting and Economics*, Centre for the Study of Regulated Industries (CRI), Bath, UK.

— (1998b), 'Deprival value and price change accounting in the UK', *Abacus*, Vol. 34, No. 1, pp. 28–30.

— (2008a), 'Fair value and the IASB conceptual framework: an alternative view', *Abacus*, Vol. 44, No. 2, pp. 139–68.

— (2008b), 'Harmonisation or discord? The critical role of the IASB conceptual framework review', *Journal of Accounting and Public Policy*, Vol. 27, No. 6, pp. 495–502.

— (2008c), 'What the 'old guys' can tell us: Edwards and Bell's *The Theory and Measurement of Business Income*', *Irish Accounting Review*, Vol. 15, No. 1, pp. 73–84.

— (2010), 'Measurement in financial reporting', *Abacus*, Vol. 46, No. 1, pp. 104–10.

— (2015), 'Fair value and IFRS', Chapter 10, pp. 217–35, of Jones (2015).

Whittington, G., Saporta, V. and Singh, A. (1997), *The Effects of Hyper-Inflation on Accounting Ratios*, IFC Technical Paper No. 3, The World Bank, Washington, DC.

Wiles, P. (1981), 'Equity values and inflation: the importance of dividends', *Lloyds Bank Review*, No. 139, January, pp. 58–59.

Wright, F. K. (1964), 'Towards a general theory of depreciation', *Journal of Accounting Research*, Vol. 2, pp. 80–90. Reprinted in Parker and Harcourt (1969).

— (1965), 'A theory of inventory measurement', *Abacus*, Vol. 1, No. 2, pp. 150–55.

— (1968), 'Measuring asset services: a linear programming approach', *Journal of Accounting Research*, Vol. 6, pp. 222–36.

— (1970), 'A theory of financial accounting', *Journal of Business Finance*, Vol. 2, No. 3, pp. 57–69.

— (1971), 'Value to the owner: a clarification', *Abacus*, Vol. 7, No. 1, pp. 58–61.

— (1978), 'Accounting rate of profit and internal rate of return', *Oxford Economic Papers*, Vol. 30, No. 3, pp. 464–68.

Yoshida, H. (1973), 'Value to the firm and the asset measurement problem', *Abacus*, Vol. 9, pp. 16–21.

Zeff, S. A. (1976), *Asset Appreciation, Business Income and Price-Level Accounting, 1918–1935*, Arno Press, New York.

— (1982), 'Truth in accounting: the ordeal of Kenneth MacNeal', *Accounting Review*, Vol. 57, No. 3, pp. 528–53.

— (2007), 'Some obstacles to global financial reporting comparability and convergence at a high level of quality', *The British Accounting Review*, Vol. 39, No. 4, pp. 290–302.

— (2016), 'The Trueblood Study Group on the objective of financial statements (1971–73): A historical study', *Journal of Accounting and Public Policy*, Vol. 35, No. 2, pp. 134–61.

# Index